With Dignity and Respect...
Dynamics of Teenage Spirituality:
How Teens May Elevate Prayer-Life

by

Philip Joseph Balest

Prestige Publishing

North Little Rock, Arkansas

Copyright © 2003 by Philip Joseph Balest
All Rights Reserved

Published by
Prestige Publishing
4271 East 43rd Street
North Little Rock, AR 72117
501-945-0866

Library of Congress Cataloging-in-Publication Data
Balest, Philip Joseph, 1949-
With dignity and respect: dynamics of teenage spirituality,
how teens may elevate prayer-life / Philip Joseph Balest
p. cm.
Includes bibliographical references.

Library of Congress Control Number: 2003106559

ISBN 0-9740208-2-6

Manufactured in the United States of America
by Prestige Press, Inc. of North Little Rock, Arkansas

Parts A of this book are a work of fiction. Names, characters, places, and incidents are either the product of the author's imagination or are used fictiously. Any resemblance to actual persons, living or dead, or business establishments, or events, or locales is entirely coincidental.

Cover design by Charles V. Bryant, Photographer
Technical Data for photo "Sunrise in Daytona Beach, Florida"
ASA 100, f 5.6, 1/60

To
My wife, Sue, and my daughter, Maria,
for their many prayers and for graciously
walking every step of this writer's journey with me.

TABLE OF CONTENTS

Preface	ix

Chapter 1: Love God...Libby Lou
    Prayers of Thanksgiving   1
A. Libby Lou   1
B. Applied Theology – Prayers of Thanksgiving   7
C. Please, Consider the Following   13

Chapter 2: Love Neighbor...Bully
    Prayers of Forgiveness   15
A. Bully   15
B. Applied Theology – Prayers of Forgiveness   21
    a. Acid Tongue   23
    b. Concept of Sin   28
    c. Sacrament of Penance and Reconciliation   33
    d. Fresh Teen Start and the Seal of Confession   39
C. Please, Consider the Following   43

Chapter 3: Gift of Life...Colin Browne
    Prayers of Adoration   45
A. Colin Browne   45
B. Applied Theology – Prayers of Adoration   56
    a. Humility   57
    b. Tension and Innocent Suffering   60
    c. Job, the Classic Innocent Sufferer   65
    d. Jesus, the Epitome of the Innocent Sufferer   67
    e. Teen Worship   72
C. Please, Consider the Following   75

Chapter 4: "Hey, Meestor, You Want to Ride My Camel"
    Prayers of Petition   77
A. Egypt   77
B. Applied Theology – Prayers of Petition   101
    a. Concept of Time   102
    b. Tweak Teen Prayers of Petitions   108
    c. Daily Need of Moses for Virtue of Fortitude   113
    d. Daily Need of Jesus for Virtue of Fortitude   118
        1.0 Roman Military Machine   119
        1.1 Roman Legion and Roman Centurion   120
        1.2 Military Training, Discipline, Battle Tactics   121
        1.3 Gladius, Sword of the Roman Legionnaire   123
        1.4 Perks of Legionnaire, Wealth of Victorious Caesar   125
        1.5 Power Dispute and Roman Empire at Time of Jesus   129
        2.0 Extreme Sufferings of Jesus from Roman Violence   131
        2.1 The Holy Shroud of Turin   134

2.2 The Scourging at the Pillar	135
2.3 The Crowning with Thorns	137
C. Please, Consider the Following	141

Chapter 5: Change...Good Bully
        Theology of Holy Trinity, Grace, Holy Eucharist   143
A. Good Bully   143
B. Applied Theology – Holy Trinity, Grace, Holy Eucharist   151
   a. Most Holy Trinity   153
      1.0 Divine Jesus   156
      2.0 Difficulty with Developed Theology of Divine Mystery   160
      2.1 Spiritual Process of New Testament Writers   162
      2.2 Problems with Fundamentalism and Holy Scripture   164
      3.0 Spiritual Dynamics and Symbols of Holy Trinity   166
   b. Grace   168
      1.0 Eastern/Greek Church and Western/Latin Church   170
      1.1 East-West Schism   172
      1.2 Vatican II Calls for East-West Unity   173
      2.0 Saint Thomas Aquinas and Modern Teens   175
      2.1 Mary Full of Grace   176
      2.2 Teens Full of Grace   178
   c. Most Holy Eucharist   179
      1.0 Most Holy Moment   180
      1.1 New Testament Eucharistic Institution Narratives   181
      1.2 Eucharistic Themes in Gospel of John   183
      1.3 Holy Eucharist Elevates Prayer   185
C. Please, Consider the Following   189

Chapter 6: Summary: Prayer in Action
        Service to Others   191

Bibliography   203

With Dignity and Respect...
Dynamics of Teenage Spirituality:
How Teens May Elevate Prayer-Life

Preface

I write this manuscript primarily to share thoughts, feelings, and experiences with my Teen daughter, Maria. My hope is also to help many Teens through their time of mental, emotional, psychological, spiritual changes. In many ways, I consider myself a spiritual farmer because I try to plant spiritual thoughts and spiritual feelings in the Teenage consciousness during the present time. I hope that many spiritual positives sprout in the future realities of Teens. My efforts try to tap into the audio and video mentalities of modern Teens with stories that spin into a theology of Teen prayer. I define theology as the study of God and Teen prayer as communication in the Teenage relationship with God.

The basics of the stories are experiences from teaching blind students in London, England. But like a good fish story, I definitely use poetic license to enhance the stories. On the other hand, the substance of the theology is the product of research, thoughts, and feelings about the historical Jesus and the 2000-year traditions of the Catholic Church. Teens, please, understand that I try my best to tell a good story in Part A of the chapter. Then I try my best to write the truth in the theology of Part B. I add a Part C to start the process of applying the moral of the stories and the theology of prayer into the lives of modern Teens.

However, understand also that the study of the Most Holy God of Antiquity is the study of the Divine Mystery. Jesus Christ shares the most accurate information about the human relationship with God the Creator. It is negative pride and manipulative ego for any writer to think that personal interpretations have the totality of understanding and knowledge about the Divine Mystery. Teens, writers, theologians need faith and trust for the journey through the Divine Mystery to the Most Holy God of Antiquity.

I utilize the combination of story + theology in imitation of Jesus and his teaching technique which tapped with his parables into the mentality of the people. Jesus utilized parables because: (1) people easily remembered his stories and therefore his spiritual teachings; (2) people reflected on his stories and then had responsibility for a personal decision to accept or reject his teachings; (3) his parables "probably reduced specific grounds for contention by hostile listeners" (New Oxford Annotated Bible, NRSV, Mt.13: 1-52, fn.; all Bible quotes from this NOAB/NRSV version unless noted). I try to help and teach Teens with stories and prayer for the same reasons that Jesus taught.

The linguistic purists may immediately note that I freely choose to capitalize the "T" in Teenager. The capital "T" indicates a dignity and respect for the individual Teen and for Teenagers as a corporate group. I believe in the spiritual potential for holiness in every Teen. I think and feel strongly that the word "Teen" designates a very special individual and a special group of people within the human race. I base my opinion on 25 years of experience working with Teenagers that includes 17 years in Catholic Youth Ministry, 5 years with Boys & Girls Clubs of America, 15 years of sharing theology in structured classrooms, and 15 years in Teen Tutoring Programs.

I want to thank my wife, Sue, and my daughter, Maria, for their many prayers and for graciously walking every step of this writer's journey with me. I also want to thank Divine Providence for allowing me five years to concentrate on theology of prayer to the Most Holy God of Antiquity.

>	Philip Joseph Balest
>	North Little Rock, AR
>	May 2003
>
>	University of Notre Dame, '75
>	 Bachelor of Arts, History
>	Loyola University New Orleans, '96
>	 Master of Pastoral Studies

With Dignity and Respect...
Dynamics of Teenage Spirituality:
How Teens May Elevate Prayer-Life

CHAPTER 1

LOVE GOD...LIBBY LOU
PRAYERS OF THANKSGIVING

A. LIBBY LOU

Let me give Teenagers one good reason to love God with whole mind, heart, soul and to love neighbor as yourself: Libby Lou.

Libby Lou was a student at Linden Lodge School for the Blind in London, England. She was a beautiful young person and ten years old. She had a magnificent smile, shoulder-length brown hair, petite body, friendly personality. As a nine-year old, Libby Lou had sight. Unfortunately for her, she was in a terrible car wreck. She and her Mom traveled on a motorway (interstate) when a drunk driver lost the control of his car, jumped the median, and smashed at a high speed head-on into Libby Lou's car. When the dust settled, the intoxicated man was unscratched, and Libby Lou's Mom had few broken bones. Libby Lou had no scratches, no broken bones, and no eyesight. The police report on file at the School for the Blind testified to the violent wreck. The best guess of a medical examiner was that the impact of the collision threw Libby Lou into the front windshield with her head hitting first. She double-clutched back into the car, and then blasted through the windshield again. The police found her on the hood of the car, and medics discovered that Libby Lou was alive and blind.

Libby Lou's parents were incredibly rich. Her family owned many factories in England, Scotland, and Canada. The family had the best insurance, and Libby Lou received the best treatments. None of the doctors restored Libby Lou's eyesight. When money from insurance played out, the family spent almost a half million pounds, about one million dollars, out of their own pocket jetting in many specialists and psychiatrists from all over the world. Nobody found physical reasons for Libby Lou's blindness. Professional consensus on file at the Blind School was that the car wreck created a severe traumatic experience in Libby Lou's mind and her brain shutdown the sight of the trauma. The hope was for an instant recovery. Meanwhile, it was time after 1½ years for Libby Lou to learn how to walk with a white stick.

Libby Lou was at the Linden Lodge School for the Blind for about two weeks before I arrived to teach a class. The combination of her personal tragedy, her fear in the new environment, and a beautiful personality made her the instantaneous darling of the Blind School. I came off the streets during a year of vagabonding Europe to help the blind children in London. We connected as the two new kids on the block, and we learned together about blindness in a real world. The foremost and harshest lesson, which we suffered together, was the fear of fire.

The Linden Lodge addressed this primary fear of all blind people with many fire drills programmed into the academic curriculum. The Headmaster (the Principal) consistently pushed the fire drill buttons, and he constantly worked the students into an automatic response. His theory was that the blind students could not see the width or the length of a fire. As a result, students did not know if safety was left, right, or through the fire. When students felt the intensity of flames, their natural reactions were individual fears leading to a corporate fear, chaos, and death. The Headmaster conquered fear by working the individual and corporate psychology of the blind students with fire drills. The hope in a life-death situation was individual safety through the self-discipline of automatic pilot. Trust was the foundation of the entire process. Every fire drill at Linden Lodge School for the Blind was strict business to the nth degree.

In all fire drills only one person talked. The Headmaster stood at the second floor exit, and he spoke with authority to the two hundred fifty students lining the halls in pairs. He gave precise instructions concerning the exits to use. The student body responded in seconds precious to all. If the Headmaster was not available for a fire drill or the real thing, Mrs. Green with her twenty-seven years of teaching experience took his place at the head of the stairs. I was the teacher at the bottom of the seniority list for the teaching staff and number thirty to talk. The administrative staff reminded all teachers before each fire drill that talking out of turn and helping of students during fire drills resulted in automatic docking of paychecks. Because I was a volunteer, my penalty was immediate dismissal from the premises never to return as teacher. The fire drills were very serious business at the Linden Lodge School for the Blind.

Libby Lou knew the procedures for a fire drill, but she had no real experience of an actual drill as a blind person. The teachers and the students helped her to walk through the entire process multiple times before her first fire drill. She understood that fear and chaos were the real enemies. Libby Lou knew well that trust in people and in a dependable procedure helped to control the negative situations. She tested her understanding of love, self-respect, friendships as applied to a potentially dangerous experience. She mastered the practical details of the system: (1) automatic and total silence when the fire bell blares; (2) reach left or right before leaving desk to find partner; (3) partner closer to walls holds the pair at arm's length from walls while "walking" right hand along the walls to find corners and doors; (4) person away from wall "hooks-on" to inside of partner's left elbow with right index and middle fingers; (5) each pair joins line of pairs rotating counter-clockwise out of the classroom into hall; (6) the pairs turn right into hall as class line joins other classes doing the identical procedure; (7) all partners stop and wait silently and patiently for the Headmaster's exit instructions. Libby Lou knew all about fire drills including the philosophy, psychology, and the nuts-and-bolts routine.

Knowing something and acting on the knowledge are two entirely different things.

When I first arrived at the Blind School, the Headmaster and I talked for nearly three hours. He then consulted Mrs. Green and Mr. McMillan, the English teachers. They handpicked a class for me to teach. I taught twelve students aged ten to nineteen years old. The Headmaster asked me to simply tell stories to the students about my travels in different countries. He wanted me to incorporate history, philosophy, and cultural impressions. The students then composed essays on their Perkins, which were the six-keyed Braille typewriters producing the raised dots for letters. Mr. McMillan read and graded the essays as part of his English class.

Life was good, but the work exhausted me. Teaching the blind students was and is a very special vocation. I struggled constantly with the simplest things. Each basic choice of a word was critical to meaningful teaching. For example, any word describing a color was meaningless to the blind students because they only saw black with the absence of light. When I described sitting in shade of Egyptian pyramids and watching beautiful sunsets over the Sahara Desert, I mentioned the brilliant colors quickly as only a passing thought. I had to concentrate on using more vivid words to describe emotions and thoughts generated by sunsets. Words descriptive of the experience included feeling the heat of the sun at dusk versus at noon or in the shade. I found myself continually changing words in mid-sentence and filling out thought patterns with a different choice of words.

The students challenged all poorly chosen words describing the simplest thoughts. I distinctly remember working mobility with Mr. McMillan. The school was in Wimbledon up the hill from the tennis courts, and we worked mobility off the school's property on sidewalks of a very nice neighborhood of London. We usually worked with ten students walking with their white canes. Mr. McMillan and I were all business when we reached the curbs at the ends of the blocks and practiced safely negotiating the traffic. We relaxed the atmosphere in the middle of the blocks, and we allowed the students to practice walking on their own or in small groups. Mr. McMillan and I always had students around us listening to us talk. He was from Northern Ireland and spoke with a thick Belfast accent. I'm from Arkansas and speak with a southern drawl. The students asked us in their Queen's English to describe the homes in the neighborhood. Our group was something to hear.

When we walked in Libby Lou's favorite block, she asked me to again describe her "very favorite sounding house." I talked about the humongous house with the two floors, ten windows across the front of the top floor, the two chimneys on each end of the house, double front doors, flowers everywhere. After we returned to our classroom hours later, Colin Browne asked, "Beg your pardon, Sir, beg your pardon, but what exactly are two chimneys?" Everyone in class, all blind from birth except for Libby Lou, waited patiently for the answer.

So, the class and I marched down to the Arts and Crafts classroom where the teacher had a small model farmhouse on display. Colin Browne felt the clay roof and discovered a chimney. He shared his discovery with the class, and the student s took turns feeling the clay roof of the model farmhouse. Colin Browne said that he knew about fireplaces and heard about chimneys in literature but never exactly connected the two. I thought often at the Linden Lodge School for the Blind that the concepts of wisdom, knowledge, Divine Revelation were sometimes in the simplest of thoughts.

Libby Lou and Colin Browne quickly became best friends. Their relationship was special, and the students heard them everywhere together. Colin Browne took Libby Lou under his wing from her first day at the school as he did with most new students. They always sat side-by-side in class. They ate lunch together, and they shared their afternoon tea together. Linden Lodge was a boarding school, and their laughter mingled together as they eased around the property every evening. When Colin Browne finally admitted to himself that he loved the sound of Libby Lou's voice, Colin Browne was the only one surprised. All students, teaching staff, administrative staff were very happy with the budding love relationship. Libby Lou seemed to adjust well with the help of Colin Browne to the Linden Lodge system of daily life and education. Colin Browne, who was the most popular student on campus, had a girlfriend.

Libby Lou was not alone in her love for Colin Browne. Everybody loved Colin Browne. He generated love all around him in his daily life. But daily living was difficult for Colin Browne. He was blind from birth, and he had a gimped-up left side. He had a deformed left arm that ended in a little claw. He had a partially paralyzed left leg, and he had to drag it along behind him. His balance was terrible, and the least amount of pressure against his body knocked him hard to the ground. Colin Browne was a complete physical wreck and the most loved person on the campus. He never complained. He always tried to the very best of his abilities. His thirteen-year-old mind was most curious intellectually. The entire teaching staff always appreciated his beautiful smile. He wasted his smiles on his blind peers, but his golden laughter always put everyone in a good mood. Colin Browne connected with all people because he was alive and full of love.

The Headmaster scheduled a fire drill at the end of my first week of teaching the blind students. It was Libby Lou's third week at the school and her first fire drill without her eyesight. The Headmaster informed the teaching staff at 8:00 a.m. on Friday that the drill was in a few hours at precisely 11:00 a.m. He again threatened disciplinary action for any speaking out of turn, for helping students through the traumatic experience, for revealing the time of the drill. He asked me to closely observe Libby Lou as part of the responsibilities for a post analysis by the school psychologist.

There were twenty-two desks in our classroom. The desks were small tables side-by-side with individual chairs. They formed a basic squared-off, upside-down U with the teacher's podium in the open end at the front of the classroom. The ten students in the class sat anywhere on the outside of the U and faced into the center. When a person stood at the podium, the windows were to the right, and the door was to the left in the corner behind the podium. There were no permanent structures along any of the walls to hinder the students during a change of class or a fire drill. During the normal changes of classes, students grabbed backpacks, pushed chairs under desks, reached for a wall to scramble left or right, bumped into each other, and log-jammed at the door.

Libby Lou sat next to Colin Browne in the far right corner of the classroom by the windows. Colin Browne always sat on the right in a desk farthest from the door and the chaos during a change of class. He rationalized, "I feel sunshine during class and walk civilized with Libby Lou to our next class." His positioning meant that Libby Lou was also very far from the door for her first fire drill as a blind person.

I was nervous for that particular fire drill. I tried to teach while my mind raced through my checklist: check the clock on back wall, door open, walls clear of obstacles, check clock, windows closed, empty chairs pushed under desks, check clock, scan students and count heads, backpacks under desks, books off floor, check clock. Colin Browne was no help for my frayed nerves. I narrated a disjointed cultural story about living in New York City. I described standing one hundred floors above ground on the observation deck of the Empire State Building. I babbled something about seeing on clear days the green expanse in Central Park to the north, the gray Brooklyn Bridge to the east, the metallic Statue of Liberty to the southwest. I used too many sight-words. Colin Browne often challenged my poor choice of words for clarification.

I tried again and focused on feeling the swirling winds at the top of the Empire State Building and on hearing the traffic far below. I finally got on a descriptive roll, and the story line developed nicely. Again Colin Browne's good right hand went up. He asked the most serious question, "Beg your pardon, Sir, beg your pardon, but what exactly would a person do if you were up one hundred floors on the observation deck, and let's say there was a fire on the 80th floor?" I looked around the classroom into sightless but alert eyes of twelve people, and I was humbled. Colin Browne asked the question in all of their minds just minutes before a fire drill that discombobulated me as a sighted person. They stared at me and waited to hear the truth.

It became a theological and a special teachable moment for me. I did not share pragmatic things learned from my uncle, a New York City firefighter with a specialization in upper floor escapes. I talked about basic trust in God and in people to not abandon an individual in negative times. I mentioned the need of all people, not just blind students, to develop a strong faith in the help from God during every difficulty. I suggested that hope in God's help was also a key virtue to spiritually cultivate. In a catastrophe hope kept a person focused until help arrived. I spoke about the love of God for each individual and about the love of individuals for others resulting in the assistance during emergencies. The remarks introduced the concept of prayer voiced before experiencing horrible tragedies as part of a spiritual self-discipline and character development. I asked the students to think about my talk during a silent three-minute meditation.

I stood at the podium and silently looked at the second hand tick towards 11:00 a.m. When the second hand hit the number twelve exactly, the fire alarm blared. It produced a loud obnoxious sound of a gong that made me jump. Libby Lou was in my direct line of vision. She literally rose frightened completely out of her chair, and then she bounced back down into a sitting position. The other students went quickly and silently into automatic pilot. They paired-up and stood pushing the chairs under desks. The inside person found the wall. The outside people hooked two fingers onto insider's left elbow. The pairs rotated counter-clockwise out of the room at warp speed.

Libby Lou sat for a few precious seconds to collect herself. She reached to her left to pair-up just like in her training. Unfortunately for her, that student found a friend to his left, and the new pair circled directly behind Libby Lou while she reached left into empty space. The training manual said that if no one was to the left, reach to the right and find a partner. Libby Lou reached right as far as she could reach. Unfortunately, at that moment Colin Browne reached to his right. Because of his gimped-up left side, Colin reached awkwardly at a strange angle with his good right hand. Libby Lou only missed touching Colin Browne's back by an unseen inch. She sat straight in her desk and froze wide-eyed with fear. Blood visibly drained from her face. She wore a mini skirt with a short-sleeve white blouse, and I watched the blood drain from her arms and legs. She went from a rosy complexion to ashen white in seconds. Her skin was notably whiter than her blouse. She sat in total fear with immobile muscles and a blank stare. Libby Lou never said a word. Big tears dropped silently down each cheek.

It seemed an eternity to Libby Lou, but in real time it was just a few seconds until Colin Browne tapped her shoulder with his good right hand. Oh, Libby Lou acted like Colin Browne was Jesus Christ coming back from the dead again! Libby Lou jumped off her chair, threw her arms around Colin Browne's neck, and gave Colin Browne a big kiss. Colin Browne, totally stunned by the big kiss, desperately struggled with the extra weight around his neck to regain his balance before toppling both of them embarrassingly to the ground. He finally succeeded in unlocking Libby Lou's tight headlock with his good right hand. Colin Browne regained his balance and his ruffled composure. He grabbed her right hand and decisively put it on his left elbow. He marched into the hall dragging her and his bad left leg behind him.

The rest of the fire drill went according to the manual. At the end of class, I asked Libby Lou to stay and talk privately. I informed her with nervous frustration, "I observed you throughout the fire drill, and you should never give up, and you should never stop trying even if afraid, and besides if the gong was for a real fire, I was going to help you out of the building no matter what the bad consequence with the Headmaster." Libby Lou told me, "Yes, Sir, I understand, but I was so terribly afraid, and I will try better next time, I promise, Sir, I will." After we both finally calmed down, I asked Libby Lou to share with me the worst part of her experience of the fire drill. Libby Lou looked at me with dead eyes and said, "Sir, I sat in my chair, and I heard the chairs pushed under desks. Then I heard the tennis shoes quickly leaving the room. The very worst part for me was that I thought all my friends were leaving me."

B. APPLIED THEOLOGY – PRAYERS OF THANKSGIVING

"I thought all my friends were leaving me." People, this is exactly why all Teenagers should try their best to love God with their whole hearts/minds/souls, and love neighbors as selves. Teenagers have a tremendous sway over each other. The individual Teen and Teens in corporate groups utilize a power to sway other Teens for good and bad results. If Teens use sway power to manufacture abandonment, fear, pain on other Teens, Teenagers do not love God. If Teenagers refuse to help Teens under negative sway power, Teens love their neighbors even less. It is wrong for Teens to misuse the sway power over other Teens, and it is bad for Teenagers to use their gifts from God to hurt other Teens.

The sway power of Teenagers over each other translates into negative and positive peer pressures. All Teenagers know and feel different degrees of peer pressure from psychological, sociological, and personal perspectives. Teenagers also incorporate a spiritual perspective concerning the power to sway other Teens. However, negative sway power or negative peer pressure blasts Teens, and with the sensationalism of the press all hear and see the bad news. A positive sway power for Teens or positive peer pressure exists and quietly affects Teens deeply, but rarely do Teens hear examples in the news or see occurrences in newspapers. Jesus gave all Teens the Greatest Commandment to love God with hearts, minds, souls above all things and love neighbor as self. Consequently, Jesus put a premium on the spiritual or theological perspective of the Teen to sway or pressure self and other Teens for the positive.

Three out of four New Testament Gospels recorded the priority of Jesus to love God and love neighbor (Mt.22:34-40; Mk.12:28-34; Lk.10:25-37). Therefore, it was very important to post-resurrectional preaching of the Twelve Apostles, who spent time and energy with the historical Jesus. It was also very important to Christian writers of Gospels in the first century. But Jesus said nothing new or original to his audiences with his specific details on love. Jesus combined the ancient Old Testament wisdom from Deuteronomy 6:4 about love God with Leviticus 19:18 about love neighbor to form his new vision on how to act daily. The original genius and the new vision of Jesus were the combinations of the two ideas with the priority to love as the Greatest Commandment.

Nevertheless, it was a real trick question 2,000 years ago. There were the ancient Ten Commandments from Yahweh to Moses, and there were also 613 other laws governing everything from work on the Sabbath to strict dietary rules (Anderson, <u>Understanding the Old Testament</u>, p. 536). Jesus thwarted attempts to get him into trouble with the ruling Sanhedrin of the Temple hierarchy by putting love of God above all the commandments instead of claiming one command of Yahweh greater than the other commands. The genius and new vision of Jesus with his Greatest Commandment put the top priority on conversion of heart and mind to love of God and love of neighbor. The genius and vision of Jesus extends from ancient times to impact modern Teenagers.

Sway powers and peer pressures are at times so powerful that Teens feel a real need to communicate with God for the help to love God, love neighbor, resist negative peer pressure, foster or choose positive peer pressure. Communication with God is prayer. Bringing God into everyday Teenage existence to help with everyday Teen problems and everyday Teen decisions to stay positive with self and other Teens elevates prayer-life, jump-starts Teen spirituality, treats God and neighbor with love, dignity, respect.

However, Teenagers need to understand that Jesus commanded Teenagers to love God and one another. It is a command, not a suggestion to do whenever the Teenager feels like it. The Greatest Commandment includes all people at all times. It is not a situation where a person picks and chooses only certain individuals to love. Jesus gave the all-inclusive command, and true Christians love all people including the most difficult people. After all, even the happy pagans love their friends.

Libby Lou was a very easy person for the Teens to love because she had a beautiful personality. None of her new friends intended to hurt her. Nevertheless, a sightless Libby Lou heard, thought, felt the serious abandonment by her new friends whom blindness forced her to trust. Libby Lou saw only a wall of black during the fire drill. She analyzed later and then understood and rationalized the mental and emotional pains from loneliness, marginalization, the freeze-out from groups. It was a harsh lesson to learn at an early age. The precious seconds of paralyzing fear impacted her life and relationships. Libby Lou coped with fear of fire as a blind person. She strengthened her friendships, especially with Colin Browne, based on mutual trust and a true respect. Libby Lou understood the sway power which people have over each other. She learned that abandonment always hurts even if the intentions of friends were innocent.

It is not easy to love people who are mean to us. It is hard work in the Teen American culture to consistently love the unpopular, the powerless, and the poor. This love requires a real sacrifice of self. It necessitates a bowing of the individual will to the command of Jesus. Jesus showed this type of love to us in three years of public ministry. His unselfish love for all people culminated in the crucifixion. From the cross Jesus asked God the Father to forgive all people who hurt him. That request for forgiveness included the Pharisees, who set Jesus up for death. The Pharisees thought that they were good by maintaining the status quo of the Hebrew religion at the expense of Jesus' physical life. Jesus' request to God the Father for forgiveness of mean people also included Roman soldiers who pounded spikes into his flesh and speared him in the side for the sake of the Peace of Rome, the Pax Romana.

About 2,000 years after his death on the cross Jesus challenges all Teens to exhibit a holy love for God and other people. This holy love requires so much trust in God that it is too difficult to do alone. Teens must ask God for help to love enemies and the marginalized. This communication with God is prayer. Jesus prayed with people to God the Father during his public life, and his example teaches Teens the need for public prayer. When he was alone among friends at his agony in the Garden of Gethsemane before his arrest, Jesus prayed, and his example teaches Teens the need for serious private prayers during all serious circumstances. Jesus epitomizes the spiritual role model for Teenagers concerning the real necessity of prayer. But Teens must elevate individual prayer-life above a kindergarten level, if Teens are to love as Jesus loved.

Observe a kindergarten child of God. Note how little persons ask for things: "Gimme this, gimme that." Kindergarten prayers fit into the same mold. Teenagers in the American culture have many years of experience with this type of prayer. Teens are excellent at asking for stuff from God because they continually do prayers of petition. Teens are excellent at the "gimme this/gimme that" type of prayer, and the list is almost endless:

- God, give me an A on the test,
- God, give me a boyfriend/girlfriend,
- God, give Dad a better job so he doesn't yell as much,
- God, give us a new car so "old banger" doesn't embarrass me,
- God, give us a better house in the right neighborhood,
- God, give me $150 tennis shoes instead of blue light specials,
- God, give Grandpa a cure for cancer,
- God, give Mom and Dad love again so they don't get a divorce,
- God, give Mom a life so she'll get off my back,
- God, give me a spot on the cheerleaders' squad,
- God, give me a starting position on the football team,
- God, give me a last second shot and let me make it,
- God, give me popularity with the right crowd,
- God, give me lots of money,
- God, give me the right fashions and labels on my clothes,

- God, give me an invitation to the right party,
- God, let my team win and be No. 1,
- God, gimme this, gimme that, please, please, etc.

When my daughter, Maria, was in kindergarten, we shared our night prayers by filling in the blanks. I said, "God, please bless ___." Maria said, "Daddy." I repeated, "God, please bless ___." Maria replied, "Mommy." I continued, "God, please bless ___." Maria yelled, "My dog, Sally," and giggled. There seemed no end to the "God blesses" and the fill in the blanks. When we tired, we stopped our prayers.

There is nothing wrong with the gimme-this prayer and the fill-in-the-blank prayer. Simple prayers from Teenage hearts are always beautiful communications with the Almighty God. The Holy Spirit of Jesus teaches Teens the "Our Father." It includes a premium prayer of petition for "our daily bread" which embodies all Teen needs. The Holy Spirit of Jesus also teaches Teens to "ask and receive" and to "seek and find" and to "knock and open" which are prayers of petition (Mt.7:7-8). However, is it best to only do prayers of petition with the kindergarten formula? Nobody wants the Teen body of a young lady or a young man to remain the same physical size as a kindergartner. Nobody wants the Teenager's psychology to stay the same as the kindergartner. Isn't it a shame if the spiritual life of a Teen stays on a kindergarten level? Spiritual growth necessitates elevating individual prayer-life of the Teen above a kindergarten level. To love perfectly, as Jesus loves, compels the individual to grow spiritually. A quality response to the command to love God and neighbor intertwines with spiritual growth.

Teens, please, allow me to insert a disclaimer at this point in the manuscript. My intention is not to degrade or belittle the prayers of kindergarten people. Even less do I want to disparage any Teenage prayer by calling a Teen's prayer on a kindergarten level as if there is something wrong with the Teenager or with the Teen's prayer. My intention is not to judge Teen prayer as if a Teen's prayer is not good enough. My intention is not to lay spiritual guilt on Teenagers. God knows, Teens know, and I know that too much guilt is already laid on Teens by some hypocritical characters. I define prayer as a spiritual communication with God. Consequently, my intention is to empower all Teens with the understanding that the Teen has the potential to communicate spiritually through prayer with the Most Holy God. My intention is to encourage all Teens with the realization that the Teen is in relationship with the Most Holy God. My intention is to help all Teens with the perception that a spiritual relationship with the Most Holy God has potential to go from good to better to best because of the love of the Most Holy God for Teens. My intention is to help all Teens with the realization that the Teenager has freedom of choice to choose to pray to the Most Holy God.

Regardless of my best intentions and of my manner in phrasing sentences, by the Teenage years people who pray are excellent at prayers of petitions. Nonetheless, Teenagers know that it is rude for people to never say, "Thank you." Teenagers know that proud and arrogant people rarely say, "I'm sorry," and mean it. All Teens know that people should only worship God, the Creator of everything seen and unseen, known and unknown, non-living and living. Prayers of thanksgiving, forgiveness, and adoration are also legitimate types of prayer alongside petitions. When Teens say "thank you" to God, do Teens really mean thanks or is it just phraseology? When the Teen says "I'm sorry" to God, is the Teen truly sorry for breaking the laws of love and for offending God/neighbor, or is the Teen just sorry that the Teenager got caught too close to the negative action? Do Teens honestly bow to God's will and worship God above all things, above power, above status, above money? If the Teen wants meaning and value in prayers, the Teen must experience a conversion of heart. If the Teen wants "I thank God" or "I'm sorry God" or "I worship God" to mean something other than lip service, the Teen must experience a conversion of mind.

It is a conscious and individual choice to pray. Prayer is a part of the individual's faith journey which spirals upward to God. Prayers represent a way of life. It sometimes takes a lifetime to develop a meaningful growth in prayer and to maintain an upward spiral to the Most Holy God. Teens may not realize the start for the conversion of mind and heart to God. Teens definitely realize the conscious effort to elevate prayer-life and the hard work to maintain a positive attitude towards prayer. Individual choices, conscious efforts, ongoing hard work do not necessarily equate with "prayer is drudgery." A person, who is excellent at sports, experiences the same three things as a way of life without bemoaning every little ache or pain. An individual choosing to elevate prayer-life is not alone and does not live in total isolation. All humans have a holy longing for the Most Holy God. All humans have an inner desire and the need to pray to God especially during hard times. Prayer taps into the life of God, the All-Powerful Creator of everything. Prayer generates a relationship with the Holy Spirit of Jesus. Prayer produces enough grace to love not hate.

Whenever a Teenager decides to elevate his or her prayer-life, a suggestion is to start with the individual's level of religious knowledge and spiritual understanding. Test and retest thoughts and feelings about familiar prayers. For example, Teens are excellent at prayers of petition. Teens can shift the focus of their petitions by asking God for the help to jump-start their spiritual lives. God freely gives Teens the grace to spiritualize themselves. Shifting focus of petitions may include requests to God for virtues such as the spiritual strength and courage to offset the negative peer pressure and the negative sway power to abuse sex, drugs, and alcohol. No one knows if or when a Teen prays for virtues to offset potential vices. Prayer is between the Teenager and God. God knows and God responds when a Teen concentrates on lifting mind and heart to God.

If a Teenager within the Catholic theology chooses, the Teen has access to Mass and Holy Eucharist to elevate prayer-life. The Mass is the premium prayer incorporating all the descriptions of prayer. It includes prayers of thanksgiving, adoration, forgiveness/healing, and petition. Mass expresses concepts of a corporate spiritual character, which helps the transition from the individual worship to a community worship of God. The Mass fuses Holy Scripture with the Holy Spirit of Jesus. The Holy Eucharist is the most legitimate source of grace and holiness to elevate prayer-life and the spiritual communication with God. If Teens don't get anything out of the Mass and the Holy Eucharist, Teens need to try worshiping God by putting personal and individual prayers into the Mass and into a Holy Communion with the Most Holy God.

If a Teenager has a gripe against the man in the Priest or against other Christians in a worshiping community, especially with hypocrisy of saying one thing and doing another, please remember to cut the people some slack. All people are on individual faith journeys, and everybody is at a different spot in a difficult journey. Some are further along the spiritual journey than others. Individuals on this side of the grave are all incomplete since nobody experiences the totality of the awesome God before death. So, Teens, cut the incomplete person some slack just as Teens want God to cut them some slack for their failures and omissions.

A gripe against any individual is a lousy reason for the Catholic Teenager to shy away from the Mass and the Holy Eucharist. It is unwise to let the judgments of individual surface sanctity negate the grace and holiness of God. Mass and Holy Eucharist are parts of a two thousand-year tradition that offers billions of people a response to a Holy God. Teens, who nitpick a few individuals and block their own personal responses to Almighty God, do not love God above all things and neighbor as self. Two basic facts become important to prevent bogging down individual spirituality: (1) God is a unity of love for each individual Teenager, (2) God also has faith and hope in the individual Teen to choose love of God with whole heart, mind, soul.

The easiest way for the Teenager to elevate individual prayer-life above a kindergarten level is to simply concentrate on thanking God for all blessings without petitioning for anything new. God blesses all individuals. Teens know that God blesses each person differently. Some Teenagers are great athletes, and others are great at math. Some never seem to study. Others are rich. Some are physically beautiful. Other Teens are popular. Some are intellectually brilliant. Other Teenagers have beautiful smiles and are happy. Some can float in or out of any clique of Teens and are welcomed by all. Other Teens have good and holy parents, but some have parents who beat up their Teens. God blesses a few Teens with the maximum number of positive blessings.

Regardless of the quantity of blessings, God blesses all Teens with a quality in the blessings. Most Teens, like most people, take these blessings for granted. Teens take their eyesight for granted. When was the last time the Teenager thanked God for the gift and the blessing of eyesight? Libby Lou's parents spent over one million dollars to buy back her eyesight, and they failed. Colin Browne was not only blind from birth but also had a gimped-up left side. When was the last time the Teen thanked God for the gift and the blessing of the ability to run? Teenagers take blessings for granted. Can you imagine, men, a world without seeing beautiful ladies? Ladies, can you imagine a world without seeing young men smile at you? Can any Teenager imagine a world without the sight of sunsets, flowers, rainbows, other Teens? Is it time to elevate the individual prayer-life above a kindergarten level? Is it time to thank God for the ability to see before asking for more stuff? Is it time to love God and neighbor as Jesus loves?

C. PLEASE, CONSIDER THE FOLLOWING:

(1) Do a three-minute meditation with eyes closed, racket blocked out, thoughts/feelings concentrating on, "Thank you, God, for my eyesight"...
(2) Create a list with people, places, things that you thank God for... i.e. eyesight, ability to run, ability to feel, ability to think, boyfriend, girlfriend, best friend, T. V., telephone, sound system, Mom, Dad, brat brother/sister, sports, snow-covered mountains, lakes, rivers, smiles, laughter, pizza, burgers, cars, malls, dances, rainbows, video games, internet, music, beach, movies, trees, sunsets, flowers, sun, stars, Teens, cheese dip, electricity, Grandparents, lights etc., etc.
(3) Compose a home-made prayer of thanksgiving to almighty God which you can think and feel several times throughout the day... remember, it's between you and your God...
(4) Try loving God and neighbor above your own will... and with kindness...

CHAPTER 2

LOVE NEIGHBOR...BULLY
PRAYERS OF FORGIVENESS

A. BULLY

Let me give all Teenagers another good reason to love God and neighbor: Bully. Both Bully and Colin Browne were blind from birth, and that is exactly where the similarities stopped. Everyone loved Colin Browne. Nobody loved Bully.

Bully was thirteen years old, five feet tall, about three feet wide. Bully was totally obnoxious and mean. He was a big, fat, old bully. Bully chose meanness because he felt unloved. Bully was not only blind from birth. He also had a very rare blood disorder. According to his medical records, there were only seven people in the world at the time with the same blood disorder. The others were dead by the time they were ten years old. Bully became part of medical history by living for thirteen years. Bully's parents signed off his legal rights to some pharmaceutical companies for money. Bully was a guinea pig for the new wonder drugs. Research scientists changed pills and dosages regularly as they tried to figure out Bully's longevity. One week, Bully sat comatose in a corner looking like a big fat toad frog. The next week, he pinged off the walls. The only constant throughout the mood swings was that he was always mean.

Whenever Bully got into trouble, it was the same old routine. The teaching staff marched Bully to the Headmaster's office. Bully sat in the big leather chair reserved for honored guests. The Headmaster started talking civilized, but ended ranting and raving. Bully always sat quietly until the Headmaster exhausted his frustrations. Invariably the Headmaster asked the ending question, "Why do you always act like a big bully?" Bully always sighed and answered, "What's it matter — nobody loves me — and besides, I should be dead."

Bully had a very distinct advantage over the other blind students. Bully could "see." He wore very thick glasses, and he distinguished shades of darkness. On bright sunny days, Bully closed his bad left eye, opened wide his good right eye, and moved his head quickly in all directions. He saw different shades of black to the point that he picked out a motionless person against a wall. He did not know who the person was until the person talked, but he knew the person was there. Bully considered small people fair game, and his nasty attitude made him dangerous. The teaching staff did not worry as much on cloudy days or after dusk. However, on bright sunny days the staff's constant question was, "Where is Bully?"

Bully's favorite foods were french fries and Snickers candy bars. Beware of Bully whenever french fries or any Snickers candies were around the school! The blind students went to the cafeteria every school day during afternoon tea to practice eating different kinds of foods. Nobody wanted to sit next to Bully after he went through the chow line. Teachers monitoring Bully's table did not worry if the day was overcast or if peas were on the menu. Bully hated peas. Peas rolled around his plate, and he could not shovel enough peas into his mouth. He left teatime predictably hungry after trying to graze on the peas. Unfortunately, the teachers always had real problems if the cafeteria served french fries on a sunny day. Bully lost his common sense and became a terror.

The feeding scenario was the same routine on the bright sunny days. Bully started eating his fries in a civilized manner under close scrutiny. The teacher watched him use his fork to locate, pierce, eat one fry at a time. Lulled into a sense of false security, the teacher usually turned to work responsibilities at another table. Bully instantly went into a feeding frenzy. He closed his bad left eye, opened wide his good right eye, moved his head quickly in every direction. Bully used smell and natural radar to locate all fries. Bully quickly stabbed with his fork two or three fries from the student's plate on his left. The teacher rotated to work Bully's table, and Bully serenely ate one fry at a time simply languishing in culinary delight. The teacher turned to the other table, and in a heartbeat Bully speared three or four fries from the student's plate on his right. The teacher turned to check on Bully, and again noticed Bully thoroughly savoring another fry. But Bully's mound of french fries was similar to Jesus' loaves and fishes because his pile of fries grew instead of diminishing. Bully was slick, and the interplay continued throughout teatime.

The interactions ended when Bully ate all french fries or when he overstepped propriety. Greed was his downfall. Bully usually went after somebody's last french fry, and he ended by stabbing someone with his fork. Whenever Bully drew blood, all hell broke loose with loud screams of pain and the real tears. Bully totally destroyed the English civilized prim and proper tea at the blind school. A teacher helped the innocent sufferer with bloody hand to the School Infirmary for a bandage and an extra-strength aspirin.

A second teacher marched bad Bully to the Headmaster's office for the usual harangue. Bully always sat silently in the big leather chair reserved for honored guests, and the frustrated Headmaster went through his spiel. Bully's grand finale only came when the tired Headmaster ran out of steam. He ended with the simple question, "Why do you always act like a big bully?" Bully always sighed and answered, "What's it matter — nobody loves me — and besides, I should be dead." Again, Bully made his point.

Bully never drew blood when he munched on his other favorite food, Snickers candy bars. The blind school had an elongated closet that the students called "Candy Store." Bully was the best customer, and he spent all his weekly allowance on Snickers bars. His money usually played out by midweek, and then Bully stole the candy. The door to the Candy Store had a solid lock in the handle of the door. Bully picked it at night in seconds. Whenever the student workers complained about a low inventory of Snickers bars, the Headmaster confronted Bully. Bully smiled from ear to ear and always said, "Must be that big, old, fat rat I keep hearing in the middle of the night."

At the special request of the Headmaster, the maintenance crew installed a big heavy hasp on the door of the Candy Store. It came with a high-dollar padlock and only the one key. The most pragmatic Headmaster secured the key in the locked desk drawer in his locked office. The set-up barely slowed Bully down on weekends when he needed a fix on Snickers.

The Linden Lodge School for the Blind was a boarding school. The 250 students stayed on campus throughout the week. On the weekends, the local students from London went home. They invited classmates home for the weekend. Students went home on Friday at noon and returned to school on Sunday by 8:00pm. Colin Browne went home with someone different every weekend. Bully, who lived in Liverpool, never went home with anybody. Bully usually spent the weekends by himself at the school.

As a matter of fact, Bully rarely went to his own home even on the holidays. Bully spent the prior Christmas at the Headmaster's home when his parents made really lame excuses about no money for transportation. Bully spent the regular school holidays with Mr. McMillan, the English teacher, and Mrs. McMillan, the school nurse. They lived in the caretaker's cottage at the entrance of the school. Bully seldom left the campus. He was alone on the weekends. He prowled the buildings and property. Bully knew every nook, cranny, and hiding place. Day or night did not matter to the blind boy looking for adventure with the freedom to rove the campus on the weekends. The school hired an old retired man for weekend security to watch the property and Bully. The security man lived at the school on the weekends, and Bully checked in with him at mealtimes. The guard was no match for a free Bully especially after dark when the playing fields were equal. Bully was alone and free.

When Bully worked up an appetite for a weekend Snickers bar, he simply helped himself to the case in the Candy Store. By the time church bells tolled the midnight hour on Friday, Bully stashed enough Snickers to last the weekend. He ate all the incriminating evidence as the fuel for his personal freedom. When confronted on Monday morning by the Headmaster, Bully smiled from ear to ear and went into his big-fat-rat dialogue. After the installation of the hasp and the high-dollar lock, the Headmaster truly wondered about rats in school.

Bully made his nightly commando runs without leaving a trace of evidence for the burglaries at the Candy Store. His weekend stealth routine was simple and brilliant. Bully switched off the lights at the main breaker box in the administration building. When the security guard went very slowly and carefully with his flashlight into the dark basement to check the breakers, Bully raided the Candy Store. The hasp and padlock were no problem for the Junior James Bond, alias Bully the slick and hungry one. He never messed with the high-dollar padlock side of the hasp on the door. Bully left no evidence of any tampering with the padlock or with the hinged metal strap that fit over the staple secured by the lock.

Bully's secret was that he took a screwdriver to the other end of the hasp. Bully took out three screws holding the hinged part of the hasp to the doorjamb. Voila! The door opened in seconds without a scratch on the high-dollar padlock with only the one key under tight security in the Headmaster's office. Bully scoffed up a Snickers bar while he filled his backpack with his weekend stash. He replaced the three screws in the hasp and skedaddled at warp speed. He scarfed down rewards from yet another successful undetected commando run throughout the weekend. Bully ate candy at his leisure with a big smile on his fat face. Bully was free to roam totally energized by his second favorite food. Bully almost forgot that he was alone on the weekends.

None of the students or the teaching staff forgot the two favorite foods of Bully or his preferred game. The favorite game of Bully was "airplane," and it was dangerous. He knew the property and all the hiding places to sneak in a game of airplane. He gave no clues for the start of his hazardous action. The only inkling of a hint for a start time was the perfect combination of weather and Bully's meanness. Bully only played his game of airplane on bright sunny days when it was advantage Bully. The optimum time for the maximum in Bully meanness and pain was the end of the school day at 3:00pm. It got to the point where everyone, except Bully, dreaded 3:00pm on bright sunny days. Let me explain the logistics for Bully's game of airplane.

Linden Lodge School for the Blind was historically a rich man's house on nearly seven acres of property in the London suburbs. For hundreds of years the huge estate passed from father to the first son until a final generation had no direct heirs. The last character deeded all property and the buildings to the blind school. The main building was a fifty-room mansion in the old days. The school renovated the bottom two floors into administrative offices and the upper two floors into the dormitories and bedrooms. The classrooms were in the new separate rectangular two-floor building about seventy yards behind the main building. Buildings strategically placed around the back of the property housed the indoor swimming pool, the School Infirmary, a gym, and other dorms. The original Caretaker/Gatekeeper Cottage at the front gate was a renovated home for Mr. McMillan (the English teacher) and his wife (the school nurse). I lived in a spare bedroom upon their kind invitation and with the approval of the Headmaster.

Wide sidewalks connected all buildings. The landscaping was impeccable with flower gardens, playing fields, foliage interspersed throughout the property. The girls especially loved the smell of the bloomed flowers, but the blind students never saw the sheer physical beauty of Linden Lodge. The layout of the land and especially the high quality of education made the Linden Lodge School for the Blind truly a showcase for innovative responses to special needs of blind students. Professional visitors both nationally and internationally were always on the campus to observe and to hopefully duplicate the excellent system in other areas of the world. When Bully played his favorite game of airplane, he repeatedly sent injured blind students to the Infirmary. Bully always gave a black eye to the entire Linden Lodge system of progressive blind education under the national and international microscopes. Everybody except Bully hated airplane.

A primary sidewalk from the two-floor school building to the main building was extra wide to accommodate the heavy foot traffic. That sidewalk had about a 1½ inch raised lip on the outside edges. None of the students used white canes to motor around school property. The students used canes only when they left the campus to work on mobility or to go home for the weekends. They utilized raised lips on the outside edges of the sidewalks to go between buildings. Students closest to the right edge let the tennis shoe on his or her right foot hit the raised lip every other step. The perfected technique always kept that person to the right. The second student hooked with two fingers onto the left elbow of the first student. Both students stayed to the right of sidewalks as long as the outside person tapped the raised lip with the right foot on every other step. People rarely bumped into the oncoming traffic because everybody stayed to his or her right.

The busiest time for the sidewalk traffic was 3:00-3:30pm when the school staggered the dismissal for the day. The vast majority of students were on the primary sidewalk between the school and the main building at the same time. Some hustled to the dorms to drop off books and change clothes. The early-outs returned quickly from the dorms on their way to favorite free-time activities. The primary sidewalk safely handled three Teens hooked together going slowly in one direction and four little people hooked together coming slowly from the opposite direction.

At the start of the free time, five or six Teens might hook together while seven or eight little people hooked and scurried towards them. The three o'clock freedom generated a warp speed and an incredible volume of noise on the primary sidewalk. There were few bumps or bruises as long as the students flared their lines backward from the person on the right edge and inward towards the center of the busy sidewalk. The entire scenario changed horribly on bright sunny days when Bad Bully decided to play his favorite game of airplane.

Bully usually hid in the rose garden next to the school's double doors on a bright sunny day at 3:00pm. Bully hunkered down in the roses, and he stealthily listened with his total focus on the noise level from the primary sidewalk. Mean Bully waited patiently for laughter and the happy sounds to increase to maximum decibels. When the sidewalk was totally full of students, Bully sprang into action. Bully closed his bad left eye, opened wide his good right eye, and moved his head quickly in all directions.

Bully jumped nimbly out of the rosebushes and onto the primary sidewalk. He raised his two arms straight out from his body to the height of his fat shoulders, and he screamed the bloodcurdling word, "Airplane!" Bully waddled down the middle of the sidewalk as fast as his fat legs could go. He thumped the students with the "wings of his airplane" in the back of the head and in the chest. Bully bopped and whacked some others off the sidewalk with his wide-bodied aircraft. His loud obnoxious sounds of jumbo jet engines blasted fear into the minds of the blind students as he closed in on his terrified victims. Bully acted like the primary sidewalk was his personal runway, and it was a total cataclysmic destruction for anyone in the way of Bully's take-off and landing.

In a few microseconds, Bully totally destroyed all semblance of the three o'clock fun and happiness for the entire school. Laughter turned into shrieks of real pain as blind students got squished in the logjam at the doors on both ends of the sidewalk. Little girls jumped in fear off the sidewalk into the big thorny rosebushes. When they eventually regained the sidewalk, they were muddy and bloody with blouses torn into shreds. Airplane was a complete catastrophe. The aftermath of Bully's airplane always included long lines of students at the School Infirmary for large Band-Aids and extra-strength aspirins. Throughout the fiasco Bully just laughed and laughed and laughed.

Bully screeched airplane to a halt when the teachers marched him with a maximum security to the Headmaster's office. Bully sat silently in the big leather chair reserved for the honored guests while the irate Headmaster ranted and raved at him. It was the same old routine ending with the Headmaster's same old question, "Why do you always act like a big bully?" Bully always sighed and answered, "What's it matter — nobody loves me — and besides, I should be dead." Bully was two-thirds right as he made his point again.

All the blind students hated Bully's game of airplane, and they hated Bully because he was so mean. Bully never said that he was sorry for hurting the blind people emotionally and physically. Oh, the Headmaster made him apologize to the students, but the students knew that Bully did not really mean it. He just said that he was sorry to get out of hot water. Bully's negative actions spoke louder than his fake words, "I'm sorry." Bully constantly looked for opportunities to deal another merciless blow. The dangerous situation deteriorated to the point that all the teachers checked the weather at 2:00pm and actively tracked Bad Bully from 2:30-3:30 on the bright sunny days. Bully so terrorized the blind students with his dangerous game that even on a cloudy day without moving an inch Bully yelled the word, "Airplane!" and little blind girls dove for the big thorny rosebushes. Bully remained a bully until he responded to love.

B. APPLIED THEOLOGY – PRAYERS OF FORGIVENESS

People, Jesus commanded Teens to love God above all things and love neighbor as self. It is most difficult to love the bullies of the world. The example for Teens is the prayer of Jesus from the cross for God the Father to forgive all people who hurt him. The example of Jesus is difficult to imitate and emulate. It is possible only if Teens pray from the pain and the sorrow caused by other people for God's special help. Teen peace of mind and spirit, instead of revenge and anger, comes from the God of All Power. There is nothing above or beyond the power of the One True God including a Teen attitude of defensive posturing. No longer is "an eye for an eye and a tooth for a tooth" an acceptable Teenage attitude (Mt.5:38-42; Lk.6:27-36; Ex. 21:23-25; Lev.24:19-20; Deut.19:21).

God commands Teenagers to evolve their spirituality above the human desire for revenge. God commands Teenagers to love their enemies, the bullies of the world. It is a conscious individual choice, accomplishable only with the help of God, to change the Teenage attitude towards the bully. The attitude adjustment and the behavior modification starts with each individual Teen utilizing his or her free will to choose to ask for God's help to forgive. It starts with prayers of forgiveness. It does not start with waiting for bullies of the world to eventually offer kindness to a Teen, and then the Teen responds to the kind bully. The command to love is now, immediate, present, not in the future with all kinds of self-imposed stipulations.

Prayers of forgiveness are personal two-tiered communications with the Most Holy God: (1) individual Teen asks/begs God to forgive self for his/her offenses against the laws of God; (2) individual Teen asks/begs God for the help and the grace to forgive other Teenagers who break Jesus' laws of love towards the individual Teen. These two concepts intertwine throughout the New Testament, but the most poignant tie is in the "Our Father." Jesus taught Teenagers to pray to God the Father: "...forgive us our trespasses, as we forgive those who trespass against us" (<u>Catechism</u>, n. 2759, 2838-45; Mt. 6:12; Lk.11: 4).

"As" is the little two-letter word that makes forgiveness a serious business for all Teens. In the Our Father the individual Teen asks the Almighty and All Just God to forgive the individual as the individual forgives other Teens that hurt him/her. If the individual Teen does not forgive other Teens, the individual asks the Almighty and All Just God to not forgive him/her. The individual Teen condemns self out of his/her own mouth in prayer to God. When Teens pray the Our Father, "as" alerts Teenagers unwilling or too pig-headed to bury the hatchets and to forgive other Teens about the theological connection between personal salvation and forgiveness of others. God's mercy is just, and Teens need awareness of Jesus' connection in prayers of forgiveness between God's mercy to the Teen and the Teen's mercy to other Teenagers.

Teens, please, pray with careful minds and cautious hearts to avoid blurting out or regurgitating memorized prayers without really thinking and feeling what you say. If a Teen is not going to forgive other Teens, it is probably better for the Teen to fall silent with the word "as" in the Our Father. Jesus is a serious spiritual teacher of prayer in the phrase to forgive us as we forgive others. When the Teenager understands the implications of the word "as" in the Our Father, semantics and splitting hairs over the meaning of the words become a very dangerous game to play with the All Knowing God. There is no wiggle room for misinterpretations of the vision of Jesus concerning Teen interactions. Love is the command of God for Teen actions, and forgiveness is the demand of God for Teen reactions. It is much better for the Teen to forgive other Teens for all hurts. The spiritual healing of Teens starts with the love of God for all Teens.

Rational humans eventually and unfortunately break down their spiritual relationships with God and others. Jesus demands with his laws of love that all Teens try to the best of their ability to eliminate the number of breakdowns. The ultimate question becomes a dual personal question: Am I going to truly say, "I am sorry," when I break down, and am I going to truly forgive others when they break down with me? Bully never really meant his "I'm sorry" because he never changed his negative actions until he experienced love. When others hurt him, Bully always held a grudge, sought his revenge, and got his retaliation. Is the Teenager also a hypocrite when the Teenager asks forgiveness and grants forgiveness? Is there any truth and value in the Teen's "I'm sorry" and in the "I forgive you" of the Teen?

Jesus came to save Teens not to condemn. Jesus offers Teens the opportunity to rejoice that God is near each individual. If Teens present their two-fold prayers of forgiveness to the God of All Mercy, Teens have the potential to repair breakdowns in their relationships with the Most Holy God and with peers/neighbors. Experiences in the restorations of friendships dismiss most anxieties from the minds and hearts of Teens as Teens relate to people and to God in peace. Saint Paul suggested that people pray and "then God's own peace, which is beyond all understanding, will stand guard over your hearts and minds, in Christ Jesus" (Phil.4:7). It is the desire for the peace of God that allows individuals to direct all thoughts to truth, honesty, dignity, respect, God. Prayers of forgiveness from the mind and the heart of the Teen lead to God's peace.

When Teens choose to elevate prayer-life above a kindergarten level, prayers of forgiveness become experiences of God's power in responses to Teenage prayers. Some natural tendencies of various Teens are to say wishy-washy prayers of forgiveness and to commit pressure-related common sins. Some supernatural tendencies of certain Teens are to say holy prayers of forgiveness and to perform holy actions. It is the power and love of God that bridges the gap between the ordinary and the supernatural. It is the power and love of God that activates the finest potential of the Teen. It is the Teen's choice to follow natural tendencies and/or supernatural tendencies.

For example, the Headmaster busted Bully for hurting the other students. On the surface for all to hear Bully always said, "I'm sorry." Maybe Bully elevated the words to God in a wishy-washy prayer of forgiveness, and maybe his words indicated a change of heart. But his actions indicated that Bully only said the words to get out of big trouble. Bully chose to commit his pressure-related common sins that continued to break down relationships with his peers/neighbors.

In the American culture, Teens often do the same. Teenagers have a tendency to commit pressure-related common sins. Catholic theologians define a "sin" as any offense against the laws of God, Jesus' laws of love, that ruptures or breaks relationships with God and/or neighbors (<u>Catechism</u>, n.1849-50, 1855-57, 1862-63). Some Teens abuse their bodies with drugs/alcohol, and the abuse breaks down their relationships with peers and parents. Other Teenagers abuse their sexuality, and the abuse breaks down love relationships especially between boyfriends and girlfriends. A lot of Teens commit the brag-and-drag-down-people sins when they lord money, power, status over peers. Numerous Teenagers act like psychological and mental bullies in their relationships with peers. Consequently, Teens commit the pressure-related common sins of pushing and shoving the psychologies and mentalities of other people until they get their way. Manipulation, domination, control freak are not holy words to describe love relationships with people!

a. Acid Tongue

However, the "acid tongue" used by Teens is the most common negative natural tendency and the most common pressure-related sin against neighbor. Certain acids eat through almost everything including steel. Teens say certain words that eat through the spirits of other Teens. By the Teen years, all people experience the wrong side of an acid tongue. It hurts. It is not funny. It destroys existing relationships. It eliminates potential friends. It breaks down spiritual relationships. It creates hate. It stings people in love relationships. It draws out numerous negative reactions. So many negatives spin out of the Teen's acid tongue especially when Teens tag team the weak and the marginalized. The personalities of many Teens are fragile with emerging sexuality and first love of the opposite sex. Teen acid tongues retard the growth of Teenage personalities and spiritualities. The acid tongue does not love peer/neighbor as self, and that makes the acid tongue a sin/offense against the laws of God and against Jesus' laws of love.

The acid tongue is a Teen offense that ruptures and breaks the Teen relationship with the Most Holy God and with neighbors/peers. Unfortunately, offenses of the acid tongue compound and complicate the negative within itself in two other areas to make the breakdown of Teenage spiritual relationships even worse: (1) Teenage sins of omission, (2) bad example of Teenagers for the little people.

The offense of the acid tongue compounds its negatives in Teen sins of omission (Catechism, n. 1853). These sins are offenses of spiritual neglect towards God's laws of love. The omissions leave notable positive spiritual efforts undone possibly because of apathy (lack of spiritual interest). Numerous good and talented Teenagers commit the pressure-related common sins of omission when they do not try to the best of their abilities to be holy. Acid tongues cause a fear in most individual Teenagers. If the acid tongues of a Teenage crowd debilitate another Teen's efforts to be holy, spiritual problems intensify for all involved. God expects much spiritual effort from all Teenagers to always shine spiritually (Mk.4:21-25; Lk.8:16-18; Mt.13:10-12). The more Teenage talents bestowed as gifts from God, the more Teenage spiritual efforts expected as a response to the love of the Most Holy God (Lk.19:11-26; Mt.25:14-30).

The expectations of God for all Teenagers include the use of an individual free will to choose to devote time and energy to the quest for holiness. The individual quest for holiness is not just for Grannies getting ready to die and trying to make their peace with God before judgment. The call to holiness is the challenge of God to elevate the spiritual life and to make a faith journey. By the time a young person reaches Teen years, it is too late for Mom and Dad to fix all spiritual things for their Teenager. Parents can not buy junior and missy into heaven with their dollars or with their parental sanctity and holiness. Parents certainly pray to God for their Teens to make good choices, and they beg God to have mercy on their Teens. Nevertheless, only the Teen gets himself/herself into Heaven.

If a Teen wants to see and enjoy the face of God for all eternity, the Teen must utilize his/her free will to choose holiness. The Teen may not want peers to tag him/her holy, but God needs to tag a Teen holy for the Teen to see the face of God for all time. Teenage sins of omission neglect spiritual duties such as genuine choices to make the best effort to be holy. Teen sins of omission leave certain positive spiritual efforts undone. God calls all Teens to go above and beyond the ordinary. God calls Teens to Himself. If the acid tongue weakens or enfeebles any efforts of the Teen in a personal quest for holiness, the acid tongue is wrong, bad, and unholy. Acid tongue is an offense against God's laws of love. The acid tongue is the pressure-related common sin that forces other Teenagers to sometimes abandon their quest for holiness. The Teenager, who spits acid with trash words at other Teens, needs to slow down and think about his/her actions. A

Teenager, who allows the acid tongue to neutralize a personal quest for holiness, needs to slow down and think about his/her reactions.

Each Teen is accountable and responsible for the acid tongue and for sins of omission. When a Teen fails to say positive spiritual things and fails to try his/her spiritual best, the individual Teen needs to consider the truthful examination of his or her conscience. Every Teen conscience knows right from wrong, enjoins the Teenager to do good and avoid evil, judges all Teenage choices as good or bad (Catechism, n. 1777, 1778-94; Rom.2:14-16, 1:32; Flannery, Vatican Council II, Vol.1., Gaudium et Spes, n.16, all Vat. II quotes in this version). The Teenager "must always obey the certain judgment of his (her) conscience," and the Teen is responsible for eliminating all moral ignorance (Catechism, n.1790-1). Teens know if their lack of spiritual efforts and their acid tongues involve sins/offenses against the laws of God and Jesus' laws of love.

Some Teenagers are good at arguing with their own shadows. However, no time is good for the Teens with aggressive acid tongues and passive sins/offenses of omission to spilt theological hairs with God. It is a much better time for prayers of forgiveness to the God of All Mercy. In the Penitential Rite at the beginning of a Catholic Mass, Teens pray a form of the ancient "Confiteor" (in Latin, "I confess"):

> I confess to Almighty God, and to you, my brothers and sisters, that I have sinned through my own fault, in my thoughts and in my words, in what I have done and in what I have failed to do; and I ask blessed Mary ever virgin, and all the angels and saints, and you, my brothers and sisters, to pray for me to the Lord our God.
> Stravinskas, Catholic Encyclopedia, p.247-8

A priest responds, "May Almighty God have mercy on us, forgive us our sins, and bring us to everlasting life." From Teen acceptance of the responsibility for negative words and neutral spiritual efforts at the beginning of Mass, Catholic Teens move through the mercy and the forgiveness of God to the Most Holy Eucharist and to the positive reception of Holy Communion with the Most Holy God.

However, the offense of the acid tongue also compounds and complicates the negatives within itself in the bad example of Teens to the little people. Kindergartners look up to Teenagers. Teens are the heroes and heroines of the little people. Teens are bigger and stronger than the little people. Teenagers throw the balls farther and catch the balls more often than the little people. Teens run faster and jump higher than the little people. Teens are kind, loving, and funny to the little people. Teens give the little people good hugs. Teens reach stuff on a top shelf. Teens get big scores on the video games. Teens log on the Internet without their parents. Teenagers read big books. Teens add and subtract numbers without using their fingers.

Teenagers are supermen and superwomen to the little people. Little people love Teenagers. Little people want to grow up just like their favorite Teenagers. When the Teenagers utilize acid tongues around the little people, little people want to act just like their favorite Teens...bad problem...big bad problem. I have a good friend whose two sons aged six and eight got kicked out of day care for cussing and cursing other little people. When he asked his sons the meaning of the words, they did not know the meanings, but they heard their favorite Teens use the words. The offence/sin from the acid tongue in all forms compounds negatives with bad example for little people.

Jesus addressed concepts of bad example and of scandal, the worst form of bad example from religious leaders to simple believers (Mk.9:42; Lk.17: 2). Jesus also instructed the disciples on the value of little children. He said that the kingdom/rule of God belonged to them and to enter the kingdom of God the individual must accept the rule/reign of God as a little child (Mt.19:13-5; Mk.10:13-6; Lk.18:15-7). However, Jesus combined his answer to the disciples concerning the question of the greatest person in God's kingdom with a harsh warning against bad example and the scandal of leaders to innocent believers:

> He called a little child over and stood him in their midst and said: 'I assure you, unless you change and become like little children, you will not enter the kingdom of God. Whoever makes himself lowly, becoming like this child, is of greatest importance in that heavenly reign. Whoever welcomes one such child for my sake welcomes me. On the other hand, it would be better for anyone who leads astray one of these little ones who believe in me, to be drowned by a millstone around his neck, in the depths of the sea.' Mt.18:2-6 (N.A.B.)

A millstone in first century Palestine was a basalt rock weighing hundreds of pounds. A donkey usually pulled the stone around the mill to grind the grain into flour. To suggest such an alternative to bad example and scandal meant that Jesus was most serious about avoiding those offenses/sins.

And Teens also make no mistake where Jesus stood on the acid tongue. Jesus declared to the hypocritical Pharisees:

> The mouth speaks whatever fills the mind. A good man produces good from his store of goodness; an evil man produces evil from his evil store. I assure you, on judgment day people will be held accountable for every unguarded word they speak. By your words you will be acquitted, and by your words you will be condemned. Mt.12:34-38 (N.A.B.)

Teens, think about the tendency to commit the pressure-related common sins of the acid tongue. In this passage from Holy Scripture, the evangelist of Mathew's Gospel emphasized final judgment based on the spoken words of the individual. Some biblical scholars think that the concerns of the author were the trash mouths of his time and the problems from abusive language. Possibly, the evangelist/author took the linguistic high ground reflecting an intellectual and a verbal bias against certain words and expressions.

However, when the biblical scholars fast-forward the Gospel of Matthew 2,000 years into our modern times, the theologians interpret more seriously the intent of the evangelist in recording the words of Jesus Christ. Biblical scholars and theologians suggest "a moral and religious sensitivity that one can kill with words, one can sin against the Spirit" (Brown, <u>New Jerome Biblical Commentary</u>, p.654). Teens feel and know the degradation from the reception of the acid tongues and the trash mouths. The fact remains that the harsh words of an individual Teen humiliate, debase, kill another individual's spirit. The acid tongue brings down both the Teen recipient and the Teen user. Although God the Holy Spirit is less sharply defined historically, the individual Teen with acid/trash words directed towards neighbors and peers offends and sins against the Holy Spirit of Jesus.

Teenagers, please note that the divorce of natural parents many times brings Teenagers down to ugly and unholy levels of existence. Divorce is a situation that begs the Teen's prayers of forgiveness and not more gasoline on an open fire. Please, Teens, do not lay guilt on self from the divorce situation. The divorce of natural parents is not the fault of the Teen. Divorce is a breakdown in the love relationship of the parents. The Teen loves both natural parents, and the Teen many times does not understand why both natural parents no longer love each other enough to continue living together.

Teens need to reason from their experiences and to remember the difficulty of maintaining love and longevity in a relationship with the opposite sex. When Mom and Dad love the step-authority in the Teen's life, it is unholy for the Teen to use the acid tongue, a silent treatment, severe mood swings, etc. to agitate the home front. As much as the Teen wants more not less freedom in his/her life, butting heads with the step-authority in the Teen's life is not the best way to get more freedom. Constant head butts make the step-relationships miserable for all in the household. Teens, consider your example in front of the little people also stuck with step-authority in their lives.

Instead of the constant negative Teenage attitude towards the person natural Mom and natural Dad chooses to love, Mom and Dad may need a Teen "friend" to help the new relationship of the natural parent with the step-authority. If the Teenager chooses friendship with natural parent and step-authority, the Teen may need to take the first step to change a child-relationship into a friend-relationship. Teens, please, realize that after the first step a Teen may offer time, energy, emotional strength, courage, and spiritual strength to a new parental relationship. Older Teenagers may offer special healing in relationships with natural parents. The Teen may spin off the deep psychological/emotional/spiritual hurt of divorced parents into a living prayer of forgiveness.

Jesus had the step-authority of Saint Joseph in his life. Jesus and Saint Joseph knew hassles and a deep love in their relationship with a step-authority. Neither hurt Mother Mary. Neither broke their relationship because of step-authority. Neither sinned because of step-authority. Jesus, Saint Joseph, Mother Mary were a holy family because they coped with step-authority in their relationships of love.

b. Concept of Sin

Within the Catholic theology of forgiveness, the concept of sin is a general term that covers many realities. For example, there exists actual sin that is the violation of the moral order. A habitual sin is the sinful state of the soul because of the bad habits from actual sins. The original sin, inherited by all humans, is the sin and evil from the disobedience/pride of the first humans, which resulted in the fallen condition from original holiness. Every sin is an offence against the laws of God.

In the Old Testament of the Bible, sin was a deliberate negative action against the established order of the One True God. Every sin verified internal pride and rebellion against the Supreme God. In the New Testament Scriptures, sins are acts that violate the moral order of God's will and indicate a heart hostile to God's love. Therefore, reconciliation with God requires the conversion of heart and mind to the Most Holy God.

In the 1994 <u>Catechism of the Catholic Church</u>, commissioned by Pope John Paul II and coordinated by Joseph Cardinal Ratzinger, it states:

> Sin is an offense against reason, truth, and right conscience; it is failure in genuine love for God and neighbor caused by a perverse attachment to certain goods. It wounds the nature of man and injures human solidarity ...Sin is an offense against God...Sin sets itself against God's love for us and turns our hearts away from it. Like the first sin, it is disobedience, a revolt against God through the will to become 'like gods'...In this proud self-exaltation, sin is diametrically opposed to the obedience of Jesus, which achieves our salvation. n.1849-50

The 2,000-year Catholic tradition evaluates and categorizes sin according to its seriousness as mortal sin (spiritually death-dealing) or venial sin (slight). A fundamental distinction and difference is that a mortal sin destroys the love and charity in the heart of a man or a woman by the grave/serious violation of the law of God (Catechism, n.1855). Mortal sin involves a radical rupture in the union of God and the individual man or woman. A venial sin is also an offense against the laws of God, but venial sin is less serious. Venial sin does not necessarily turn the individual irrevocably away from God with the preference of inferior good to the God of All Love, who is the ultimate end of all humans. However, it is a flippant effrontery, a shameless boldness, to conclude that offense against the love of the Most Holy God is "only a venial sin."

In traditional Catholic theology, the offense against God requires three conditions together to make the offense a mortal sin: (1) grave or serious matter, (2) sufficiently full knowledge, (3) full consent of the will (Ibid., n.1857). An offense against the laws of the Most Holy God is a mortal sin if the three conditions exist simultaneously at the time of the negative action.

When one out of the three conditions is absent, the Teen offense is a venial sin, not a mortal sin. A correctly formed Teen conscious is crucial in the spiritual process. It is not a time for the Teen to take a chance by toying with the three conditions determining a mortal sin against God. This is not a mind game. The consequences are too serious. Physical death with a mortal sin, a serious offense against laws of God that breaks love relationship with God as determined by God, means a spiritual death in hell for all time. Hell is the absence of the Most Holy God of All Love.

If a Teenager has any question or doubt about the seriousness of the negative action, this is no time to gamble. Teens, please, say immediately to the God of All Mercy from your heart and your mind with truthful meaning that you are sorry for your offense against God. Then, go with humility and ask without negative pride the Catholic priest for spiritual counseling and for his thoughts with regard to the seriousness of your negative action. This is not the time to gamble away your eternity, and this is most definitely not a mind game. The priest trains long years in the seminary to help the Teen through this moral moment. The priest helps the Teen make the correct spiritual interpretation of God's laws in reference to the three conditions for committing a mortal sin. The priest helps the Teenager repair the spiritual damage to the break in relationship between the Teen and the Most Holy God of All Love.

The first condition, which makes a negative action a mortal sin, is serious or grave matter. The Ten Commandments specify serious or grave matter (Ibid., n.1858, 2072-3). They are 10 Commandments of God, not 10 suggestions from God. Jesus did not come to abolish the Ten Commandments, but to fulfill the law and the prophets (Mt.5: 17-20). The seriousness of sin is contingent on the specific negative action and on the wronged person. Moral theologians consider both the action and the harmed person to determine the seriousness of the matter in sin and offense against God's laws. It is not necessarily easy or straightforward work.

For example, murder is more serious than theft. Both negative actions are offenses against God's laws, but not necessarily mortal sins every time there are offenses. The moral theologians question differently the seriousness of the action and the seriousness of the wronged person in the following two scenarios: (1) Is it murder and a mortal sin to defend yourself and your family against a violent armed person when self-defense ends with the death of the intruder? (2) Is it a mortal sin to steal the last $10 of the homeless person when the person living on the streets in the cold of winter has no other money and the theft leaves the homeless person totally destitute without the hope for immediate survival? Hmmm, "Thou shall not kill," and the intruder is dead; "Thou shall not steal," and a homeless person may die of cold or starvation. Without denying the seriousness of death or the lightness of only $10, Teens see the moral complexity in the first condition to make a sin mortal. Contingent on a negative action in relation to a wronged person, the offense against the law of God is a mortal sin when the matter is grave or serious and when the other two conditions exist simultaneously.

The second necessary condition to recognize a negative action as a mortal sin is sufficiently full knowledge. Full knowledge affects the gravity and seriousness of the offense (Ibid., n.1859). If a person does not have full knowledge that the offensive action is in a serious opposition to the laws of God, the sin is not mortal. However, Teen ignorance of the serious offenses against the laws of God is not a very good excuse in a modern Teen age of instant knowledge and instant communication.

Furthermore, principles of the moral and the natural law, written by the One True God in the conscience of every man and woman, exist for Teenagers today. The Ten Commandments, given by the One True God Yahweh to Moses on Mount Sinai in 1280 B.C. about 3,280 years ago, exist for Teenagers today. The laws of love, given by the One True God the Father's Only Son Jesus to his historical contemporaries about 2,000 years ago, exist for Teenagers today. There is only One God. The God of All Love is the God of All Truth and the God of All Justice.

Teenagers fake out parents and peers by rationalizing loopholes in the laws of God just like a Pharisee. But Teens can not fake out the God of All Truth who knows the intentions of the individual's heart and mind. Every Teenager has the God-given conscience to help make distinctions between good and evil. Responsibility of the Teen for individual and corporate actions does not diminish because of a feigned ignorance (Lk.16:19-31) and a hardness of heart (Mk.3:5-6). Teen honesty with self is a key virtue to knowing God through God's laws of love.

The third condition for making a sin mortal is the full consent of the will. Teens must choose to give a deliberate "yes" as full consent to a serious or grave negative act with full knowledge of the gravity and seriousness in the negative action. When the three conditions exist together, the commitment of a serious offense against the laws of God radically destroys and totally ruptures the love and grace of God in the relationship of God and Teen. Offenses against the laws of God committed with malice and a deliberate choice of evil are very serious sins (Catechism, n.1860).

Full consent of the individual's will to a grave or serious violation of God's law involves fundamental human freedom. God is not going to force any Teenager to obey laws because God gives humans the gift of fundamental freedom to choose between good and evil. The Teenager has the capacity to choose evil just as the Teen has the ability to risk love. Fundamental freedom is the fundamental option between selfishness and love. The choice is between self and God, who is the ultimate destiny of individual self. Fundamental freedom allows the option to reject the love of God that is alive in the essence of a man or a woman. This is never a good choice for any Teenager. Rejection of the God of All Love in the depths of the individual's soul is most serious because this type of deep rejection denies the Divine Presence of the Holy Spirit of God. Such a denial surfaces as the pigheaded rejection of the ability of the Almighty God to forgive.

However, the flip side of the rejection and denial of God's love is also a choice of fundamental freedom. A Teen utilizes fundamental freedom of choice to give a full consent of his or her will in the open response to love of God. The resultant plus choice of fundamental freedom has a positive triple potential for the Teen.

First, the Teenager experiences a spiritual growth process that avoids excessive and debilitating guilt trips. The stress is not on the analysis of the full consent to mortal or venial violations of God's law. Focus of spiritual life is on deepening the individual disposition of a Teen soul in relation to the love of God.

Second, the Teen fundamental choice of full consent in an open response to God's love avoids "quitting" the spiritual growth process of the Teen. Teens quit the quest for greater spirituality because of a relative happiness with the status quo of the Teen spiritual journey or because of pressure from other Teens to quit. Avoiding mortal sin makes a good Teenager, but zero mortal sin is not the equivalent to a justification before God, the Judge of all spiritual life. The Judge wants more from the Teen. The Judge wants a conversion of heart and mind stemming from the fundamental Teen freedom to choose God's love and laws over self. Positive results from this Teenage choice are a basic optimism and the inner joys in the Teen spiritual life. However, inner peace from the Divine Presence of God within a Teenage soul necessitates a "no-quit" spiritual attitude. The no-quit spirituality requires continual and positive response to a supernatural tendency of Teens.

The third positive potential from openness to God's love is the nonjudgmental stance toward peers. Surface actions of Teens are not guaranteed signs of interior dispositions of the Teen soul. Is the individual Teen utilizing fundamental freedom for opposition to the laws and love of God or for his/her conversion of heart and mind to the laws and love of God? That is a good question for the Judge. No knowledge of the answer to that question is a good reason for Teens to delete the acid tongues since the sometimes-fragile spirituality of a Teen is at stake. A fragile spirituality is a very good reason for the Teen choice of a nonjudgmental stance and a pure spiritual attitude toward the peers/neighbors/bullies whom Jesus challenges the Teen to love. Teens, please, leave the judgment of Teenagers to the God of All Truth and All Knowledge!

When Teenagers sin by committing voluntary transgressions of divine laws, it is time to elevate prayer-life and to choose prayers of forgiveness. It is time for spiritual healing of the Teen soul, peace of the Teen mind, a fresh Teen start. It is also the time for the ancient virtue of fortitude which is spiritual strength and spiritual courage. It is not a time for negative Teen pride to block repairs of the spiritual ruptures in the Teen's relationship with the Most Holy God.

The penalty for dying in a spiritual condition of mortal sin is hell, and the main punishment of damnation in hell is eternal separation from God (Catechism, n.1033-5, 1861). God is All Love, All Peace, All Truth, All Power, All Wisdom, All Intelligence, All Understanding, All Good, All Dignity, All Respect, All Holiness. Does any Teen really want to choose separation from God for all time? The final penalty for dying in a spiritual condition of venial sin is purgatory which is the final purification in cleansing fire "to achieve the holiness necessary to enter the joy of heaven" (Ibid., n.1030). Heaven is the perfect life with God the Most Holy Trinity. Heaven is a face to face communion of life and love with God the Father, God the Son Jesus Christ, God the Holy Spirit, Mother Mary, Saint Joseph, all angels, all the saints. Heaven is the "ultimate end and fulfillment of the deepest human longings, the state of supreme, definitive happiness (Ibid., n.1024).

When the Teenager dies, the time to accept or reject God ends. According to traditional Catholic theology, the One True God of All Justice, All Knowledge, All Wisdom judges the individual human soul in a particular judgment that results in heaven, hell, purgatory. It is not a trifle situation. This side of the Teenage grave is the time for forgiveness from God and reconciliation with God. Death ends the fundamental Teen option to choose good or evil. The other side of the Teen grave is the time for heaven, pit stop in purgatory, hell for all eternity.

c. Sacrament of Penance and Reconciliation

The Sacrament of Penance and Reconciliation exists within the 2000-year tradition of the Catholic Church. This sacrament is for the Teen who ruptures love relationships with God and peers/neighbors. The Sacrament of Penance is the evolved ritual of the early Catholic community that reconciles sinners with God and Church through the ministry of bishops and priests (Ibid., n.1461-2). The power of God the Holy Spirit to heal is the essence of this Sacrament of Penance and Reconciliation.

If a Teenager chooses to spend time and energy studying Holy Scriptures, the Teen finds concepts of reconciliation and forgiveness on numerous pages of the New Testament Gospels (e.g., Mt.9:2-8; Mk.2:5-12; Lk.5:20-26). Jesus taught the essential message of the divine forgiveness for sinners throughout the three years of his public ministry in his healing the sick and in his parables. The good news of God's gift of reconciliation and forgiveness directly connected the death and the resurrection of Jesus.

However, the sacramental ritual of Penance and Reconciliation evolved in the Catholic Church over the past two millennia into the liturgical rite of today. Teenagers, remember that Jesus Christ was not the president and CEO of an international corporation, and that Jesus left no exact blueprint for the success of day-to-day operations (Jerome, p.1339-40). God the Father and God the Son Jesus shared God the Holy Spirit with the Catholic Church to keep an eye on all things and to direct spiritual matters. Imperfect humans as church leaders sometimes blurred spiritual history with attempts to govern the physical church. The longevity of the physical church solidifies thoughts not only for the need of the corrective directions from God the Holy Spirit but also for the need of the Sacrament of Penance and Reconciliation for everyone.

The Catholic Church utilizes two specific passages from the New Testament Gospels to substantiate divine origins for the sacramental ritual of Penance:

> (A) He said to them, 'But who do say that I am?' Simon Peter answered, 'You are the Messiah, the Son of the living God.' And Jesus answered him, 'Blessed are you, Simon, son of Jonah! For flesh and blood has not revealed this to you, but my Father in heaven. And I tell you, you are Peter, and on this rock I will build my church, and the gates of Hades (hell) will not prevail against it. I will give you the keys of the kingdom of heaven, and whatever you bind on earth will be bound in heaven, and whatever you loose on earth will be loosed in heaven.' Mt.16:15-19
> (B) Jesus said to them again, 'Peace be with you. As the Father has sent me, so I send you.' When he had said this,

he breathed on them and said to them, 'Receive the Holy Spirit. If you forgive the sins of any, they are forgiven them; if you retain the sins of any, they are retained.' Jn.20:21-23

The two passages are foundation stories about the commission of leaders and the postresurrectional authority in the Catholic Church (Jerome, p.659, 984; see also, Mt.18:15-18, 28:18-20; Lk.24:47-8; 2 Cor.5:18). These verses give an enormous power and a tremendous authority to Peter and subsequent leaders of the Catholic Church. The parallel binding/loosing and forgiving/retaining are theological passives. This means that God in Heaven binds, forgives all which Peter on earth binds, forgives in the Catholic Church. It is the same result in Heaven and in the Church for the parallel dual formula of the loosing and retaining. Today's ritual of reconciliation developed with time, but the parallel double formulas express the power of the Holy Spirit in the Catholic Church to isolate and negate sin in the earliest times of Catholic church history (McBrien, Encyclopedia, p.1083).

The historical Jesus had the power and the authority to forgive sins and to heal ruptured relationships with God the Creator. Jesus walked and talked with Peter and the Twelve Apostles for the three years of his public ministry. Jesus groomed his chosen followers to forgive offenses and heal spirits through love, faith, trust in Almighty God. Jesus conferred the power and authority to bind and forgive on Peter, the Apostles, and their successors by extension. The historical ministry of Jesus written into four Gospels showed that Jesus always forgave and healed people who sought the forgiveness of sins and reconciliation with God the Father. The Sacrament of Penance and Reconciliation ultimately returns the modern Teen to God and God to the Teenager within the mystery of forgiveness from the Holy Spirit of Jesus. The fidelity of the Catholic Church to the salvation history expressed in Jesus' forgiveness of sins underpins the development of the Sacrament of Penance and Reconciliation.

The concrete form of the sacramental ritual "varied considerably" during the 2000 year traditions of the Catholic Church (Catechism, n. 1447). There is little written material recording ritualized forgiveness of sins in the early church of the first through the third centuries. The Catholic Church has the words remembered as Jesus' institution of the Sacrament of Penance and Reconciliation in Gospels. However, the same Gospels are silent on exactly how the Apostles/disciples performed the ritual of the sacrament. The argument of silence does not concern the validity of the early-ritualized forgiveness of sins. Silent Gospels concern the fact of no stark written evidence in New Testament Gospels about the public presentation of a specific ritual or rite. The Apostles and disciples understood Jesus to command them to forgive sins and to heal the broken relationships with God. The Jewish system of education in first century Palestine may help to fathom a modern lack of details about the original liturgical ritual or rite of forgiveness.

Teenagers, please, understand that there was no printing press to disseminate any information on a wide scale until the invention of Johann Gutenberg in 1450. The most important concepts became a part of the oral tradition. Ordinary people usually heard the important ideas before they saw the written expression of the same ideas. The expense of writing on paper (i.e., Egyptian papyrus) and parchment (i.e., skins of goats) often reserved books for the rich and scrolls for religious organizations. Reading, writing, and structured education were generic privileges of the rich and powerful. There was a great value in the written word because books and scrolls were rare for the ordinary people. There was a great value in oral tradition because it was the historical memory of the people in their own language.

During the time of the historical Jesus, the Hebrew people did a better job of educating Jewish children than most pre-printing-press societies. The main reason for Jewish education was the influence of the Hebrew religion. All pious Jews taught their children to read in Hebrew so that children had a knowledge of God, "the sum total, the sole object of his (her) education" (Edersheim, Sketches of Jewish Social Life, p.117, 113-128). Although "writing was not so common an accomplishment as reading" and many Rabbis disapproved "the same amount of instruction being given to girls as to boys," every synagogue with at least 25 boys paid for the schoolmaster (Ibid., p. 122-3, 126-7). Consequently, the school attached to the synagogue was the primary/elementary school for all six-year-olds to study the Hebrew Scriptures. The accomplished male student continued his religious studies in the academy school ("beth hammerdrash") or in the classroom of a Rabbi or in the discussions of the Sanhedrin, the epitome of advanced studies (Ibid., p.124).

The home teaching that began at age three was before entry into the synagogue school. If the historical Jesus had the typical Jewish education, Saint Joseph was the most responsible from ages 3 to 6 for his early education. However, the first training of Jesus was from his Mother Mary (Deut.11:19). Both parents shared the oral tradition of Israel's religious history with the children, and the religious leaders repeated the same oral tradition at the festivals and in synagogues. Boys and girls learned the Hebrew alphabet, and they memorized Scripture verses, the benedictions, the wise sayings with mnemonic rules to help their retention. Five-year-old students read from Hebrew Scriptures starting in the book of Leviticus to learn the "ordinances." The foundation of the entire Jewish educational system was on the individual student remembering/memorizing the oral traditions of the religious history and reading/memorizing the written Torah, the Law in the Hebrew Scriptures.

The basic system of Jewish education for children in first century Palestine produced in all probability many Jewish adults in the time of the historical Jesus with excellent memories for religious details. Many first "Christians" were the descendents/alumni of the Jewish educational system. I posit that the earliest Christians did not need written directions or the written descriptions on how to do the ritual of penance and reconciliation as it developed into a liturgical rite. And because reproduced written words were often expensive, Christians wrote only the most important information like the content of the four Gospels. The Apostles/disciples simply forgave sins and healed the ruptured spiritual relationships on the verbal command of Jesus. It was an important verbal command because in Jewish theology only God forgave sins. So the Christian authors wrote the command from Jesus the Christ, Son of God, in the Gospels. Apostles/disciples did the forgiveness ritual, and then they did it again based on the strong oral tradition from the command of Jesus. But written directions and written descriptions of the forgiveness ritual/rite were unnecessary for religious people with good religious memories. Need for an exact ritual/rite came later in the church history because of the tremendous number and the influx of the Gentile Christians without the traditional Jewish educational basis.

Moreover, Father Brown suggested in The New Jerome Biblical Commentary that the life patterns of the earliest Christian *koinonia* (community) showed its strong heritage from Israel in the teaching of the Apostles (p.1340-1; Acts 2:42). The first followers of Jesus held the Hebrew Scriptures, especially the Law and the Prophets, as the theological authority. Father Raymond Brown stated:

> ...points of unique importance mentioned in the NT are like the tip of an iceberg, the bulk of which is the unmentioned, presupposed teaching of Israel...Points where Jesus modified or differed from the law or from the Pharisee interpretation of the law were remembered and became the nucleus of a special teaching... this teaching of Jesus and of the apostles ...was more authoritative in regard to the restricted points it touched. When such teaching was eventually committed to writing, those writings had within themselves the possibility of becoming a second set of sacred Scriptures (the NT). This canon-forming process was especially sharp in the late 2d cent. p.1341

The ritual/rite of forgiveness in the Sacrament of Penance and Reconciliation is a legitimate point of difference between Jesus and Jewish laws of forgiveness because Jesus commanded humans to forgive sins in the name of God. Pertinent words of Jesus' command are in the New Testament Gospels, and a developing ritual/rite was in the everyday life of the Apostles. The people had a real need for the forgiveness of their sins, not for written directions or the written descriptions of a rite.

Most biblical scholars discern that the final editing and the final writing for the Gospel of John was in 90-100A.D. (final Matthew circa 85A.D., Luke ca. 75A.D., Mark ca. 70A.D.). Authors of the four Gospels wrote their memories of Jesus' historical ministry about 40-60 years after Jesus walked with the original Twelve Apostles. The Gospel of John does not describe a ritual or liturgical rite for the forgiveness of sins. The evangelist does not say exactly how the chosen followers of Jesus exercised the power to forgive sins. However, the very fact that John's Gospel mentions receiving the Holy Spirit and forgiving sins (20:21-3) shows the power exercised in John's community as a continuation of Jesus' healing ministry (McBrien, Catholicism, p.837). The model for the Church in the past and today is Jesus the forgiver of sins, the reconciler, the healer, and consequently, the "sacrament of Reconciliation does what Jesus does" (Ibid., p.843).

The Catholic Church developed the ritual/rite for the Sacrament of Penance and Reconciliation after the deaths of the Apostles (Ibid., p.837-43; Encyclopedia, p.1083-7; Catechism, n.1447). Christians, who sinned after baptism in the early Church, received forgiveness in a public ritual/rite only once during a lifetime. The penitent did public penance, which sometimes lasted years for a serious public sin such as idolatry, murder, apostasy, and adultery. A reconciliation rite for forgiveness and the length of public penance for serious sins varied from region to region and from sin to sin. Some of the local churches prescribed a ritualistic process for grave sins that lasted three years. The forgiveness and reconciliation process for murder sometimes lasted fifteen years. The Church's forms of penance for less serious sins were prayers, almsgiving, fasting, charity to poor and sick.

The Western Church, more so than the Eastern Church, added a most rigorous additional penance for serious sins. Penitents had to remain celibate for the remainder of their lives. Teens may assume that celibacy was a little better than stoning to death, the penalty for adultery under the law of Moses during the time of Jesus (Jn.8:3-11; Lv. 20:10, 18:20; Dt.22:22). However, a penitential lifelong celibacy caused the breakup of marriages. Teens can imagine the resistance of the laity to the Church's very rigorous discipline including no sex for penance after receiving reconciliation for serious sins. The laity deliberately postponed a Sacrament of Penance and Reconciliation until they were near death. When the laity factored in such severe penance, only once in a lifetime confession/reconciliation of sins, the length of time for penance, inclusion of celibacy for a serious sexual sin, the Church's Sacrament of Penance and Reconciliation became the laity's sacrament of the dying.

Widespread death of Christians magnified the situation. Until the Emperor Constantine I declared the Edict of Milan in 313A.D., there were the on-again off-again persecutions of the Christians. When to receive only one reconciliation/forgiveness was a dicey decision with eternal implications. If the sinner received the only once-a-lifetime reconciliation and then committed a publicly known serious sin for a second time, Christians in the community prayed for the sinner. The community prayers continued at the deathbed of the sinner, but the Church denied the sinner the three Sacraments of Reconciliation, the Anointing of the Sick (Extreme Unction), Holy Eucharist. Bishops at the Council of Nicea (325A.D.) curtailed the influence of the rigorists. They decreed that all the dying Christians receive the Sacraments of Penance and Holy Eucharist. Bishops at the Fourth Lateran Council (1215A.D.) officially ended public once-a-lifetime rite of Penance in the Western Church. They decreed that baptized Christians confess sins and receive Holy Communion at least once a year.

It was the influence of the Irish monks hundreds of years before the Fourth Lateran Council that resulted in annual confession. The Celtic monks of the late sixth century developed a specific form of spiritual direction. Monks discussed their sins and need for personal reform with their abbot. The discussions were private, frequent, and listed the personal sins. Irish monks were missionaries to continental Europe in the early seventh century, and they brought their form of the Sacrament of Reconciliation with them.

The Irish form of Penance became widespread and popular with the laity, but Celtic reconciliation clashed with the Roman Catholic form of Penance. The Roman form of reconciliation was public and available only once in a lifetime with severe penance. The Irish form of reconciliation was private and frequent with the penance selected from a developed code of penitential practices. The penitential books ("libri poenitentiales") listed every sin with the appropriate penance. In the Roman form of Penance, a minister of the sacrament was the healer and reconciler. In the Irish form, a priest was the judge. From the seventh century to our own day, about 1400 years, the Western Catholic Church did the Sacrament of Penance and Reconciliation in secret between penitent and priest.

Catholic theologians discern the same "fundamental structure" in a Sacrament of Penance and Reconciliation throughout the centuries (<u>Catechism</u>, n.1448-60). Under the changes in discipline and form is the fourfold process: contrition, confession, satisfaction, absolution. Contrition is the "sorrow of the soul" and the resolution to not sin. A confession is the disclosure of personal sins and taking responsibility for offenses. Satisfaction is the repairing the harm of sin and doing penance imposed by a priest (prayers for mercy, service to neighbor/ peer, voluntary self-denial, sacrifices). Absolution is the granting the penitent pardon and peace by God through the priest's sacramental absolution/formula. Bishops at the Second Vatican Council in 1962-5 preserved the four ancient theological concepts when they mandated a renewed ritual for the Sacrament of Penance.

Over 2,600 bishops from all over the world at Vatican II called for the revision of the rite and ritual for the Sacrament of Penance. <u>The Constitution on the Sacred Liturgy (Sacrosanctum Concilium)</u> of

Vatican II established criteria for the revision: "The rite and formulae of Penance are to be revised so that they more clearly express both the nature and effect of the sacrament" (n.72). The bishops at the Vatican II Council declared the sacred nature of the sacrament in the Dogmatic Constitution on the Church (Lumen Gentium): "Those who approach the sacrament of Penance obtain pardon from God's mercy for the offense committed against him, and are, at the same time, reconciled with the Church" (n.11). Vatican II bishops defined the Church as "...'the People of God' (1Pet.2:9-10)... the Church of Christ (cf. Mt.16:18)...All those, who in faith look towards Jesus, the author of salvation and the principle of unity and peace, God has gathered together and established as the Church" (Ibid., n.9).

The bishops implemented the new revised rite/ritual in 1973. It is this new Rite of Penance that Teens access today for the sacrament of forgiveness for sins. The new rite has four distinct and legitimate forms: (1) individual ritual with individual confession and individual absolution; (2) the communal ritual with the individual confession and individual absolution; (3) the communal ritual with general confession and general absolution; (4) abbreviated emergency ritual when death is imminent (Catechism, n.1482-4). The Bishop of each diocese has the authority to determine the specific form to emphasize (The Code of Canon Law, *Canon 961*— §2).

The rite/ritual for the first three forms include: prayer of welcome, the reading from the Word of God, a reflection on Sacred Scripture, confession of sins with an expression of sorrow, the priest's prayer of absolution, the prayer of praise and dismissal (Catechism, n.1480; Catholicism, p.841-2). The emphasis is on prayers of forgiveness. Catholic theology underscoring the new rite/ritual is a dual concept with the same basic effect: sin is offense against God and against neighbor (community/church); so reconciliation is with God and with neighbor (community/church) (Encyclopedia, p.1086). A priest in this new revised rite/ritual is a healer more than a judge.

d. Fresh Teen Start and the Seal of Confession

Formulas of absolution, recited by a Catholic priest in a Western and Eastern Church, express the essential elements and mystery of God's forgiveness in the Sacrament of Penance and Reconciliation:

> (A) Western (Roman/Latin) Church...
> God, the Father of mercies, through the death and resurrection of his Son has reconciled the world to himself and sent the Holy Spirit among us for the forgiveness of sins; through the ministry of the Church may God give you pardon and peace, and I absolve you from your sins in the name of the Father, and of the Son, and of the Holy Spirit.
> Catechism, n.1449

(B) Eastern (Byzantine) Church...
May the same God, who through the Prophet Nathan forgave David when he confessed his sins, who forgave Peter when he wept bitterly, the prostitute when she washed his feet with her tears, the Pharisee, and the prodigal son, through me, a sinner, forgive you both in this life and in the next and enable you to appear before his awe-inspiring tribunal without condemnation, he who is blessed for ever and ever. Amen. <u>Catechism</u>, n.1481

It is a truly beautiful thought pattern to know, believe, and trust that the words of absolution from a Catholic priest in the Sacrament of Penance and Reconciliation restore to the Teen the grace and love of the Most Holy God!

Restoration of God's grace to the Teenager means a fresh start for the Teen. It is the ministry of the Catholic bishops and priests to return Teenagers to God and God to Teenagers. The bishops and the priests are the "moderators" for the Sacrament of Penance and Reconciliation (<u>Lumen Gentium</u>, 26:3; <u>Catechism</u>, n.1462). The main emphases of the sacrament in a post-Vatican II Church are healing and conversion of heart. The primary focus of priests in the ministry of reconciliation is not to bust a Teenager. A priest works within the sacrament to help the Teen turn away from sin and return to the God of All Love and Compassion. The priest will not blab the Teenager's private business learned in confession. The priest will not squeal or snitch to Mom and Dad about the Teen's sins against God learned in confession. The Catholic Church is very serious about imposing a "seal of confession" on all priests and all bishops.

<u>Catechism of the Catholic Church</u> states in most certain terms:

> Given the delicacy and greatness of this ministry and the respect due to persons, the Church declares that every priest who hears confessions is bound under very severe penalties to keep absolute secrecy regarding the sins that his penitents have confessed to him. He can make no use of knowledge that confession gives him about penitents' lives. This secret, which admits of no exceptions, is called the 'sacramental seal,' because what the penitent has made known to the priest remains 'sealed' by the sacrament.
> n.1467

The Catholic Church expects and demands that all bishops and all priests go to their graves without blabbing the private business of the Teen heard in confession.

<u>The Code of Canon Law</u> is the specific book that contains all the laws governing the operations of the Catholic Church in the United States and throughout the world. There are 1,752 canons or laws in

the book. The Church laws in The Code of Canon Law pertaining to the priest/confessor in the Sacrament of Penance and Reconciliation are most specific regarding confidentiality of confession and violation of confessional seal:

> Canon 983 – §1. The sacramental seal is inviolable; therefore, it is a crime for a confessor in any way to betray a penitent by word or in any other manner or for any reason.
> p. 691
>
> Canon 984 – §1. Even if every danger of revelation is excluded, a confessor is absolutely forbidden to use knowledge acquired from confession when it might harm the penitent. Ibid.
>
> Canon 1388 – §1. A confessor who directly violates the seal of confession incurs an automatic (latae sententiae) excommunication reserved to the Apostolic See; if he does so only indirectly, he is to be punished in accord with the seriousness of the offense. p. 927

All the Catholic bishops and priests have a copy of The Code of Canon Law. All Catholic bishops and priests know and understand the seriousness from the seal of confession. All Catholic bishops and priests know and understand that the penalty for directly breaking the seal of confession is automatic excommunication. Excommunication means that the Pope as the Apostolic See kicks the guilty bishop or priest out of the Catholic Church. All Catholic bishops and priests know and understand that excommunication of a bishop or a priest because of the very serious offense of directly violating the seal of confession means the potential loss of the individual soul to the fires of hell for all eternity.

All Catholic bishops and priests as moderators for the sacrament utilize a copy of the same official Church book for the Sacrament of Penance and Reconciliation. The book reminds bishops and priests briefly and forcefully of the sacramental seal:

> Conscious that he has come to know the secret of another's conscience only because he is God's minister, the confessor is bound by the obligation of preserving the seal of confession absolutely unbroken. Rite of Penance, p.10d;
> cf., Code of Canon Law, p.691

When a Teen asks the Catholic priest to go to confession and to receive the Sacrament of Penance and Reconciliation, the Teen can rest assured that the priest will not blab his or her private business. The seal of confession is the Church law that all priests and bishops understand despite pressures put on them. A Catholic priest and bishop will go to his grave without revealing the sins of the Teen.

It is difficult for Teens to love God above all gifts from God. It is difficult for Teens to love neighbors/peers especially the bullies of the world. It is difficult for Teenagers to accept responsibility for every word, action, thought. It is possible for the Teenager to overcome all difficulties if the Teenager asks the Almighty God for help. When the Teen succumbs to the difficult and breaks down relationships, the Teen has the free choice to say prayers of forgiveness. If a Catholic Teen controls pride and humbles self after spiritual breakdowns, the Teen has the Sacrament of Penance and Reconciliation to restore the grace and love of the Most Holy God. A natural Teen tendency kowtows to negative peer pressure and spews, "I'm sorry," to get out of trouble without the loss of friends. A supernatural Teen tendency chooses holiness. All Teenagers have the ability to eliminate little offenses against the laws of God and to produce a holier self. Every Teen has the freedom of choice to choose God.

Remember, Teens, Jesus suffered great pain and died a horrible death as his offering of perfect obedience and total love to God the Father. The historical Jesus utilized his personal freedom of choice to love God the Father above all things, including his physical life, and to love neighbors/Teens even through his physical death of self. His "reward" for total obedience and total love was his Resurrection of self and the spiritual forgiveness/reconciliation/salvation for all neighbors/Teens whom he still loves.

Also remember, Teens, the sinful woman who washed the feet of Jesus with her tears. She was sorry for her sins, and she expressed sorrow in her actions. She utilized her personal freedom of choice to show love of God above all things with her actions of sorrow for her sins against God and neighbor. Jesus said in response to her free choices of love and sorrow for sins: "I tell you, her sins, which were many, have been forgiven; hence she has shown great love... your faith has saved you; go in peace" (Lk.7:47,50). Her reward for love of God and sorrow for sin was spiritual forgiveness/salvation/peace.

If the Teen wants to elevate prayer-life off the kindergarten level, the Teenager may utilize his/her personal freedom of choice to love God above everything and to love their neighbors/peers including the bullies. If Teenagers break down spiritual relationships with God and neighbor, Teenagers may choose active prayers of forgiveness like the sinful woman washing the feet of Jesus. Teen rewards for a total love of God and for the sorrow of sin have the same value of spiritual forgiveness/salvation/peace. A Teenager may also be so sorry for offenses against the God of All Love that the Teen chooses a most difficult change of mind and heart from old ways of sin to new ways of love and obedience to God just like Jesus. This Teen conversion of heart and mind to God is a most worthy prayer of forgiveness and a most worthy personal offering to the supernatural and eternal God.

C. PLEASE, CONSIDER THE FOLLOWING:

(1) Do a three-minute meditation with eyes closed, racket blocked out, thoughts and feelings concentrated on the focal point: I'm sorry, God, for my offenses against you and against my neighbors/peers... please, forgive me...

(2) Create a mental list of specific offenses against the laws of God, and then ask for forgiveness from God the Most Holy One of All Mercy...(acid tongue against peers, failure to try with best effort to be holy, putting more emphasis on money/power/status/popularity/fame/fashion than on God and people, psychological bullying of people, hypocrisy, pushing/shoving people until get own way, bad example for little people, negative pride, quitting personal faith journey, abuse of body/mind/spirit with drugs/alcohol, magnifying problems with the step-authority in life, abuse of fundamental freedom, letting personal ego control/dominate life/decisions to the detriment of others, failure to forgive those who hurt individuals, sins of omission, failure to love the "Bully" in personal life, etc.)...

(3) Compose a home-made prayer of forgiveness to Almighty God that you can think and feel several times throughout the day... remember, it's between you and your God...

(4) Try loving God and neighbors/peers to the point that you ask and give forgiveness whenever spiritual relationships rupture...

CHAPTER 3

GIFT OF LIFE...COLIN BROWNE
PRAYERS OF ADORATION

A. COLIN BROWNE

All the Teens and pre-Teens at the Linden Lodge School for the Blind hated Bully. Teens, pre-Teens, teaching staff, administrative staff, gardeners, janitors, cooks loved Colin Browne. Colin Browne was a thirteen-year-old physical disaster. He was not bitter about his body. Colin Browne was alive with the gift of life. Everybody loved Colin Browne because Colin loved everybody. Colin Browne even offered love and friendship to Bully whom responded with focused meanness. Colin Browne had a million-dollar smile for the sighted and golden laughter for the blind.

Unfortunately, Colin Browne's body did not cooperate with his spirit. It was sad to observe his blindness from birth, gimped-up left side, deformed left arm ending in a little claw, partially paralyzed left leg dragging behind him, lousy balance. People just wanted to cry and hug him every time they saw Colin Browne picking himself off the ground. More than once, I shook my fist at God and demanded to know why the innocent Colin Browne had to suffer so much pain! God usually answered through Colin's laughter. When Colin Browne realized that I saw him fall, he frequently said, "Beg your pardon, Sir, beg your pardon, but I bet I look totally ridiculous with all this mud on me." Colin Browne laughed until I laughed.

Colin Browne never let his severe handicaps prevent him from trying to the best of his God-given talents. Colin enjoyed listening to music. One day he was in the school's music room listening to the London Symphony Orchestra on the good sound system. The music teacher at the school was with Colin Browne, and they had the music on full blast thoroughly enjoying themselves. All of a sudden Colin asked the music teacher, "Beg your pardon, Sir, beg your pardon, but what's that sound?" The music teacher responded, "Colin, what in the world are you talking about—the sound is a whole symphony with every instrument taking a part." The undeterred Colin Browne listened closely and said, "That sound." They both listened intently with Colin Browne saying "that sound" each time he heard the clear note. The music teacher finally figured out that a trumpet made "that sound." He switched to a solo of a trumpet for Colin Browne.

Colin Browne listened quietly for a long time to the music of the trumpet. Finally, Colin Browne said, "Beg your pardon, Sir, beg your pardon... that is such a beautiful sound...I'd like to make that sound... will you teach me to play the trumpet, please?" The music teacher laughed in Colin Browne's face. He explained that a person needed two good hands to play the trumpet because of the construction of the instrument. Then the music teacher laughed in Colin Browne's face again.

Colin Browne taught himself to play the trumpet. Colin Browne never complained, and he never felt sorry for himself. Colin went to the music practice room after school during his free time. There was a piano with a high back and a flat top in the practice room. Colin Browne borrowed a trumpet, cassette player, and a small stool from the school's music supplies. He scooted the stool with his gimped-up left leg next to the side of the high back piano. Colin Browne slowly and carefully stepped onto the stool, and with his good right hand, he put the cassette player on the flat top of the piano. Colin placed a special tape in the player that had a person talking about the finger positions for the different notes on a trumpet and then blowing the musical scales for the proper sound of the notes. He stepped down slowly and carefully from the stool to collect his borrowed trumpet.

Colin again stepped slowly and carefully onto the stool with the trumpet in his good right hand. He strategically placed the trumpet on the piano top with the mouthpiece hanging over the side edge. He balanced his gimped-up left side precariously on the small stool. He could only raise his weak left arm about halfway to the height of his shoulder. Colin Browne grabbed his bad left arm with his good right hand, and he raised the bad arm high enough to drape it over the piano top and the back of the trumpet. Colin Browne worked the three trumpet stops with his good right hand while his bad left arm steadied the trumpet and himself. Colin practiced as long as he did not loose his balance and fall off the stool. The set-up process took about forty-five minutes for a one-hour practice. Things usually went well without too many bruises or hobbles to the School Infirmary for Band-Aids.

The whole process totally exhausted him. Colin suffered quietly through the negatives without any complaints because he wanted to play the trumpet. Colin Browne eventually taught himself to play a few songs on the trumpet. Oh, Colin wasn't very good, and he was never ready for prime time. But Colin Browne taught himself to play the trumpet after the music teacher laughed in his face twice. Colin did not teach himself to spite the music teacher. Colin taught himself to make "that sound" because the sound of a trumpet was beautiful.

Colin Browne exhibited positive character and spiritual strength especially when he suffered physical pain trying to play sports. Mr. McMillan, the English teacher, and I gladly substituted anytime for the PE teachers. Our standard choice of games was cricket with the students in the gym. Colin Browne hated cricket. Bully loved cricket.

Cricket is similar to American baseball. It is a game with a bat and small hard ball. There are two teams with usually eleven players on each team, and they play the game on a large open field. There are two wickets about waste high to a Teenager that look like T-ball stands. The positions of the two wickets are at the spots in American baseball of home plate and second base. A pitcher takes a running start and throws the hard ball overhand and fast at the "home plate" wicket. A batsman with cricket bat defends the "home plate" wicket. A typical cricket bat looks like an American baseball bat where you grip it on the handle with two hands, but the bulk of the bat looks like a five-inch flat board where you hit the ball. The batter hits the fast ball, runs and touches the "second base" wicket, then runs back and touches the "home plate" wicket to score runs. The team with the most runs wins the match.

A blind school version of cricket was a crisscross between dodge ball, football, jungle ball, roller derby, a visit to the circus, and a field trip to the zoo. Mr. McMillan and I never played cricket with the blind students without Band-Aids, extra-strength aspirin, a red alert to the School Infirmary. The students, except for Colin Browne, thoroughly enjoyed the excitement of the game. The biggest negative in cricket was always Bully who wanted to hurt whomever he was mad at for the day. Bully, however, acted about half-civilized in the morning if there was an opportunity to play cricket in the afternoon.

Cricket was the only time that any student wanted Bully on their team. Bully was very good at cricket especially on the bright sunny days. Bully never tried to hurt his teammates because the teacher without fail marched him to the "penalty box" and refused to let him finish the game. Bully's team usually won the cricket match unless the teacher threw Bully out of the game for hurting someone on the other team. Captains always choose Bully first and Colin last. Colin Browne never made any excuses to get out of playing cricket, and he never quit a game in progress. Colin suffered through cricket while Bully basked in the glory of the sport. Colin thought victory was the end of the PE class without any broken bones. Bully knew victory was on the scoreboard within his grasp if he just didn't get caught throwing too many elbows at the opposing team. Bully always smiled from ear to ear, and Colin Browne always cringed, as Mr. McMillan yelled, "Play ball!"

The Linden Lodge School for the Blind version of cricket wasn't exactly like what you see on T.V. Mr. McMillan and I used a soccer ball instead of the official small hard ball. Batters hit with oversized cricket bats. Wickets had extra rubber for the students' protection. We only played cricket in the gym where the four walls corralled any lucky hit. If a batter hit the ball onto the stage at the far end of the gym, it was an automatic "home run." Mr. McMillan was the pitcher for both teams, and I was the catcher. When it was time to pitch the ball, Mr. McMillan yelled, "Silence." Everybody in the gym stopped talking, froze in place, and listened intently. It seemed quieter in the gym than in the school halls during a fire drill!

Mr. McMillan pitched the soccer ball so that it bounced one time between himself and the batter. Everybody listened for the bounce. A batter had to time his or her swing to meet the ball. Whenever the batter thought the ball bounced waist-high at his/her side, the batter made a mighty swing or a vicious cut at the ball. If the batter hit the ball, both teams heard the hit and listened in total silence for the ball to bounce somewhere on the gym floor. As soon as the team in the field knew which direction to go for the ball, all hell broke loose. The batter, cheered with much volume by teammates, started his/her run to find the wicket at "second base" and then the return run to find the "home plate" wicket. The team in the field ran yelling and screaming in the general direction of the bouncing ball. If anyone found the ball, the person threw it at the batter. The batter was "out" if the ball by some miracle hit the batter instead of a teammate during the run for the wickets.

Mr. McMillan and I were notorious for beefing-up the action. He pitched the ball so that the bounce was usually slow and waist-high to the batter, except for his pitches to Bully. For improved timing on the first and second pitches, I yelled, "Swing batter," except for Bully. On the third pitch, I helped the batter grip and swing the cricket bat, except for Bully. When a batter hit a ball, Mr. McMillan yelled some directions above the pandemonium to help the team in the field. He screamed, "Libby Lou, go to your right for the ball, and throw towards home." Mr. McMillan often got caught up in the fast action and only yelled, "Go right." All fielders facing him went to their right, and all fielders with their backs to him also went to their right. The blunder meant that everybody in the field banged into each other and tripped over each other and scrambled for the ball on their hands and knees. All the highlight films were absolute chaos. It is truly a wonder that Mr. McMillan and I did not take Bully's place in the big leather chair reserved for the honored guests in the Headmaster's office.

Cricket was simply not the game for Colin Browne. Every cricket match was dangerous for him. He usually stood a few paces from Mr. McMillan for protection. Every game of cricket was a real test of Colin's physical stamina, positive character, and spiritual strength. On the other hand, Bully reveled in the sport. Bully took a major ego trip off every game of cricket to the point that he acted halfway right on the mornings of the cricket matches. Bully even tried to bribe Mr. McMillan and me with his precious Snickers bars to play cricket more often. Mr. McMillan and I tolerated Bully's bravado before and after each match just to get a peaceful morning. Mr. McMillan didn't stick his leg out very often to trip Bully on his run for the wickets to shut him up. We did use the real threat of culling Bully off the team to expand Bully's morning window of good behavior. We had a mixture of success depending on the medicines Bully took for the week.

Bully knew that Mr. McMillan and I bluffed about culling him off the team. Bully understood that we enjoyed watching him excel in cricket matches as long as he did not hurt anybody. The three of us really felt good when the other students wanted Bully on their team. We three felt even better when the captains chose Bully first. But we three felt best when Bully cracked a "home run." Bully always did his jelly belly victory dance. It was completely wasted on the other blind students, but Mr. McMillan and I always laughed as we watched the dancing Bully. Then we laughed even louder as Bully did his encore version of his jelly belly victory dance. The other students laughed at us laughing at the dancing Bully. After every home run and jelly belly victory dance, Bully sat quietly on the gym floor. Bully's eyes glazed over; a genuine smile spread from ear to ear; and silent tears were in his eyes as he relived the glory of a home run in the instant replay of his mind. It was as close to love as Bully chose to get.

Bully had the process of hitting home runs down to the perfection of a fine art. There was a row of windows at the top of the gym, so Bully was at his best on a bright sunshiny day. He stepped up to the home wicket. He leaned his cricket bat against his leg and took off his thick glasses. He slowly cleaned his glasses on his dirty shirt while glaring a blind stare at Mr. McMillan, the pitcher. Bully put his glasses on his head with determination, griped his bat tightly, and wound himself up like a pretzel. He closed his bad left eye, opened wide his good right eye, and rocked his head viciously waiting for the pitch. Mr. McMillan yelled for silence.

Everybody tensed ready for the pitcher-batter duel. Mr. McMillan bounced the soccer ball fast, high, low, curved, but never slow. It did not matter because Bully was so focused. Bully put his big, old, fat self behind the hit and whacked the ball hard. All players listened in silence for the loud thump of the ball high on the gym wall and the ricocheting thump back on earth. When the ball finally hit the floor, the uproar began. Bully quickly waddled to the wickets bulling over anybody in his way. If the fielders hastily found the ball, there was a good chance that they could throw and hit the big, old, fat Bully. The drama was intense every time Bully went to bat. On the brightest sunshiny days, Bully had the ability to whack the soccer ball and hit the stage at the far end of the gym. If the students in the field heard the ball land far behind them on the stage, they sounded a stereo chorus of oohing and aahing. That was an automatic home run, and both teams stood to cheer Bully's feat of glory.

Colin Browne never had a moment of glory in any cricket match. Colin Browne had too much character to squirm out of cricket using his handicaps as excuses. Colin always showed up for the cricket matches dressed in dark trousers, a long sleeve white shirt, and a tie. He commented, "Beg your pardon, Sirs, beg your pardon, but I think a man ought to look like a gentleman even if he has to play this barbarian game." The barbarian game was almost the death of Colin Browne in one of Bully's less than finest moments.

That particular day started well for Bully and Colin Browne. Colin was sky-high because Libby Lou expressed her fancy for him in front of mutual friends. Bully was on his very best behavior because it was a rainy day with a cricket match scheduled by Mr. McMillan and me for the afternoon PE class. Unfortunately, Bully's doctors upped the mid-morning dosage on his new steroid-based guinea-pig medicine. Bully was pinging off the walls by lunchtime. We came so close to benching Bully for the game. Mr. McMillan and I decided exercise might do him some good, and besides it was a cloudy day.

The cricket match progressed safely until Bully's third time at bat. He muffed his other attempts to hit the ball, and he blamed the lousy medicines as much as the lousy weather. He scared his teammates with his trash talk, and he sat by himself darkly mulling over his ill fortune. When it was his turn to bat, Bully positioned himself by the home wicket. All of a sudden, the sun broke through thick clouds. The entire gym filled with bright light. Bully could see. He quickly dispensed with his usual rigmarole and went directly to the pretzel position. He closed his bad left eye, opened wide his good right eye, rocked his head most viciously waiting for the pitch in broad daylight.

Mr. McMillan and I looked at each other, and we both shook a "no" with our heads. We called time-out to stall. While Mr. McMillan and I talked things over, the students felt the increased heat in the gym from the sunshine. All knew the exact circumstances. Bully's teammates yelled and pumped him up for a big hit. The fielders took a few steps backwards. Colin Browne, usually in the shadow of Mr. McMillan, took a few steps back and away from the imagined path of Bully to the second base wicket. Colin's move meant even more separation from Mr. McMillan. We continued to stall, but the sun did not go behind any clouds. The noise reached a frenzied intensity.

Mr. McMillan and I talked options. We could force Bully out of the batter's box on some trumped-up charges. Bully was just as likely to loose all self-control, pop a vein, and sling the cricket bat. We could inspect the cricket bat to get it out of Bully's hands and then kick him out of the game on false charges. Bully would roar his disapproval, and then try to really hurt another student sometime during the day away from authority figures. We could tell Bully the truth that he was too dangerous to bat with the hyped-up medicine. Again, we thought that it was just a matter of time before Bully got his revenge for our no-bat call by seriously hurting another student.

Mr. McMillan and I checked the sunlight and the time to the end of class. There was too much in both categories. Mr. McMillan and I talked pitches. If we threw the high fast inside ball to crowd Bully's swing, he would probably hit hard into left field directly at Libby Lou and most of the girls. If we "accidentally" hit Bully with the high fast brush-off pitch, he could pop the same vein and catapult the cricket bat. If we threw fast down the middle, he might hit a harmless fly ball to the stage, but a miss-hit with velocity was a real danger. All slow pitches were completely out of the question because the change-up gave Bully too many seconds to zero-in on the pitch. We agreed that our safest pitch was low, fast, outside. We hoped for a strike-out, or a lazy pop fly to right field, or a harmless dribble to right field. Our greatest worry with a lazy type of hit was Bully bowling over innocent fielders on a run for the wickets. At that point, "accidentally" tripping Bully became a viable option. Mr. McMillan and I checked the bright daylight, shook our heads in major disgust, and halfheartedly yelled, "Play ball."

While I walked slowly to the catcher's position, Bully adjusted his thick glasses carefully and wound-up quickly into the pretzel position with no wasted motion. He closed his bad left eye, opened wide his good right eye, slowly and confidently rocked his head. The sunshine was brilliant, and Bully was ready. Mr. McMillan yelled, "Silence," and there was utter stillness. The pitch was very, very good. The hit was excellent.

The pitch was low, very fast, and outside. All heard the ball skip on the gym floor. All heard the instantaneous crack of the bat. All heard a dull thud of the soccer ball hitting human flesh. Milliseconds later, all heard the deadly thump of a body hitting the gym floor. All stood in utter stillness listening for any sound to identify the person on the floor. Only Mr. McMillan and I saw the good pitch, the totally focused Bully step across the wicket into the pitch, a hit with all his Bully weight and his Bully morning frustrations behind the ultimate swing. Bully hit a powerful line drive directly at Colin Browne. The soccer ball hit the unsuspecting Colin Browne squarely in the face. The hit lifted Colin Browne completely off the ground and threw him backward about three feet. The back of Colin's head was the first thing to land on the gym floor. He lay motionless, flat on his back. I stared at his chest and saw no movement and no sign of breathing. Colin had blood dripping from his nose and mouth. Blood already pooled in a large crimson stain on the front of his long sleeve white shirt. I instinctively made the sign of the cross. I thought that Colin Browne was dead. All students listened intensely to hear who was hurt. Everyone seemed frozen in time and place.

After an eternity of seconds, Colin Browne finally let out a huge, "Ooohoohoh!" The students knew instantly that it was Colin's groan. Everybody jumped into action bumping into each other while trying to help Colin. Mr. McMillan and I looked at each other, shook our heads slowly, and semi-wheezed a sigh of relief. I said a few silent prayers of thanksgiving for Colin's life. Mr. McMillan and I calmed down the class while attending to Colin Browne. Then Bully went berserk in a hysterical apology, "I am so sorry, Colin Browne— it was an accident — I didn't mean to hurt you— truly I didn't— I am so sorry, please, forgive me, Colin Browne, please, forgive me." It was the only time I saw Bully express genuine sorrow for hurting anyone. Colin Browne forgave Bully from a daze and added, "These things happen when gentlemen play barbarian games."

Mr. McMillan and I checked for broken bones and a concussion. Colin Browne had neither. So we stood him up and held him until he stopped swooning. When he regained his balance and stood alone,

Colin Browne said a most remarkable thing, "Beg your pardon, Sirs, beg your pardon, sorry for the delay, but is it time to play ball?" Mr. McMillan and I tried to persuade him to go to the School Infirmary. Colin Browne simply said, "Beg your pardon, Sirs, beg your pardon, but I think it is best if I finish the class." Colin Browne finished the PE class. He stood next to Mr. McMillan and swayed from side to side. He wore the crimson stain, which only Mr. McMillan and I saw, on the chest of his long sleeve white shirt with honor, dignity, courage, respect, spiritual strength. When a bell finally rang to dismiss class, Colin Browne said simply, "Beg your pardon, Sirs, beg your pardon, but I don't feel so good—I think I better go to the School Infirmary."

Colin Browne never seemed to loose his keen sense of humor no matter how tragic he appeared to sighted people. He had a quick but respectful wit. Colin Browne generated love through laughter. He usually got his way with the teaching staff through his quick wit and his million-dollar smile. However, the one area on the blind school campus "verboten" to Colin was the indoor swimming pool. He had half-dozen doctors warning him and the school's staff of the extreme danger from deep water. Of course, swimming intrigued Colin. One day Colin pumped-up all his courage to ask Mr. McMillan and me, "Beg your pardon, Sirs, beg your pardon, but would you, please, take me swimming just to see why Libby Lou loves swimming and what the fuss is all about?" Mr. McMillan and I immediately went into our harangue about the need for two good arms to float in deep water. Colin Browne listened calmly until we ran out of protests. He said quietly, "Beg your pardon, Sirs, beg your pardon, but you sound just like the music teacher." Oh, man, he had us there. Mr. McMillan and I looked at each other, shook our heads and our fists in silence, and sighed in unison. We deferred the decision to the Headmaster.

Colin Browne made an official appointment with the Headmaster. When we went into the Headmaster's office, Colin sat comfortably and politely in the big leather chair reserved for honored guests. Mr. McMillan and I stood respectably behind Colin Browne at attention. Colin Browne made his request to go swimming, and immediately the Headmaster lectured us on the dangers of the deep water for a person without two good arms and two good legs. Colin Browne, Mr. McMillan, and I listened calmly until the Headmaster ran out of his best protests. Colin said quietly, "Beg your pardon, Mr. Headmaster Sir, beg your pardon, but you sound just like the music teacher." The Headmaster was speechless. He looked at Mr. McMillan and then at me. He silently shook both his fists at both of us. We in unison threw our opened hands silently into the air and shrugged our shoulders. We looked at each other and then at Colin in a thoughtful silence. We knew perfectly well that Colin Browne quite cleverly bamboozled us into a corner. The Headmaster eventually gave his blessing for Colin to go swimming with a list of precautions about a mile long.

Mr. McMillan and I reserved the pool and checked Colin Browne out of class so that we had the swimming pool without competition from the other students. The pool was indoors, heated, about forty yards long and twenty yards wide. Students climbed up and down one of four ladders strategically positioned at the corners. The depth of the pool sloped from four feet to eight feet. The locker rooms were opposite the shallow end. The pool had a stainless steel rail at the edge of the water and completely around the inside of the pool. Most students hung on the safety rail and had a blast working hand over hand around the perimeter of the swimming pool.

Libby Lou and Bully were the best swimmers. Libby Lou had the experiences from her sighted days in the family pools and in oceans. Bully was like a baby whale. He had so much blubber that he bobbed around like a cork and did not sink. However, Bully rarely made it to the end of swim time. The lifeguards usually kicked him out of the pool for swimming underwater and pinching the girls. Sometimes he got the boot for doing a huge cannonball on top of whoever headed his personal hate list for the day.

However, the swimming routine was a totally new experience for Colin Browne. Mr. McMillan and I started our protective coverage by reserving the whole swimming area for our special project. Worries began at the pool doors. The brave Colin Browne with his terrible balance had to navigate the tiled floor, slippery from condensation, without cracking his skull.

One of the longest walks of my life was the short distance from the locker rooms to the shallow end of the blind school pool. Colin Browne tightly clutched the elbow of Mr. McMillan with his good right hand. I walked a few steps behind them. It was the first and the only time that I saw Colin Browne without a long sleeve white shirt, shoes, socks, trousers. Colin Browne was horribly deformed. His left arm ended in a claw, and his left leg ended in a clubfoot. Both shriveled into nothingness. It was sad to see his body and hear him joyfully thanking Mr. McMillan and me for giving him the opportunity to swim. Again I shook spiritual fists at the God of All Power and demanded to know the purpose of the innocent Colin Browne suffering so much pain. Again God answered me through the light-hearted laughter of Colin Browne. The concept of innocent suffering was my theological problem, not Colin's.

Colin only slipped twice going to the far ladder. Mr. McMillan had him in a strong grasp, so Colin Browne did not fall. Understanding the dangers began to dawn in Colin when he realized the tiles were as slippery as ice for a person with lousy balance. Colin heard my jump into the water and swim to a far ladder. I stood in the water and held Colin at his waist while he tried to slowly back down the ladder. Mr. McMillan was on the deck and held Colin by his good right wrist. Colin also learned and understood that a jump or push into the water meant he did not have the arm and leg strength to climb a ladder by himself. Without help and complete trust in others, a swimming pool was a dangerous trap for Colin Browne.

Colin Browne hung on the pool's safety rail with his good right hand, kicked with his good right leg, and quickly tired. He worked his way with the help of Mr. McMillan along the rail to the deep water. I positioned myself about six feet from the side of the pool. We asked Colin to breathe in and hold a lot of air, push away from the poolside with his good right arm and good right leg, and do the dog paddle to me. Colin Browne said he was ready for his first swim.

As soon as Colin Browne released his grip on the rail, he sank to the bottom of the swimming pool. He went down faster than a tote sack full of rocks. A three-month old baby taking a bath in a half-full kitchen sink swam better than Colin Browne. Colin Browne was a terrible swimmer. The half-dozen doctors were 100% correct about the extreme danger from deep water for Colin Browne.

I swam down to the bottom of the pool and collected Colin. We surfaced with my left arm around his waist and with his good right arm in a tight death-grip around my neck. I draped my right arm over the rail and waited for him to stop spitting and sputtering. The first words out of Colin's mouth were, "Beg your pardon, Sirs, beg your pardon, but am I swimming yet?" Mr. McMillan and I broke all tension with our laughter. Finally, I said, "No Sir, Mr. Colin Browne, you were not swimming, you were drowning." Colin Browne stared at me as if he could see. Moments later he said quietly, "Sirs, I understand your laughter, and I do understand what all the fuss is about, but if Libby Lou could see me now, I bet that she would hug my neck because I look like a wet puppy dog." And then Colin Browne laughed until his golden laughter echoed throughout the Aquatic Center. I just had to give him a big bear hug with both my arms. We immediately sank underwater. We surfaced together spitting, sputtering, laughing, and asking Mr. McMillan if we were swimming yet.

Most new experiences did not make Colin Browne nervous. He enjoyed the gift of life, and he was a most welcoming person. Colin was intellectually sharp and blessed with intellectual curiosity. Each day was a new day for Colin to learn new things. The teaching and administrative staffs were the ones who hoped Colin's new learning were not more lessons about pain. Colin simply lived each day to its fullest. He was truly a grace-filled Teenager. His life was a continual praise and glory to the wisdom of God because so much good went to others from Colin's handicaps and from the negatives in his daily life. Colin Browne simply rocked along enjoying the gift of life, and good stuff spun out of his existence. Colin never complained, and things didn't bother him to the point of bringing him down. However, Colin Browne had a real case of the nerves with the new experience of his first official date with Libby Lou.

The very articulate Colin Browne could barely string a sentence together when he thought about a date with Libby Lou. He sought counsel from Mr. McMillan and me before he actually asked her out. We encouraged him to go for the gold. We observed him for a week dragging his bad left leg to the most isolated places on the school campus. Colin constantly mumbled to himself. Mr. McMillan and I presumed that he was practicing his lines and pumping himself up. Libby Lou did not help his nerves at all. She kept asking him why he was walking by himself all the time, and what was wrong, and what did he say when he mumbled. Colin Browne was an emotional wreck by the end of the week of deep pondering without much sleep. He seemed completely out of character. His eyes were bloodshot; his hair was messed-up; his socks were mismatched; the buttons on his long sleeve white shirt were in the wrong buttonholes.

Mr. McMillan and I knew minutes after Colin finally summoned his courage and asked Libby Lou for a date. Colin found us leaning against the school wall and plotting privately. The slicked-out Colin Browne boldly interrupted and loudly proclaimed, "Beg your pardon, Sirs, beg your pardon, but I thought that you might like to know that I have a date with Miss Libby Lou." Colin Browne accepted our hearty congratulations with a sheepish, or maybe a roguish, grin from ear to ear. Colin casually but conspiratorially remarked, "Sirs, I could drop by the office of Mr. McMillan later, and we three might discuss where a gentleman brings a lady on a date nowadays."

The good news of "The Date" spread faster than a wild fire on a plain of parched sagebrush. The entire campus buzzed with happy expectations. By the time Colin dropped by the office to discuss all matters, the pressure to develop the perfect date was intense. Colin Browne had frayed nerves again. It took three drops by the office to finally settle on "The Plan" for the much-ballyhooed date. In the wise words of Colin Browne, "The Plan" was simple and elegant.

The outline for "The Plan for The Date" included:
(1) Pick Libby Lou up at her dormitory at 7:00pm,
(2) Swing by the Candy Store for Snickers and Cokes,
(3) Head to the gym to see what's happening,
(4) Stroll down the path by Headmaster's house to smell Libby Lou's favorite flowers,
(5) Pit stop at music room to listen privately to some trumpets on the good sound system,
(6) Back to Libby Lou's dormitory by curfew,
(6A) Goodnight kiss.

The 6A part was the addendum from Mr. McMillan and me that we did not mention too often because of the frayed-nerves business. The premium throughout the night was uninterrupted private time to listen to Libby Lou because Colin Browne loved to hear the sound of her voice.

I was with Mr. and Mrs. McMillan in the caretaker's cottage at the front gate of the Linden Lodge on the night of the date. At precisely 6:30pm there was a triple knock on the front door. When we opened the door, there stood Colin Browne dressed impeccably in his best long sleeve white shirt, best tie, best trousers, best sports coat, best shoes shined to a very high gloss. Colin Browne spoke with a calm confidence, "Beg your pardon, Sirs and Mrs. McMillan, beg your pardon, but I was wondering if I might borrow the mirror over the sink in your front bathroom?" Mr. McMillan and I looked at each other and silently raised our eyebrows.

After securing the proper permission from Mrs. McMillan, Colin Browne made his way carefully to the front bathroom. The blind from birth Colin Browne turned on the light above the mirror over the sink. We three adults crowded into the small hallway to watch in silence. Colin Browne stood erect and stared into the mirror. He slowly turned his head to the right while he kept eyes glued to his reflected image. He carefully brushed with his good right fingers a couple of imagined unruly hairs on the left side of his perfectly coiffured head. He slowly turned his head to the left continuing to lock his eyes on his mirrored image. Remember, Teens, that Colin Browne was blind from birth and had no use for a mirror or the light above the mirror. The right side of his head passed a meticulous inspection of his hair. He next looked directly into the mirror and straightened his tie that already had a perfect Windsor knot. Colin Browne picked with his good right hand an imaginary piece of lint off the left shoulder of his sports coat and flicked it into space. We watched in silence while Colin Browne fastidiously dusted both lapels of his sports coat. He took a final look at himself in the mirror and turned to us. Colin Browne spoke with a quiet confidence, "Beg your pardon, Sirs and Mrs. McMillan, beg your pardon, but as you know I have a date with Miss Libby Lou in just a few minutes, sooo, how do I look?" Oh, Mrs. McMillan broke down crying happy tears and then went to get her camera. We three men-folk stood hitching-up our trousers and philosophizing how men had to put up with this kind of stuff when a real man got involved with a woman.

Colin Browne regained his royal stature and left the caretaker's cottage smiling and humming to himself. Colin's date with Libby Lou went exactly according to the planned outline, including 6A. The next day Colin Browne had a sparkle in his blind eyes and a high bounce in his uneven steps. Colin Browne also had a roguish, not sheepish, grin from ear to ear.

B. APPLIED THEOLOGY – PRAYERS OF ADORATION

People, the story of Colin Browne has an application to prayers of adoration. If the Teenager wants to elevate prayer-life above the kindergarten level, the living a prayer of adoration is an ultimate and attainable goal between the Teenager and Almighty God. There is the mystery of God involved in applying worship of God the Creator and the Theology of Adoration to daily living. Colin Browne was a good example of a living prayer of adoration to the Most Powerful, Most Mysterious, Most Holy God. Colin Browne never bemoaned or whined about his severe handicaps. Colin simply lived the gift of life with love. He was a grace-filled and holy Teenager who never called himself holy or full of grace. Colin Browne simply loved neighbor and God, and his love showed in his everyday actions.

Good went from Colin Browne through his harsh daily existence to the people around him. Colin Browne exemplified the mystery of God (why Colin Browne's pain) and the wisdom of God (good from Colin's handicaps) in his daily life. God "nurtured" the life of Colin in the righteousness of God; God "instructed" the life of Colin in God's laws of love; God "reproved" the life of Colin in the wisdom of God (2Esdras 8:12, NOAB/NRSV, p. 321, AP; = 4Esdras 8:12 in the Latin Vulgate Appendix). Therefore, the daily crippled life of Colin Browne gave a majestic glory to God the Most High and praise to God the Most Holy Love. The gift of Colin Browne's life was a constant living prayer of adoration to God.

a. Humility

Prayers of adoration and the praise of God do not always involve pain and suffering like the living example of Colin Browne's crippled body coupled with his love for the gift of life. Nevertheless, prayers of adoration always involve the virtue of humility. It is not wise for any human to go before the God of All Power in prayer acting like a stubborn jackass and demanding or expecting certain things in return for cooperation. Humble adoration of God is not a false bow to God based on God-given stuff in return. The humble adoration of God is a positive attitude of the mind and heart that focuses a dignity and a respect on the One True God of Antiquity. Teens are most capable of adoring/worshiping God with humility.

Jesus Christ bluntly told his Apostles that the greatest person in the Kingdom of God is the least person. Humility is a prerequisite for salvation. Jesus Christ said intentionally, "Truly I tell you, unless you change and become like children, you will never enter the kingdom of heaven. Whoever becomes humble like this child is the greatest in the kingdom of heaven" (Mt.18:3-4; see also, please, Mk.9:33-7; Lk.9:46-8, 18:17). Jesus utilized a real child as a symbol for humility.

Teens, who have little "brat" brother or "brat" sister, know that little children are not naturally humble. Little children are sometimes selfish and stuck on themselves. However, they are most dependent on their parents. Little children simply trust and openly love parents.

Jesus never condoned negative childish behavior. Jesus cleverly pointed to childlike relations with the parents to symbolize a humble relationship between self and the Divine Presence. The recognition of dependency on God the Father is the key to all humble prayers of adoration. To choose a change and to become like children is a shift from self-chosen wants to the need for a truly humble relationship with God the Father. A simple and humble trust in God is a concrete factor shared by all saints in the Kingdom/Reign/Rule of God.

A person may humble oneself without degrading self. Humility recognizes that the individual has a lot to learn regardless of age and intelligence. Humility does not take anything away from the spiritual or intellectual self. A person who humbles self before the Almighty God is an individual who sets limits on self. As Teens assume more responsibilities for their own selves, they experience the arrogance and pride built into all positions of authority. The self-imposed limits and the self-regulations of a humble person help to check tendencies towards arrogance and a negative pride. Various forms of rebellion occur where there is no humility. It is a bad choice for a Teen when the rebellion is against the Almighty God of Divine Love.

Humility before the Divine Intelligence is the basis for all prayers of adoration and for worship of the Most Holy God. From the lands of sunrise and sunset at the ends of earth there is praise, worship, awe, joy of God (Ps.113:1-3; Mal.1:11; Ps. 65:8, NOAB/ NRSV; Ps. 65:9, NAB). The gaze of the Teen from a green valley to permanent snow above the timberline of a mountain raises the consciousness of majestic glory to the worthy adoration of God. A Teen's stare at the ocean from the broad expanse of water on the horizon to constant waves hitting the uncountable grains of sand on a deserted beach invokes a finite human to worship the Infinite God. A Teen's look up into a clear night sky summons adoration of the Almighty and humble respect for the dignity of God. There are many reasons around all Teens to choose humble prayers of adoration for the worship of the Almighty God. All involve the mystery of God.

Take, for example, stars in the night sky. Beauty from the light of stars may help Teens to raise their minds and hearts to adore God, the Creator of the mysterious universe. When a Teenager looks at the awesome night sky and returns thoughts and feelings to God, the joy and happiness of the Teen from the mental and heartfelt bow to the Creator is holy worship of God. That is very good stuff from the theological perspective for two reasons: (1) a Teen's worship of God the Divine Creator taps into the divine mystery of God expressed in ancient Theology of Salvation History and the Theology of Prayer; (2) Teens carry on the worship/prayer traditions for themselves and future generations.

If a Teenager wants to utilize the night sky to "get heavy" about humility before Almighty God with prayers of adoration, the Teenager only needs to research the knowledge base and educated guesses of mankind concerning stars in space. When Teenagers look into the night sky, Teens see about 8,000 stars with the naked eye (4,000 in both the Northern and Southern Hemispheres). Astronomers up the number of the viewed stars when they utilize the Hubble Space Telescope (launched in 1990) and the largest computer-enhanced optical telescope (a 387-inch telescope at Mauna Kea Observatory in Hawaii). A best guesstimate of astronomers for the number of stars sighted at the beginning of the third millennium include: (1) the Milky Way Galaxy with our sun and solar system has hundreds of billions of stars; (2) the Milky Way Galaxy is only one of several hundred million galaxies in a viewing range of modern (2002A.D.) telescopes; (3) next nearest galaxy to us is the Andromeda Galaxy that has a hundred billion stars and is approximately 2½ million light years from the Milky Way Galaxy ("Star," Microsoft Encarta '98 Encyclopedia.).

The man-made concept of light years is also humbling before the intelligence, glory, majesty of God. A light year is the distance that a ray of light travels through space in a solar year. Light travels at the speed of 186,282 miles per second (300,000km per second). One light year equals 5,880,000,000,000 miles (Ibid., "Light Year"). Our sun is roughly 30,000 light years from the center of the Milky Way Galaxy. The galaxy is disk-shaped and looks like a huge saucer. The central bulge is 10,000 light years thick, and the diameter of the disk is about 100,000 light years (Ibid., "Milky Way").

Andromeda Galaxy is about 2½ million light years from our Milky Way Galaxy. The Hawaii telescope reveals galaxies as far away as several billion light years. The Hubble Space Telescope confirms the existence of quasars, which are very small but brilliantly luminous extragalactic systems. The light from quasars takes several billion years to reach earth traveling at 186,282 miles per second.

Milky Way Galaxy rotates around an axis at its galactic center. In the area of our sun and solar system, one rotation takes about 200 million years traveling at the speed of approximately 130 miles per second (Ibid., "Astronomy"). A galactic rotation is in addition to our earth rotating around the sun and the moon rotating around earth. The age of our earth is about 4.7 billion years (Ibid., "Earth"). The oldest known star is about 16 billion years; a big bang theory for the age of the universe is about 20 billion years (Ibid., "Cosmology").

From the theological perspective, Catholics/humans credit God with the creation of all physical existence. We give God the honor and the glory from the laws of astrophysics. God is the Creator, and God = the First Cause = the Ultimate Cause. God makes the laws of gravity and astrophysics. God owns the "cosmic library" where the humans tap into the Divine Intelligence as human knowledge of math and physics grows. Teens worship the One True God of Antiquity with prayers of adoration.

Stellar numbers and the astronomical theories boggle the mind and humble the spirit. The educated guesses broach the subject of metaphysics and an ontological argument. From humble theological perspectives, Teenagers admit that Teenagers do not know all things absolutely. Teens take a leap of faith, and Teens trust that all truth abides in the mystery of the Almighty God. For the sake of minds and spirits, Teens define God as the Creator, the First Cause, the

Ultimate Power, the Most Holy Mystery. God is Divine Presence in the eternal instant and in the eternal present. God has no teachers. God has no counselors (Is.40:10-7; Wis.9:13,17; Rom.11:33-6; 1Cor. 2:11). God is Divine Intelligence. God is All Knowledge. God is All Truth. And the Almighty God loves each Teen. Look into the clear night sky and ask yourself if God is worthy of worship. Teenagers, please, look up with humility and offer prayers of adoration to God the Most Holy Divine Intelligence.

Admitting limits in the human intelligence allows true worship and pure adoration of God the Creator. The laws of astrophysics, spatial density, and gravity are man-made words to describe concepts that exist as laws of God's truth for 20 billion years. Vast brainpower and cumulative technologies of mankind reach a miniscule understanding of Divine Intelligence. Humility before God allows the Teen to see the beauty of God everywhere. Recognition of God's beauty helps to lead the Teenager toward true worship of the Creator and prayers of adoration to God. If a Teen opens humble eyes to the beauty of God, even a drop of water may raise the Teen mind and heart to God.

For example, focus on an individual drop of rain during the next sprinkle. A drop of rainwater gathers its weight to form a drip from a housetop. The tiny raindrop is part of the beauty and glory of God in the present moment. With more rain, the drop is lost in a downpour. With less rain, the drop of water is gone from sight. But let a single ray of sunshine hit the drop of rainwater, and the sparkle will truly lift the soul. The splash of colors is magnificent. Only the human, who sees and understands drops of water, can choose to give more glory to God than a single raindrop acting as a prism of light. Scientists tell us the past and future of the raindrop with a complicated history of cycling water vapors. A humble person sees the beauty of God in the simple present. The human spirit enjoys the glory of God in the beauty of a raindrop refracting a natural light. With mind and heart lifted to God, a Teen may give thanks to the Creator of a tiny drop of rainwater who is full of wisdom, honor, intelligence, power, beauty, life. A Teen may choose to worship not the reflection of God in the beautiful drop of water splashing the colors of the rainbow. A Teen may choose to adore God directly as the Creator of all beauty and as the Most Holy Spirit fulfilling a humble joy in the natural human spirit.

b. Tension and Innocent Suffering

The worship of the Divine Creator and prayers of adoration to the Most Holy God experience a tension generated by humanity. Colin Browne's life was a living praise and adoration of the wisdom of the Almighty God. Wisdom of God is the active cause of all goodness including a real good spun out of the real negative of Colin Browne's broken body (Wis.3:4-6; Brown, New Jerome Biblical Commentary, p.514). However, humanity often creates the tension between the concept of the God of All Good and the observation of the innocent sufferer. Tension sometimes blocks the prayer of adoration to God the Creator and the worship of God the Divine Intelligence. It takes faith and love to release tension so that prayers of adoration flow as worship to the One True God.

There is always tension in the lives of young women and young men. Only the graveyard has no tension. If the Teen is alive, there is tension: worship God vs. worship the mundane (popularity, money, power, status, fashion), good vs. evil, right vs. wrong, love vs. hate. Eventually a person reaches the point where the tension is between good and better or between better and best. This may very well exist as a point of wisdom or a point of sainthood. It is certainly the focal point for the conversion of the mind and heart to God. The tension exists within a good person to either retreat into the mediocrity of a comfortable goodness or to risk total love. The command and the example of Jesus to love God demands that individuals choose to risk total love. Prayer helps in this conversion process to fire mind and heart with love of God. It is a real temptation to remain within the smugness of a pretty good person.

Wasn't that part of the critique from Jesus directed at the smug Pharisees? They knew the Ten Commandments of God to Moses. And yet the smug Pharisees overdeveloped a nitpicky list of minor laws (613 other laws or casuistic rules in Torah) that endangered the comprehension of the essential love and worship of God (Anderson, Understanding the Old Testament, p.536; Lk.11:39-46; Mt.23:1-7, 13-28). For example, concerning the Mosaic command to "Remember to keep holy the Sabbath day" (Ex.20:8), the laws and the rules of the Pharisees questioned how far the true believer could walk on a Sabbath and if the true believer could rescue his donkey from injury without breaking a Sabbath. Manufactured tensions of the Pharisees blocked pure and true worship of God.

In contrast to smug Pharisees stood Saint Joseph who reflected an unconditional love of God. Saint Joseph's choice to risk total love for God throughout his life resulted in a mind enlightened by God the Holy Spirit and a heart filled with love for Baby Jesus. Saint Joseph was a premium example of faith and love dissipating all the tensions between God the Creator and man the creature. The life of Saint Joseph was a living prayer of adoration raised to the One True God. Joy of the Lord was the reward of Saint Joseph for refusing to retreat into the mediocrity of a smug faith in God the Creator. Peace of the Lord was the alternative of Saint Joseph to the debilitating tensions that break the relationship of faith between creature and the Creator. There was no block in the prayers of adoration from Saint Joseph to God because his faith and his love of God overcame all the tensions between the concept of the God of All Goodness and the observation of the innocent sufferer. The challenges of God to the faith of Saint

Joseph were not easy, but ultimately the obedience of Saint Joseph to God was faith in action.

Faith in action presupposes a complete trust in God. Faith, trust, and love are the multi-cornerstones to all prayers of adoration and all worship of God. Just like God with Colin Browne, God "nurtures" the life of a Teen in God's goodness and righteousness; God "instructs" the Teenager in God's law; God "reproves" the Teenager in God's wisdom (2Esdras 8: 12, NOAB/NRSV, p.321, AP; = 4Esdras 8:12 in Latin Vulgate Appendix).

It is precisely God's "reproving" through Divine Intelligence that draws the human reaction which breaks down the worship of God. When the individual sees the innocent person suffer, the question becomes, "Why does the All Good God allow the innocent to suffer so much pain?" The next question follows closely, "Why does the All Good God allow evil in the world?" Down the list of questions about the mystery of evil is the question, "What terrible sin did the person commit to deserve so much punishment, pain, suffering from God?" These are some ancient questions that tend to breach the faith, trust, love of God and put the worship of God on hold.

It is difficult for idealistic Teens to not ask these questions when they see ethnic cleansing, rape, prejudice, social injustice, poverty, starvation, wars, murders, death of a baby, grandpa fighting cancer, mental retardation, blindness, Colin Browne's gimped-up left side. It is not wrong for the Teen to question the mystery of pain, suffering, and evil. However, Teens, think seriously about your obligation to worship God above all things including pain, suffering, evil. Faith, trust, love of the Omnipotent God deal with obedience to God's law of love even when we do not understand the mystery of God and the mystery of evil.

Some of the holiest people and some of the best minds in human history thought and felt many ideas about the mystery of the innocent sufferer. Certainly the Teenager may research the ideas of the great spiritual thinkers. Please, also consider the thoughts of David, the modern plumber. David had a son who was a very good person. The son married when he was nineteen, and all were so happy. About three months after the marriage the daughter-in-law accidentally lost control of their truck on an icy road. The truck flipped over in a ditch, and the son died instantly in the crushed passenger's seat. David, the plumber, stayed drunk for five years. David could not understand the death of his good son when lousy people live. David's constant thought was that his son told him every day, "Dad, I love you." His constant question was, "Why did God allow my son to die at such a young age?" David did not want to live until the day he looked into the mirror and saw a drunk with a very bad hangover. The thought registered that God wanted him to go to work for God. David, the sober plumber, now testifies constantly to four thoughts: (1) I taught my son to hunt and fish, but not to pray; (2) my son's death taught me how to pray; (3) I put love of my son above love of God; (4) my son's death put love of God and service to God first.

The lessons from innocent suffering are always difficult to learn because they involve faith in a mysterious God and lack of personal control over extenuating circumstances. Maybe God allows pain and suffering because God expects a person who suffers to show others the Christian way to handle the negatives. Maybe the All Just God decides the individual innocent sufferer is not so innocent, and pain cleanses/purifies the individual from temporal punishment due for the sin/offenses against the laws of God. Maybe God utilizes individual pain and suffering to elevate the spirituality of the people around the innocent sufferer. Maybe innocent sufferings show God's spiritual education of Teenagers through a corrective discipline and a test of fidelity in which God recognizes the people most worthy of God for all eternity (Wis.3:4-6; Jerome, p.514). It is harsh to think about the God of All Mercy toying with people as if humans were little puppets dangling on divine strings. Within Teen efforts to think through the cosmic implications of the innocent sufferer, theological caution is appropriate for Teens to not fall victim to the occupational hazards of theologians: some theologians forget that innocent suffering always deals with Divine Mystery.

Understanding anything about the mystery of God requires faith in God because Teenagers reach points where Teens simply do not know. However, there are three positive potentials about faith in God with relationship to the innocent sufferer: (1) the people, who usually pray with little fervor, pray with zeal to God for the innocent sufferer producing a potential for a humble dependency on God; (2) pain and suffering of the innocent bring people closer to God in their thoughts and feelings producing the potential for the real conversion of minds and hearts to God; (3) to truly worship and purely adore the God of All Goodness, people must get past holding grudges against God for not getting their way with the innocent sufferer producing a potential for true faith and pure trust in God.

The reality of innocent suffering, pain, and evil is undeniable. It is sometimes easier to accept the existence of evil, pain, suffering than to understand its meaning. According to ancient Hebrew belief expressed in the Old Testament, painful experiences and suffering were concrete signs of God's judgement. The classic statement of the Old Testament for the traditional view of "divine retribution" was that the wicked were punished and the just rewarded in this life (Ps. 37:27-29). In the New Testament culture, Jesus did not necessarily argue against the Old Testament connection between a moral good and evil/pain/suffering. Jesus said suffering represented a judgement of God; suffering was a specific call to repentance so that a spiritual catastrophe did not overcome his listeners (Lk.13:1-9). Along with his "repent or perish" message, Jesus said to love your unjust enemies, who cause pain and suffering, because God's sun shines and God's rain falls on both the just and unjust (Mt.5:43-48). Both Old and New Testament agree that pain, suffering, and evil spirits were under the sovereignty of God, the Creator of all material and spiritual things. This means for modern Teenagers that evil spirits and suffering do not control humans by suppressing the individual freedom to choose and the responsibility to worship God the Most Holy Spirit.

However, evil and sufferings exist and add to the destruction of love. As a result, all breaks in relationships with God deteriorate the worship of God. The perfectly good God calls idealistic Teenagers to join the struggle against evil and innocent suffering in every form: all social injustice, oppression, Teen school massacres, infidelity, ethnic cleansing, Teen gang murders, prejudice, Teen suicide, dishonesty. God's call is for the Teen to put faith into action and at the very least to put value on prayers of adoration to God. God already won cosmic battles ions ago between God vs. evil. God is stronger than evil. But the ancient conflict of evil vs. the sovereignty of God encompasses modern Teens. The individual heart and mind is the battleground for the conflict. The expressions and experiences of the struggle are the worldwide miseries of the innocent sufferers.

Bishops at the Second Vatican Council made a serious comment on this ancient conflict affecting the modern world. In the document <u>Pastoral Constitution on the Church in the Modern World (Gaudium et Spes)</u> written by the bishops and signed by Pope Paul VI in 1965, they said:

> ...the hierarchy of values has been disordered, good and evil intermingle, and every man and every group is interested only in its own affairs, not in those of others. So it is that the earth has not yet become the scene of true brotherhood... The whole of man's history has been the story of dour combat with the powers of evil, stretching, so our Lord tells us, from the very dawn of history until the last day. Finding himself in the midst of the battlefield man has to struggle to do what is right, and it is at great cost to himself, and aided by God's grace, that he succeeds in achieving his own inner integrity. n.37

God won the ancient cosmic battle between good vs. evil. God is sovereign over evil, pain, and suffering. However, evil constantly fights the dominance of God, and as a result, God wars against evil in all times. It is the real conflict between good and evil that snares Teens in the modern times. The Teenager has a free will, which is a gift from God, and the Teen uses his/her free will to choose between good and evil. The will of God is for the Teen to use his/her free will and to choose love of God above all things including pain, suffering, evil. But God does not force the Teen to choose God. A Teenager may in fact use his/her free will to choose evil, and consequently, evil instead of love of God spreads in the modern world. God is the first to know if a Teenager chooses adoration of God above all things or adoration of lesser entities.

The choice-conscious Teenager identifies three principle options in the response to recognizing evil and especially innocent suffering (McBrien, Catholicism, p. 345). First, the Teen may choose rebellion and revolution against God. The Teen may choose to rebel, revolt, shake the angry fist at God when the Teen sees so much pain and suffering in individual lives and in the world. A Teen spiritual temper tantrum directed at Almighty God might vent Teen frustrations and give God a pretty good laugh. Nevertheless, the spiritual spitting and slobbering at the mouth will not do much good, and it might lead to major depression when the Teen runs out of energy.

The second option is resignation. A Teenager may try to bear up stoically to the horror of evil and the innocent sufferer. A Teenager may get tight-lipped and avoid the question, "Why is there evil and innocent suffering?" Teenagers have the ability to go into a spiritual stupor or a metaphysical shock. Teenagers simply accept what they neither understand nor have the power to instantly change. However, resignation spiritually stuns Teens.

The third option is trust and hope in God. The basic paradox is the same for a modern Teen as for the entire historical human race: to worship the perfectly good God who mysteriously allows evil and especially innocent suffering. Prayers of adoration require trust and hope in God. It was a complete trust and hope that Job of the Old Testament and Jesus in the New Testament had in God the Creator. Both were innocent sufferers, and both asked the question, "Why?"

c. Job, the Classic Innocent Sufferer

The Book of Job had an anonymous author and unknown date of origin. Job was the classic example of the innocent sufferer in the Hebrew literature from the sixth century B.C. to modern times. Job was a holy man and Oriental aristocrat with land, riches, good health, family, wisdom, friends, sons, much respect (Jb.1:1-5). The serious theological hassle in the Book of Job was the meaning of suffering in the life of the just and innocent man, not in the life of an evil bum. The doctrine of divine retribution (God rewards good people and God punishes bad people) was basic to the ancient Hebrew wisdom. The emphasis on the good life (riches, power, social status, large family with sons, good health, respect) was the almost infallible equation that wisdom = life of virtue = success in life (Jerome, p.466-7). The writer of Job did not ridicule the ancient doctrine of divine retribution. However, readers recognized the author's challenge of inadequacy to traditional doctrine in light of the mystery of God and the mystery of the innocent sufferer.

A cynical Adversary/Satan/Accuser expressed the fundamental theme in the Book of Job with the penetrating question to the Lord, "Does Job fear God for nothing?" (Ibid., p.469-70; Jb.1:9). In other words, do human beings serve God because of what they receive from God? "Fear God" meant the realization of one's relationship to God the Creator by showing reverence and obedience to God. "For nothing" meant out of love without expecting rewards or payments (i.e., money, power, status, good health). Did Job worship God for the love of God or for the "goodies" from God? God allowed the evil Adversary to withhold the gifts of God from Job and to demonstrate if Job's love centered on the gifts or the Giver of the gifts (Jb.1:12).

Job lost everything. Job was the innocent sufferer. He definitely questioned, "Why?" (Jb.3:11-26), but he maintained his integrity and his innocence. Job did not curse God because of his misfortunes. Job persevered in his faith that God loved him. But Job experienced bewilderment concerning the goodness of God. He even questioned God's gift of life, which was no gift, when his life was so miserable (Jb.3:20-2; Jerome, p.471). He sunk to the verge of nonexistence, and all abandoned him (Jb.19:19-20). His closest friends stuck to their "commercial morality" because their motives for serving God were the fear of punishment and the hope of reward (Jerome, p.479). Job was utterly alone in his serving God for love.

Job searched for God's presence and was downhearted when he could not find God. Despite Job's fidelity, God was remote and inaccessible. Job experienced a dark night of the soul (Jb.23:16-17; Jerome, p.480). His feeling of total abandonment by God was the sharpest torture. Job loved God, and Job regularly experienced the Divine Presence in early morning worship and prayers of adoration (Jb.1:5). His feeling of God's absence from his life was horrible. Job knew that he was totally innocent of any wrongdoing. He had a clear conscience. Job was steadfast in his faith that God loved him even in his misery (Jb.27:6). He trusted in God's help and redemption from his miserable existence (Jb.19:25-7). Job hoped for a relief from his feelings of abandonment with the restoration of the close relationship with the Divine Presence in his life (Jb.29:2-6).

Job had no answer to his problem of innocent suffering because any answer tapped directly into the mystery of God's wisdom. Job found that there was no debate with the God of Divine Intelligence. Job knew little of the origins for natural and familiar phenomena such as stars, land, and sea. However, Job understood that the majestic glory of God and the mysteries of God were everywhere. The Divine Intelligence involved a series of unanswerable questions (Jb.38:1-42:6). Job did not understand the deeper mystery of God's treatment of people who love God (Jerome, p.486).

Modern people are in the same position as the ancient poet of the Book of Job. Modern knowledge bases about the mechanics of stars, land, and seas are greater than the ancient understanding of the author. Nevertheless, the same mysteries of God exist for Teens today. Secrets of Divine Intelligence remain elusive and challenge our trust, hope, and faith in God. Teens should not reject worship of God because they lack understanding of God's treatment for people who love God. That is a human problem from antiquity based on the transcendence of Divine Wisdom. However, modern Teenagers may learn from the ancient Job.

Job realized that answers involved a search for wisdom, which is a gift from God (Jb.28:1-28). For Job, just understanding stuff was not true wisdom. The author of Job let God explain, "Truly, the fear of the Lord, that is wisdom" (Jb.28:28). Job had no fear of the power of God in Mother Nature: earthquakes, hurricanes, tornadoes, floods, and volcanoes. Job chose "fear of the Lord" from his mind and heart. Job had a dignity and a respect for the awesome God that translated into reverence, obedience, piety, service. Throughout his innocent suffering, Job never lost faith that God loved him. Job had a special relationship with God the Almighty Creator based on a mutual and reciprocal communion of love. Job had fear of the Lord based on the dignity and respect of true love for God. Therefore, Job had wisdom.

The Adversary/Satan/Accuser asked the serious question, "Does Job fear God for nothing?" Job chose to answer "yes" by living his life in good and bad times for the dignity of God, for the respect of God, for the love of God. Job worshiped God for love not for God's goodies. Job passed the test of the innocent sufferer. God of love restored all good things to Job and relieved his innocent suffering. Job anchored hope and trust in God. His prayers of adoration were pure, and his worship of God remained true. Those are lessons for all Teens of all ages to learn from the ancient Book of Job.

d. Jesus, the Epitome of the Innocent Sufferer

Teens may also choose to learn from Jesus, the epitome of the innocent sufferer. Jesus committed no sin and no offense against the laws of God the Father. Jesus was conceived holy by the power of God the Holy Spirit (Mt.1:18-22; Lk.1:30-35). Jesus was "God from God, Light from Light, true God from true God" (Catechism, "Nicene Creed," p. 49). There was no theological reason based on original or habitual sin for Jesus to suffer and die. The historical Jesus was truly the innocent sufferer. Jesus chose total obedience to the will of God the Father that included suffering, death on a cross, and resurrection from the dead. The Jesus of history is the premium teacher for true worship and pure prayers of adoration to God the Creator. Jesus is the perfect example of complete trust and hope in God the Father. Jesus is the most humble role model, who never let human tension between the goodness of God and innocent suffering block worship of God and prayers of adoration.

Although he experienced intense pain and innocent suffering, Jesus was totally loyal in his love and obedience to God the Creator. The virtue of Jesus never bogged down in self-interest. Jesus never served God for fear of punishment or hope of reward, which Hebrew divine retribution doctrine sponsored. The suffering of the innocent Jesus educated people to God's discipline, God's correction, God's test of fidelity that God used to justify people worthy of the eternal life with God (Wis.3:1-12; Jerome, p.514). The suffering of the innocent Jesus leads Teens to God through his hanging on the cross and his rising from the tomb (1Pet.3:18, 22; 2:21-25). Jesus purifies Teens with the truth of his innocent suffering. Jesus guides Teenagers with his innocent suffering in the way of holiness to the Most Holy God of Antiquity.

When the disciples saw a man blind from birth, they asked Jesus if the man or his parents sinned. They thought in the concepts for the traditional Hebrew doctrine of divine retribution, and Jesus schooled them in innocent suffering. Jesus corrected them emphatically when he said the blind man suffered not because of sin but for the glory of God. Jesus shifted focus for the ancient Hebrew doctrine of divine retribution from the cause of the blindness to the purpose of God for blindness. Jesus answered his disciples, "Neither this man nor his parents sinned; he was born blind so that God's works might be revealed in him" (Jn.9:33). Then Jesus showed the power and glory of God when he cured the man of a life-long blindness. The healed blind man told the skeptical and cynical Pharisees that Jesus was from God because God listened to the one who worshiped God and obeyed God's will (Jn.9:30-3).

Jesus was the excellent living example of not overvaluing any innocent suffering. Innocent suffering is not a bargaining chip with God. Creatures are not in a position to demand comforts from God the Creator. Jesus Christ never said to God the Creator, "I innocently suffer, so I deserve longevity of life, power, status, fame, good health from you, God the Father." Jesus made no claims on God the Father to balance his innocent suffering with worldly goodies. As a matter of fact, Jesus showed and told all Teenagers the exact opposite of overvaluing innocent suffering. Jesus gave the disciples and Teens a most serious warning about the harsh reality of demanding things from God. Jesus told the disciples to do all things commanded and then to say, "We are worthless slaves; we have done only what we ought to have done!" (Lk.17:10). Irrespective of the value of innocent suffering, a Teen relationship with God makes obedience to God an obligation not an opportunity for reward. Jesus never overvalued his innocent suffering because he never let his individual pains cause breaks in worship and love of God. If Teenagers utilize Jesus as a premium example of moral and ethical living, Teens need to negate both overvaluing innocent suffering and also putting contingencies on worship of God and on prayers of adoration.

It is easy for Teenagers to fall into the ancient trap of theological simplicity concerning daily ethical living. The ancient doctrine of the divine retribution is fantastic as long as things "rock on" your way. The good people get God's goodies, and an angry God smokes the bad people. It is difficult to coordinate true and pure worship of God with real pain and real suffering of the innocent. The ancient Hebrew doctrine of divine retribution is totally inadequate to explain the cross of Jesus. It is theological simplicity to put both pain and suffering on human scales of human justice.

It is too theologically simplistic to have a T-bar of justice with all pain and suffering on one plate balanced against God's goodies on the other plate. A theological tendency is to manipulate the scales by overvaluing the innocent suffering. The dominant spiritual attitude becomes, "I suffer too much misery and I don't have enough of God's goodies." It is like the old-timey butcher holding thumbs on fraudulent scales to make extra money by cheating his trustworthy customers. Scales of God's justice involve the mystery of God. Teenage minds and Teenage hearts can not manipulate the reality of God's justice. God's goodies are God's gifts. Teens are at the mercy of the Divine Intelligence. Teens can only pray. Pain and suffering warps simple theological thoughts about daily ethical living because all innocent suffering always involves the mystery of God.

When Teens experience pain, there is not a simple explanation. Innocent suffering is not simple theology. When Jesus experienced the pain of the cross, value from his innocent suffering was intrinsic to the human redemption from sin and to the restoration of grace for humanity. That's heavy theology because all the thoughts seriously involve crosscurrents of ideas steeped in the mystery of God. When Jesus experienced pain, he prayed. When Teens experience pain, it is time to decide who is #1. It is time for prayers of adoration to God, The #1. It is not the time to collapse theologically and spiritually. It is a time to worship God, The #1. The best example for Teenagers of coping with pain is Jesus. The best role model for Teens in prayers of adoration is Jesus. The one who rose above innocent suffering to worship God the Creator is Jesus.

Let our theological thoughts on generic pain not belittle the real physical misery in the innocent suffering of Jesus. The historical Jesus suffered real pain in his total obedience and total love of God the Father. Jesus Christ sweated blood on the night of his arrest as he prayed in mental and emotional agony in the garden (Lk. 22:44). Hematidrosis is the physiological condition of sweating blood. Bloody sweat is very rare and only occurs when the person is under extreme emotional stress. The tiny capillaries in the sweat glands break, and blood mixes with sweat.

While his closest friends slept, Jesus knelt in prayer. The normal posture for a prayer in the ancient world was to stand. Jesus knelt in humility before God the Father. Jesus prayed that God the Father remove the cup of innocent suffering from him. Jesus bowed his will in perfect obedience to the will of God the Father when he prayed, "...not my will but yours be done" (Lk. 22:42). Jesus knew that his destiny included his death in Jerusalem. God the Father willed that Jesus work kingdom ministry for all oppressed and all marginalized people. The spiritual and psychological conflicts of Jesus with the status quo of the religious and political structures were paramount and imminent. Jesus in his anguish prayed more earnestly with even greater intensity. Then, Saint Luke, the physician, stated that Jesus sweated blood.

The prayers of Jesus strengthened him to do the will of God the Father. When Judas betrayed him with a kiss of friendship and the temple police arrested him, Jesus did not resist the arrest. When a follower of Jesus cut off the right ear of the high priest's slave, Jesus healed his enemy. Jesus did not fall into the real temptation to utilize violence, and Jesus did not abandon his nonviolent ministry to fight his arrest. Jesus went to his death forgiving and loving his enemies in basic silence that stemmed from a profound trust in a faithful God the Father (Jerome, p.717-18).

The physical misery of Jesus became more intense with Roman involvement. At the command of Pilate, Roman soldiers scourged Jesus at the pillar, crowned him with thorns, forced him to carry the cross, nailed him to the cross, mocked him hanging on the cross for over three hours, watched him die on the cross, speared him (Mt.26: 47-27:56; Mk.14:32-15:41; Lk.22:39-23:49; Jn.18:1-19:37). During his entire physiological suffering under the Roman authority, Jesus had immense psychological and spiritual pain equal in trauma to his physical pains. Jesus suffered a tremendous loneliness: "all the disciples deserted him and fled" (Mt.26:56; cf. Mk.14:50); "Peter remembered ...before the cock crows today, you will deny me three times" (Lk.22:61); "all his acquaintances, including the women who had followed him from Galilee, stood at a distance" (Lk.23:49).

Jesus also had the spiritual suffering from the feeling of the total abandonment by God the Father as he hung on the cross: "My God, my God, why have you forsaken me?" (Mt.27:46; Mk.15:34). Like Job in the Old Testament Jesus questioned, "Why?" Also like Job, Jesus did not despair when faced with severe pain. Jesus prayed from the cross to God the Father to forgive the Roman soldiers: "For they do not know what they are doing" (Lk.23:34). From the cross Jesus reconciled and restored the relationship between the crucified criminal and God the Father: "Truly I tell you, today you will be with me in Paradise" (Lk.23:43). Jesus trusted the will of God the Father despite his real pain and innocent suffering.

The Roman crucifixion was a horrible death. The ordinary death sentence from capital punishment for insurgents against Rome was enslavement. The Romans enslaved the guilty to get free labor and to make revolutionaries suffer a slow miserable death. For example, the Romans sent slaves to the rich silver mines in Spain to work until death. "Condemnation to the mines" was a major capital punishment (Lewis, Roman Civilization. Sourcebook II: The Empire, p.547, 158, 163, 188-90). More often, the Romans put slaves to work on their large farms, but Romans sometimes chained slaves in the bowels of ships. Slaves rowed the Roman navy and rich Roman merchants around the Mediterranean Sea until death. Roman crucifixion was the special horror reserved for the most rebellious criminals. It was "the supreme penalty," and a capital punishment designed to totally intimidate the living (Ibid., p.547).

The Roman fiendish style was to plant a cross outside the town's busiest gate for a maximum effect from shock. All entering or leaving town saw the major penalty for loosing any face-off against Roman power. The condemned hung naked on a cross in total degradation and humiliation until death. The hanging on the cross was neither the beginning nor the end of the individual's pain. Roman crucifixion usually began with the Roman soldiers flogging the condemned to weaken the body and break the spirit of the individual. Then Roman soldiers made the prisoner carry the crossbeam of the cross through the town on the busier streets to the execution site outside the main gate. The crossbeam weighed about 110 pounds, and total weight of the cross was about 300 pounds. Roman soldiers at the execution site sometimes tied the prisoner to the cross probably like the two criminals crucified with Jesus. The rope made from hemp was more plentiful and cost fewer denarii than iron nails. However, nails in the hands and feet made a maximum negative impact of public relations. The Roman soldiers used heavy, square, wrought-iron, 7½ inch nails to crucify, and the innocent Jesus got treatment similar to the worst criminal (Wilson, The Shroud of Turin, p.35, pl.15).

The crucified died very slowly on the cross in the heat or the cold without food or water. Death took two or three days while a crucified person suffered extreme pain. When the crucified lost energy, birds usually pecked-out the eyeballs, and wild animals started eating the entrails (Barbet, A Doctor at Calvary, p.51). The crucified sometimes stayed on a cross long after death. The Roman soldiers thought that the rotting cadaver and the stench from human death deterred other potential revolutionaries against the Roman Empire. If the Roman soldiers in the execution squad had any smidgen of mercy for the crucified, two Roman soldiers lifted a spare crossbeam and rammed the kneecaps of the individual hanging on the cross. Otherwise, the Roman military staff broke the legs of the crucified with iron bars or heavy mallets (Ibid., p.134, 172; NOAB/NRSV, p.156, NT). Broken legs or kneecaps meant that the crucified suffocated in minutes. The crucified needed stiffened legs and kneecaps to put all weight on the foot nails or the rope around the feet and to lift the body for exhaling carbon dioxide. A weakened individual with broken kneecaps or legs could not hold up the body weight to breathe with only the arms tied or nailed to the crossbeam. Asphyxiation was Roman mercy for the crucified. Nevertheless, no ancient or modern historian remembered the Roman army for its mercy to insurgents.

Josephus was a Jewish historian who lived from 37 or 38 A.D. to circa 101 A.D. He wrote The Wars of the Jews in seven books and The Antiquities of the Jews in twenty books. Josephus stated in his Antiquities that a Roman army crucified two thousand Jewish rebels in 4 B.C. during riots after the death of Herod the Great (17.10.10). In Wars, Josephus said that during the Jewish revolt of 66-70 A.D. the Roman army whipped and crucified five hundred Jews every day (5.11.1). He also related in Wars that a horror of the Roman crucifixion intimidated a besieged Jewish citadel to surrender immediately when Roman soldiers set up a cross outside the walls for a popular Jewish captive "to suffer a most miserable death" (7.6.4).

Revolt against the Roman Empire meant a fight-to-death against the Roman military machine. If the insurgents capitulated before the Roman army shed its blood, the Romans dealt harshly with the rebel leaders but usually kept the local infrastructure and town intact. Total revolt meant total destruction for the losers and their cities. Romans put Caesar's governor/procurator and army in the occupied land to collect heavy taxes for Rome. As long as there were no revolts, the "Pax Romana" meant a Roman Peace based on severe taxation and perpetual occupation by the mighty and totally dominating Roman military machine. All troublemakers received Roman cruelty with no mercy. The Roman soldiers had no mercy on Jesus, the embodiment and the epitome of the innocent sufferer.

Jesus is worthy of Teen worship and adoration. The historical Jesus suffered a combination of extreme tortures from the Roman soldiers. Jesus totally obeyed the will of God the Father out of total love for God the Father. Jesus sacrificed his life in absolute trust of God the Creator. Jesus experienced excruciating pain until his death on the cross with dignity and respect for God the Father. Jesus is most worthy of Teen worship and Teen adoration because he is the epitome of the innocent sufferer for the will of God, and the only Son of God, and the second person of the Triune God. Jesus reconciled innocent suffering with worship of God the Creator through perfect obedience to the will of God the Father. The life, death, resurrection of Jesus was a living worship and a living prayer of adoration to the Most Holy God.

e. *Teen Worship*

The Holy Spirit of Jesus challenges Teenagers today to choose a life worshiping God through prayers of adoration. Colin Browne, Saint Joseph, the historical Jesus, Job made the choices to risk total love of God through a difficult daily life of faith in action. Their trust, humility, and obedience dissipated the tensions between the broken bodies of innocent sufferers and the Divine Wisdom. They did not break relationships with the Most Holy God. They simply worshiped God by living a personal prayer of adoration.

According to traditional Catholic dogma, God is the Most Holy Trinity (Catechism, n.234). God is Divine Mystery. God is the unity of Father, Son, Holy Spirit as three persons in one Godhead, divine nature, essence (Ibid., n.252-5). The Divine Mystery of the Most Holy Trinity is the central mystery of the Christian faith, the source of all other mysteries of faith, the most fundamental teaching. A traditional symbol representing the Most Holy Trinity is one equilateral triangle with three sides equal in length.

Also consider an experimental figure to symbolize the Most Holy Trinity. Tie a 12" length of string at the ends to make a circle. A Teen can make three distinct, equal, parallel lines of string out of the one circle, if the Teen's thumbs hide equidistant loops of string. Although the figure looks like three equal lines of string between the thumbs, the Teen knows that the sum of all parts is only one circle of string. The Teen might even say that the three lines are equal to one whole circle. There is one added fact to consider in the equations and all the figures symbolizing the Triune God: God the Most Holy Trinity = God the Most Holy Mystery.

If the Teen wants to elevate his/her prayer-life off a kindergarten level, consider prayers of adoration to the One True God. Prayers of adoration to the Divine Presence require a conscious individualistic choice. Humility, faith, love, trust, obedience are attainable virtues that combine in the worship of God. God the Father is the Creator and Divine Intelligence of the universe including the Teenager's earth and the Teenager's world of family and friends. God the Father, the first person of God and the Most Holy Ancient One, is worthy of Teen praise, adoration, worship. Jesus is the most obedient and the most loving Son, who experienced such horrible human pain. Jesus, the second person of God, is worthy of Teen praise, adoration, worship. The Holy Spirit is the timeless and ageless Divine Presence in the sacred history of Teen ancestors, in current minds and hearts, in future eschatological descendents. The Holy Spirit, the third person of God, is worthy of Teen praise, adoration, worship.

The Teenager has the ability to freely create space for God the Most Holy Trinity in his or her knowledge and understanding. The omnipotent God is omnipresent in the minds, hearts, virtues, positive emotions, love, cosmos, and microscopic magnifications. The Divine Presence exists for the Teenager, no matter how large or how small the space, as long as the Teen does not break relationship with God the Divine Intelligence.

When the Teen decides to make the effort to find and worship God, eyes open to the love of God. Teenagers see and know God from the complex workings of their own bodies to the goodness in each other. The choice to worship God becomes important. At the point of contact with the Most Holy God, it does not really matter if a Teen is pretty or ugly, intelligent or less gifted academically, a good athlete or less gifted athletically, rich or poor. Those are human value judgments. God's judgments value the Teenage ability to find God in science, literature, music, love, healing, sufferings, self-sacrifice, art, sharing with others, technology. God values each Teenage choice to worship without expecting to win the Florida lottery as the reward for recognizing God through primary worship. Teenage worship and adoration of God is not the exchange for making a huge monetary gain in the stock market. Teenage worship and adoration of God is more like seeing God in the beauty of a sunset and raising both mind and heart in praise of God the Creator. Teen worship and adoration of God is like hearing the silence of a rainbow and knowing silence invokes the voice of God the Most Ancient One.

The Mystery of God is the paradox in Teen understanding and knowing the Divine Presence of God. Consistently worshiping God usually leads the Teen to a positive change of lifestyles because of the impact of God's holiness. Nevertheless, some Teenagers do not want to worship God because it's "not fun." They think that God cuts down personal freedom to have fun. God's gift of freedom involves the Teen ability to choose not the guarantee of fun as the end result. However, the Teen choice to worship the Mysterious God leads to a relationship with the Holy Spirit of God which includes joy, kindness, smiles, laughter, happy dreams, love, happiness, peace of mind and heart. Every Teen knows the good feeling when another Teenager freely gives a smile and kindness. Think of the positives from freely choosing to worship and adore God and then from sharing results of kindness, smiles, joy with other Teens. Peace and quiet satisfaction discover a Teen and his or her close friends after the Teen effort to worship the Most Holy God through watching God's sunsets, seeing God's rainbows, and gazing at God's stars.

There is only the One True God with the many mysterious facets affecting the modern Teenager. Two questions remain unanswered. Does the Teenager utilize an aspect of fundamental freedom to offer prayers of adoration to God? Are the Teenage prayers of adoration a one-time deal versus continual prayers of adoration in good and bad times throughout the longevity of life? Colin Browne asked and answered the questions with his daily life. Bully did not even ask the questions.

C. PLEASE, CONSIDER THE FOLLOWING:

(1) Do a three-minute meditation with eyes closed, racket blocked out, thoughts and feelings concentrated on the focal point: I choose to give all glory, praise, honor, and worship to God the Creator, the Redeemer, the Sanctifier...

(2) Create a mental list of thoughts/feelings about God the Most Holy Trinity... worship God the Father, the Most Holy Creator of life, love, stars, earth, universe, oceans, fresh water, DNA sequencing, gravity, mountains, space, technology, family, friends, laws of physics, time, spatial density, astrophysics, rainbows, sunsets, etc. ...worship God the Most Holy Son, the historical Jesus, Redeemer from sin, epitome of love for the Father, example of total obedience to the Father, the innocent sufferer (abandonment, sweated blood, Roman tortures)... worship God the Most Holy Spirit, timeless/ageless Divine Presence, Sanctifier of people, principal author of Holy Scripture, source of all holiness (holy prayers, love, joy, peace, kindness, goodness, etc.)...

(3) Compose a home-made prayer of adoration to Almighty God that you can think and feel several times throughout the day...remember it's between you and your God...

(4) Without asking for more of God's "goodies," try loving God the Most Holy Trinity and Most Holy Mystery, and try loving neighbor/peer to the point that all personal praise, personal glory, personal honor goes to God...

CHAPTER 4

"HEY, MEESTOR, YOU WANT TO RIDE MY CAMEL" PRAYERS OF PETITION

A. EGYPT

I traveled Europe from March 1973 to March 1974. During the year I taught blind students at the Linden Lodge School for the Blind in London, England. My main reason for volunteering to help blind students formed during five weeks of travel in a side trip to Egypt. My original intent was to crawl inside the pyramids and to research the face-off of Moses against Pharaoh Rameses II resulting in the Exodus. Both things happened along with some experiences that still generate reflections, short stories, prayers of petitions.

Egypt was the only country where I experienced a cultural shock. I flew around sundown from Athens, Greece to Cairo, Egypt. Sand was the only thing that I saw from the air until the plane reached the Nile River. The Sahara Desert is west of the Nile River with the Sinai Peninsula to the east. The only breaks in the sand were two ribbons of green on each side of the Nile River. I saw many miles of sand from the plane. I immediately understood the logistical problem of fresh water for ancient armies trying to capture the land of Egypt and for Moses leading a large group of people out of Egypt. Fresh water became valuable instantly. The pilots circled Cairo and dramatically tipped the wings to the three pyramids and the sphinx built by their ancestors in c.2500B.C. at Giza. The thrill pumped me up a notch, but the reality of the differences settled almost immediately into the forefront of my conscious mentality.

A blast of hot air from the desert country hit me as I stepped out of the plane onto the tarmac to walk to the terminal. The value of all fresh water increased again. I stopped and turned on the scorched tarmac in the suffocating heat to watch the sunset over the Sahara Desert. The rays from the sun broke through heat shimmers from the desert and fired the sky. I stood in the heat, and I prayed silently to God the Creator in thanksgiving for the beauty and majesty of the sunset. I turned to see if others enjoyed the sight of that magnificent sunset. And there were the differences.

Egypt is a Muslim country and a nation of Arabs. Muslims are adherents to Islam that includes belief in Allah (God). The prophet Muhammad (570-632A.D.) had visions of the Angel Gabriel in 610A.D. While he was in a trance, the Angel Gabriel repeated three times the order to "recite." All Muslims believe that Muhammad received the "recitings" from Allah through the Angel Gabriel. When recorded in written form, the "recitings" became <u>The Koran</u>, the Arabic name for "The Recital." <u>The Koran</u> is the holy book sacred to all Muslims, and they believe that The Koran is the infallible word of Allah revealed to the prophet Muhammad by the Angel Gabriel.

Good Muslims pray to Allah in public at least six times per day. When called to prayer by the mullahs, Muslims break their routines and pray. If Muslims cannot go to the mosque for the official public worship of Allah, they stop for prayer and symbolically face east to the city of Mecca, the holy birthplace of Muhammad. While reciting lines memorized from The Koran, Muslims stand facing east, bow, kneel, touch foreheads on the ground in adoration and submission to the will of Allah.

One of the official times for all good Muslims to pray is sundown. When I turned to share the joy from a magnificent sunset in the west, I saw almost 200 people around the airport tarmac and terminal. All faced east. All had their butts to the sunset.

Although I considered myself a "veteran of the road," the sight shocked me into a realization of the cultural and religious differences in Egypt. I had to constantly remind myself that people are people regardless of the differences in cultures and religions. I learned to value laughter as a legitimate help for meaningful friendships across cultural and religious lines. When I established friendships with the native Egyptians, good laughs helped to connect and communicate in spite of differences. Most Egyptians and I treated each other with dignity and respect based on effort, friendship, and laughter.

Usually the joke was on me. My style in other countries was to immerse myself into the local culture. I thoroughly enjoyed melting into the street scenes and observing the interactions of the people. There was no way in Egypt for me to tootle with people. I stuck out like a sore thumb thumped by a carpenter's hammer. Most men in Egypt in the early 1970's had very short haircuts, no beards (except the religious leaders), and little pin mustaches. They dressed in long robes with long sleeves called gallabiyahs (sp. Ar. dial. Eg.). They had sandals on their feet and kaffiyehs or turbans on their heads. I had no beard and no mustache, but I had kinky shoulder-length hair because of no haircut during one year of traveling. I wore a T-shirt, cutoffs, mountain boots, wide-brimmed leather hat. People spotted me coming and going in a crowd. There was no place for me to hide.

I did not speak the Arabic language, and few Egyptians spoke English. Most written Arabic words looked like modern hieroglyphics to me. The only written English words that I saw during five weeks of traveling Egypt were "Welcome to Cairo" above the airport terminal. The only printed words using the western alphabet that I saw were in French on menus at the Cairo International Hilton Hotel. I sometimes went to the Cairo Hilton to eat the "Caravan Driver's Mirage," a hot fudge sundae.

Egypt was a difficult country for me to travel because there was no escape from the heat, poverty, and flies. It was about 110° F in the shade throughout the country in the daylight hours. The desert temperatures cooled at night to about 45° F, and night air felt cold with the 60-70 degree swings in temperatures. It did not cool down in the cities. At 3:00am it was still about 85°-90° F. It was difficult to get a good and refreshing sleep. The heat zapped all energy, and caution was the word for traveling the desert. A potential heat stroke and dehydration were constant realities.

Poverty worked on a person's mind just as the heat worked on the body. A gap between the rich and the poor was more extreme than the temperatures in the Sahara Desert. Most people were very poor. People swelled cities because of the Arab-Israeli wars. Many problems from the war intensely magnified negatives in the Egyptian society. War forced people into the cities for safety, jobs, housing. There simply and sadly was not enough of anything to go around.

I remember vividly a family of four living on the streets. I walked past the family twice daily on my way to and from the pyramids. The family had a patch of sidewalk on an unpaved back street. The mom, young dad, boy about three years old, and baby girl literally lived on the sidewalk. They stacked eight watermelons for sale on a narrow sidewalk in front of their straw mats. They sat all day in the heat, the dust, and dirt with their backs against the wall of a building. At night, they slept between their unsold watermelons and the wall. They tried to sell their watermelons for the equivalent of seven pennies in U.S. money. I gave them a dollar for a melon and refused the change. The mother cried big tears of relief. I shared the watermelon with a dozen young homeless boys living under the palm tree in front of the Cairo Youth Hostel. It was the only food that the boys successfully begged to eat for the day. For the price of one dollar, the seventeen people were happy for a little while. War is hell on living people.

There was no escape from the heat and wartime poverty. There was also no escape from the flies. There were flies everywhere that bit a person and sucked blood for moisture. If a person went under a shade tree to break the direct rays of the sun, the person had to fight the flies claiming the spot of shade and waiting to suck blood. There was no relief in buildings because there was no glass or screens in the windows. Glass and screens cost too much money, so windows were just open squares in the walls. At night, wooden shutters often covered the windows for security, but they trapped the flies and the heat inside. Flies swarmed in and out of buildings at their leisure. The only exceptions on my beaten path were the Cairo International Hilton Hotel, embassies, and the government buildings. Government buildings, however, had sandbags covering windows compliments of the war. A few students at the Cairo Youth Hostel slept under stifling mosquito nets to keep away the flies looking for a midnight snack.

I will never forget the open-aired cafe three blocks from the Cairo Youth Hostel. I walked past it on my way to and from the pyramids. There was a huge hunk of meat on a large skewer over the exposed low flame from the stove. The rack of meat was at the front of the cafe inside an opened window. The idea was to step from the street to the open window and order a sandwich. The cook sliced the meat directly from the 20-pound hunk of meat skewered over the fire. He made sandwiches for his customers throughout the day and night. The meat always looked black and rotted to me.

Every time a cook saw me, he tried to sell me a meat sandwich. I always said "no" very politely in local Egyptian Arabic. While bowing slightly I touched my forehead, lips, heart with my fingertips and said softly, "La, la, la." It meant the most polite "no" from my mind, "no" from my mouth for communication, "no" from my heart. If I wanted to show a special respect, after the first time through the usual la-la-la routine I continued to bow and to repeatedly touch only my heart while I said, "La, la, la, la." The cook laughed and waited for his next opportunity to sell me a sandwich.

Once after the rigmarole with my la-la-la routine I made a stupid mistake when I said, "Sayyi." That meant "bad," and I compounded the mistake by pointing to the black meat on the rack. My blunder freaked the cook out, and he went bonkers. He shouted, "La sayyi, la sayii, gayid," which meant, "No bad, no bad, good." Then the cook took his machete and whacked the side of the skewered meat. At least a zillion flies flew off the meat and out the window in a big black cloud. And sure enough, the meat was red!

The combinations of heat, poverty, flies were bad. However, the thing that got on my nerves the most was the action of the dozen young homeless boys living under a palm tree in front of the Cairo Youth Hostel. The ringleader was about sixteen years old, and the ages of the group ranged down to about seven years old. They were street people, homeless orphans, abandoned because of lost family in the war. They fought outsiders regularly with fists and clubs to keep their patch of shade.

Every time that I went down the front steps of the Youth Hostel, they ran to me. They formed a tight circle around me and held out their hands with their palms up. All the boys screamed, "Baksheesh, baksheesh, baksheesh." That is the Arabic street word for money, tip, freebee. I was totally overwhelmed. I broke through their circle while the boys grabbed and tugged at my shirt and cutoffs. I walked quickly and sometimes jogged to the bus stop about five blocks from the Youth Hostel with the boys trailing me and yelling for baksheesh the entire way. If I stopped anywhere on my five-block marathon, the boys encircled me. I had to bust through the weakest point of grabs and tugs to continue my mad dash to the bus stop. They strung out behind me always screaming, "Baksheesh, baksheesh, baksheesh."

To make all matters worse, block #2 had another dozen street urchins commanding the shade of the only palm tree. As we passed through their territory, they joined the ruckus just for fun. By the time I got to the bus stop, I was like the pied piper weaving through back streets of Cairo with a couple dozen munchkins trailing and yelling in unison, "Baksheesh, baksheesh, baksheesh." My only relief was the group of adults at the bus stop threatening the boys. Adults always heard us coming from several blocks away. When I finally made it to the bus stop, adults yelled stuff at the boys in mean sounding Arabic. Sometimes the adults threw rocks at the boys until they backed off. The adults did not necessarily want to help me as much as stop the horrible ear-splitting racket of the boys. After my rescue the ugly stares and evil eyes of the adults always transferred from the boys to me. And sometimes they held the spare rocks a little too long and stared a little too intensely at me to make me completely comfortable waiting with them for the bus. But I never missed the bus because the boys loitered in some borrowed shade just a stone's throw away waiting to pounce again.

The worst part of the daily experience was in block #3. There was the outdoor cafe in block #3 with the six Arab men sitting in the shade at the prima donna table. They were always there sipping little cups of strong black coffee. They smoked chunks of Turkish tobacco and sometimes hashish from their two-foot water pipe with six long hoses. They regularly laughed at the "stupido americano" with two dozen boys yelling for baksheesh. The third block gauntlet of verbal abuse was a daily hell for me.

It got to me. About a week later, I found the American Consulate in the Spanish Embassy Complex. U.S. supplied Israel with weapons during the Arab-Israeli wars, so the U.S. had no official embassy in Egypt at the time. The U.S. conducted business in a few offices of the Spanish Consulate. I was a rare American traveling Egypt in the years with the deteriorated political relationships from the mid-east wars. Nevertheless, I finally found the career diplomat who spoke English and excellent Arabic. He listened patiently to my frustrations and meaningless threats to leave the country in disgust if we could not find a solution to my hassle. He simply said, "No problem, the next time just turn to the boys and say, 'Kellemfarick' (sp.?), but say it with your meanest, dirtiest, and nastiest voice." I asked him what the word meant. He chuckled and said to not worry about a meaning or the spelling of the word because I was not going to find the word in any Arabic to English dictionary. Just say, "Kellemfarick."

The next morning I stopped on the top step of the Youth Hostel to fake a stretch and a loud yawn. The Palm Tree Twelve spotted me immediately and ran to beg baksheesh. I strolled into block #2 and stopped to gather the second group. I meandered into block #3 and frequently checked over my shoulder to make sure that none of the boys got lost. I cruised to a slow halt in the middle of the unpaved street directly in front of the notorious cafe. I glanced out of a corner of my eye to make sure The Six were in place at their prima donna table. Then I raised both my fists as if to hit the boys, and in my most insane, meanest, dirtiest, nastiest voice I shouted, "Kellemfarick!" with the week's worth of anger for the heat, the poverty, the flies, the baksheesh begging, the verbal abuse of The Six. Everybody froze in place. Everybody could have heard a penny drop in the dust. The eyes of the little bitty boys got big, and some cried in terrified silence. That street scene frozen in time was worthy of the best surrealistic artist's efforts. Then the Table of Six laughed. The boys laughed. I laughed. Everybody in the street scene laughed. It was the longest and loudest laughter that I ever heard.

Eventually the boys drifted back to the shade of their palm trees laughing and waving good-bye. The Table of Six invited me to join them at the prima donna table for a smoke and a toke. I went into my la-la-la routine, and they laughed robustly again. When I left the Cairo Youth Hostel the next morning, the Palm Tree Twelve waved vigorously to me, but they never left their shade. I was one of the boys. We were all friends. To this day, I have no idea what I said.

There were many eye diseases in Egypt. The street and country scenes contained so many people with glaucoma, cataracts, glazed eyes, crossed-eyes, trachoma, and blindness. Very few people wore glasses because they cost too much money. In the western countries blindness is an educational problem. Questions relate to teaching the blind people to function in the society with quality in their lives. In Egypt blindness and the eye diseases remained rudimentary health and medical problems. Water was a most valuable commodity, but the Nile River at the time was certifiably polluted. Many eye problems especially trachoma began with drinking the polluted water and living in terrible squalor.

I remember standing on a bridge over the Nile River in a village below Memphis about fifteen kilometers south of Cairo. I observed some cows drinking the Nile River water and standing in the water to cool off. Next to the cows were a few women dressed in long black robes with faces and heads covered in black shawls. They washed a load of clothes in the Nile River and beat the clothes on the rocks to wring the soapy water out of them. Next to the women were small children laughing and swimming in the Nile. Next to the swimmers were Teenagers filling large earthen water jugs with Nile River water. They balanced the full jugs on their heads and returned up the mud bank to their village with the drinking water for their families. During the previous day, I saw a chemical factory in Cairo dumping both raw sewage and chemical wastes directly into the Nile River.

Egypt simultaneously had the glory of the ancient world and the misery of current third world countries. Within sight of the pyramids were poor blind Egyptians who never saw the riches and the glory of their ancient heritage. However, I did not volunteer to teach the blind students in England because of vast amount of eye problems sadly observed in Egypt. I taught blind people in London because of one little Egyptian boy.

I wanted to go deeper into the Sahara Desert to see the Step Pyramid built at Saqqarah in 2700 B.C. I awoke at dawn to catch the first bus. When I descended the Youth Hostel steps, the most vigilant ringleader of the Palm Tree Twelve waved silently to me and went back to sleep. I cut through back alleys and headed for a different bus stop. While walking slowly in a half-sleep, I felt a soft tug on my cutoffs. Without even looking or stopping, I slapped a hand off my cutoffs. A few steps later I felt the silent tug and swatted the hand again. I stopped at the third tug on my cutoffs and turned to see a very little boy. He wore his little gallabiyah, the long robe with long sleeves. Even with his little turban on his head, he only came up to my waist. He held out his little hand with his palm open and raised upwards. The little boy said softly almost in a whisper, "Baksheesh, baksheesh, baksheesh."

I looked at his face. He was cross-eyed. You know when you have a winter cold and you sometimes wake up with matted crust in the corner of your eye. The little boy had a glob of fresh goo in the corner of his cross-eye. In the goo was a fly. The fly was alive. The fly flapped its wings trying to escape. The little boy stood there with a raised palm begging baksheesh with a fly in his eye.

He was the only little man who beat me out of baksheesh. My heart went out to him. I gave him $5 and a hug. At that moment, I vowed to myself that I would volunteer some time to help the blind as soon as I entered an English speaking country. When I arrived and settled into London, I walked into the Royal Eye Clinic to volunteer. The representative set up a fifteen-minute interview for me with the Headmaster (the Principal) of the Linden Lodge School for the Blind. The Headmaster asked my reason for volunteering to help the blind students. I shared the story of the little Egyptian boy with the fly in the eye. We talked and shared experiences for about three hours. Then the Headmaster handpicked a class for me to teach. The blind students included Libby Lou, Colin Browne, and Bully. I shared the story of the little Egyptian boy with the fly in the eye with the class. Libby Lou and Colin Browne cried silently. Bully laughed out loud. They also cried and laughed respectively when I shared the story of the Egyptian boy and his camel.

My daily routine for seeing and crawling around inside the three pyramids at Giza was the same. I rode the city bus to the last stop where the pavement ended. There was about a block of businesses geared to the tourist trade. The desert started where the businesses stopped. There was a magnificent panoramic view of the sphinx and three pyramids at that spot in the unpaved road. Everybody seemed to stop there and gasp at the glory of the ancient world. It was an incredible sight to look at such huge manmade structures built about 4,500 years ago in 2500 B.C. One of the more lucrative businesses was the last business on the left at the exact spot where all tourists stopped to ogle the pyramids. It was a ride-a-camel-to-the-pyramids business.

There was the camel tied to the last palm tree on the left. The camel munched the straw in the shade, but he was always saddled and ready to go. For $5 the tourist rode the camel about a half-mile to the pyramids. The owner was the bwana, and he walked in front holding the leash of the camel. When all arrived at the pyramids, for another $5 the owner loaned the tourist a turban and a gallabiyah. The owner snapped a picture of the dressed up tourist sitting on the camel with the pyramids strategically placed in background. It was exotic and instant Lawrence of Arabia with the Polaroid snapshot for proof. But times were tough on the tourist trade with the Arab-Israeli wars. It was easy for a tourist to haggle the camel owner down to $3 for the grand camel tour including a picture.

The camel owner spoke only one sentence in English. However, he was a very astute businessman in a very premium location. To personalize his sales pitch, the owner changed one word three times depending on the potential customer. He sat in the shade of the last building before the desert, while his camel stood in the shade of the last palm tree before the desert. He very precisely yelled from his patch of shade, "Hey, Meestor, you want to ride my camel?" If the tourist was a woman, he altered the question a tad and yelled, "Hey, Laady, you want to ride my camel?" I was young with long hair, so I was automatically a student. When I went past his patch of shade to crawl around inside the pyramids, he always yelled, "Hey, Stuudent, you want to ride my camel?"

It looked to me like the old camel could barely munch straw and stand in the shade at the same time. For the answer to his question, I always went into my la-la-la routine touching my forehead, lips, and heart. I observed that it was always a strain for the camel to carry a tourist up the slope to the three pyramids. The owner never failed to cover the camel's skin-and-bones flanks for the taking of all pictures. The camel did much better when he went downhill and headed for the shade under the palm tree. The number of camel safaris left in the beast of burden was a limited toss-up question. But the camel still held up the family's business even as the owner tried to save enough money for a younger replacement. It was very important for the old camel to make the walk to the pyramids just as the owner's one sentence in English was very important to drumming up the new business. The family's existence depended upon maximum effort.

One morning I was the only tourist on a first bus to the pyramids. I arrived at the end of the pavement at dawn. The weather forecast was for extreme heat, and I wanted to get inside the coolness of the Great Pyramid to study some hieroglyphics in relative comfort. I saw immediately that the owner of the ride-a-camel business was not at his post. His ten-year-old son sat in the owner's customary patch of shade against the building. He wore his best gallabiyah, turban, and sandals. The son was ready to accept his new family responsibilities seriously except for one thing. He was fast asleep. I tried to ease past him without disturbing his sleep, but the camel snorted loudly. The little boy opened his eyes, and he saw me getting away. In his disorientation and confusion, he made a valiant effort to do business. The young boy shouted in desperation, "Hey, Meestor, you want to ride my Stuudent camel?"

Unfortunately, the father heard the boy's mistake in the family's one and only one English sentence. The father went berserk. He ran outside the building yelling and screaming in Arabic. He was spitting and slobbering at the mouth while steadily cussing the young boy. He ran to his son and beat him with both fists closed. He picked up the boy by the shoulders of his gallabiyah and threw him in the dust of the street. The father cursed, hollered, and hit his son in the face. He kicked his crumpled son in the back and in the groin. The father continued beating his son into the ground until the father ran out of energy. He left his son motionless in the dirt and went inside spitting, slobbering curse words, cussing his son with violent verbal abuse.

The little boy eventually moaned and stood wobbly in the spot of his beating. He had a black right eye, swollen face, blood dripping from his nose and left ear. When he regained his balance, he went slowly to the camel holding his stomach with both hands. He untied the camel's leash from the palm tree. He returned to the spot of his beating and sat cross-legged. The camel stood munching straw in the shade of the last palm tree before the desert. The little boy sat in a meaningless stupor in the direct sunlight holding the camel's leash tightly with both hands. About seven hours later I returned from the pyramids to catch the Cairo bus. The little boy still sat in the direct sunlight holding the camel's leash tightly with both hands. The flies buzzed around his swollen head. He sat motionless in the direct sun when the flies landed on the dried blood from his nose and left ear. It was 114° F in the direct sunlight next to the camel's shade from the last palm tree before the desert.

The career diplomat, who spoke English and excellent Arabic, forewarned me to never interfere with any Arab man disciplining his son. Interference was a primary insult to the Arab man's pride, and it always drew a vicious response. The extreme violence stunned me into inaction. However, I cannot imagine a response more vicious than the camel man's physical abuse of his son. All the pain resulted from one misplaced word in one verbal sentence. Arabic male pride underpinned the one English sentence, and Arabic culture bolstered the vicious physical attack of the father on the son.

Egypt was essentially a male dominated country as the career diplomat explained the local situation to me. Only the adult male had any basic human rights in the reality of daily living. Young girls and women had no real human rights on their own. They had rights by the extension of the adult male, and the male expected women to be baby machines with a huge preference for baby boys. In those days of severe poverty and war, young rich girls left the country, usually to

France, to get a basic quality education. Young boys had no human rights, but eventually they grew into the adult male dominated world of modern Egypt. Young boys felt the harsh discipline involved in the tough love based on male pride. Adult male pride underpinned the entire daily culture of the Arabic society.

The extreme street scene was no wonder to the career diplomat. Nevertheless, it was one thing to study a tremendous national pride in the accomplishments of ancient Egyptians. It was a totally different thing to observe the mentality and pride of the current Arabic male in the streets. The experiences and displays of Arabic male pride never ceased to amaze me. Male pride surfaced often in Egypt and always seemed to hurt somebody. Usually a tourist coped with Arabic pride in the streets and rendered it relatively harmless. However, it often produced clashes from different cultural perspectives. Sometimes Arabic male pride in the streets was very dangerous.

I remember the incident at the Cairo Youth Hostel with Farouk, who was the #1 model student of Egypt. Farouk was eighteen years old and a student in Alexandria, which was about 114 miles north of Cairo on the Mediterranean Sea. The government declared Farouk the #1 model student for the entire country of Egypt. He was in Cairo for a week of interviews on national TV and radio. A special awards banquet was at the end of the week. A big shot in the government was on the agenda to give Farouk the award before a national TV and radio audience.

Farouk, Charles, and I were roommates at the Youth Hostel for 3½ days. Charles was an American on his way home after traveling Africa for six months. He was a seasoned veteran of difficult travels in Third World countries. I immediately made five observations about Farouk that were rare in Egypt: (1) he spoke fluent English; (2) he wore expensive glasses; (3) the government had a very comfortable future outlined for him; (4) he was a totally obnoxious braggart; (5) he choose not to jive with Charles.

Every morning for three days Farouk outlined in English his total itinerary for me. He always ended with the invitation for me to join him in his week of personal glory. I always declined with my la-la-la routine. I usually said that I wanted to crawl inside the pyramids of his ancestors. Every evening I patiently listened to Farouk brag on his honors for the day. I noticed to my chagrin that Farouk never extended an invitation to Charles. I told Farouk that Charles was my traveling partner for his last two weeks on the road. I blatantly hinted that I might join Farouk for a daily event, if he invited Charles out of common courtesy. I thought it odd that a person always bragging on himself did not want another warm body in his personal entourage.

Farouk was uncharacteristically silent on the fourth morning. As Charles left the room, Farouk formally invited me to join him at the banquet to honor him the next night. I formally declined and coldly added, "No Charles, no me." I left the room and stood in the hall by the door to let Farouk contemplate his guest list by himself for a few minutes. When I returned to the room, Farouk acted very nervous. Farouk grabbed his stuff, said good-bye, and rushed out.

I explained the strange happenings to Charles upon his return to the room. The behavior of Farouk was so odd that we suspiciously decided to check our belongings. Charles had all his stuff. Someone stole my reading glasses and my 7-inch knife in a sheath. I knew for an undisputed fact that both glasses and knife were in my backpack. My waking habit was to immediately check my stuff. I completed the inspection less than ten minutes before the robbery. To rip off my glasses and knife, the robber had to push aside my traveler's checks, $30 in local Egyptian currency, my U.S. passport worth about $1,000 on the black market. All of those items remained in my backpack.

The room only had the one door, and nobody entered the room past me from the hall. The only opened window was too high off the ground for any quick entry. Farouk was in the room alone for three minutes. There was no doubt in my mind. Farouk stole my reading glasses and my knife. The #1 model student of Egypt was a thief.

When I reported the robbery to the front desk of the Cairo Youth Hostel, the manager said that Farouk recently checked out. He said nonchalantly that he was very sorry, but there was no way to find Farouk for any questions about a robbery. I told the manager that I knew Farouk's entire schedule and I intended to track down Farouk. A threat of a public confrontation with the #1 model student of Egypt over my stolen items jolted the manager out of his complacency. He called his trusted friend in the police department for some help. The policeman spoke no English, so the manager was the translator with his broken English. We spent hours going round and round the facts. The policeman said that he would try to find my stuff, but Cairo was a very big city with many people. He also said a little too often that the important Farouk had many personal bodyguards. Both manager and policeman cautioned me and strongly advised me to not go after Farouk because of unspecified "serious consequences" for me.

Weeks later I told the story to Gamil, a very good friend. He was native Egyptian, and he spoke excellent English. I trusted that the explanation of Gamil was most accurate. Farouk took my glasses and knife because of Arabic male pride. When I innocently refused multiple invitations to join Farouk for his week of glory, I insulted his pride and his family honor. Farouk's honor also prohibited him from stealing my traveler's checks, Egyptian currency, and my passport. However, Farouk's pride demanded retribution for the personal insult to his personal honor. Glasses and knives were very personal items in the Egyptian culture. Farouk took my glasses and knife because he wanted a part of me to go with him to share his moment of glory. The only way to get back my glasses and knife was to substitute myself for my personal items.

As an example, Gamil equated the incident with taking pictures. It was O.K. in the Arab world to take pictures of the pyramids or the many people in a street scene. But taking pictures of an individual in the Arab world meant taking a part of the person's spirit. It was most polite to ask the individual before taking a picture because it involved part of the person's spirit leaving the individual and going with the photographer. Asking before taking was the way to avoid insults to pride and honor. It was a most polite way to avoid violent reactions.

Farouk asked three times for me to join him in his great moment of glory. Then Farouk took a part of me in the form of my personal glasses and my personal knife to join him in his glory. I considered the experience stealing from the perspective of American culture. Farouk considered the experience sharing his personal honor, pride, glory from the perspective of Arab culture. Gamil said that it would probably shock Farouk to call him a thief. One then worried that a statement about stealing might insult Farouk's personal pride or the honor of his family and draw a violent reaction.

I understood from my good friend Gamil that the complexities of Arab male pride made the incident more than just stealing. For Gamil it was simply a different way of life. However, I thought often about the Arab-Israeli wars. Are there brave and courageous leaders on both sides of the international war to deal honorably, intelligently, sensitively with Arabic male pride and with Israeli male pride for the sake of peace? Are Mideast Teens doomed to perpetual war and hatred because of male egos and negative prides on both sides of the bullets? Is peace among different cultures simply recognizing a different way of life?

Cultural interpretations of male pride and the differences in the concepts of stealing nearly got me killed in Cairo's Old City bazaar. I wanted to see the site designated the temporary home for the Baby Jesus, Mother Mary, and Saint Joseph. When the three Magi did not return to King Herod with the exact birthplace of Baby Jesus, Herod ordered his soldiers to massacre all the Hebrew baby boys around Bethlehem under the age of two. An angel ordered Saint Joseph in a dream vision to take Baby Jesus and Mother Mary to Egypt until the danger passed (Mt.2:1-21). Saint Joseph obeyed and went to Cairo while Herod murdered the Holy Innocents. Religious tradition located the site of their home in the Old City.

The career diplomat forewarned me about real physical dangers especially after dark in the Old City for Americans. I talked reluctant Charles into an inspection of the homesite. We had difficulties galore finding the homesite. Large crowds filled winding narrow unmarked streets. Language barriers for directions slowed us and consumed valuable time. We eventually found the site. It took even more time to exit the Old City. Congestion in the maze of streets was massive. It was late afternoon, and our exit developed the sense of urgency. Large noisy crowds stirred the dirt from unpaved streets into a cloud trapped between buildings. There was no escape from the heat and the stink of sweaty bodies. Crowds jostled, pushed, and shoved us along with all others. The street noises deafened us and dulled my ability to think. We surged through the bazaar in a sea of humanity from one block to the next. All actions seemed in slow motion.

Charles and I finally reached a street that we recognized. We were only two long blocks from completely exiting the Old City, and there was still a little daylight. Both the sides of the narrow street had covered stalls against the buildings with merchandise for sale. There were only a few breaks in the lines of stalls to enter other businesses inside the buildings. The congestion and the noise were intense. It was enough to give you a severe headache. However, we were no longer lost, and we were almost survivors of the Old City at dusk. I was almost euphoric.

Then I felt a very sharp tug on my shirtsleeve. I turned quickly and looked into eyes full of hate. The face instantly contorted into a smile. There stood the owner of a stall trying to sell me fresh fruit. He jabbered in Arabic and pointed to bowls of figs. He held my arm in a viselike grip. I released my arm and went into my la-la-la routine. He quickly picked up a bowl of figs and offered one to me. He said in broken English with an encouraging smile, "Taste free, no money." I questioned, "La baksheesh?" He said, "La baksheesh, taste free, no money."

I looked into his eyes and got a sick feeling in my stomach. He knew and I knew that it was a major insult to his pride to refuse his gift. He knew and I knew that he was a violent person. I took a tiny itty-bitty bite out of the smallest fig. It was sour. I threw the fig down and spit into the dirt. He laughed. I turned to walk away. He grabbed my arm in his vise grip and wildly yelled, "Baksheesh, baksheesh, baksheesh." I jerked my arm to release his grip. We were nose to nose. He shouted for baksheesh. I shouted, "La baksheesh, taste free, no money, la baksheesh."

I looked into his eyes and saw unmasked hatred. His face looked dark and evil. I instantly realized that I was in a no-win and a very dangerous situation. I kept pace with a few more shouts, and then I gave him seven Egyptian pennies, the price of a large watermelon. He screamed, "La, la, la." He held up ten fingers, and flashed them twice. Then he hit me in the face with a big glob of spit.

I froze in place. I silently felt my pride and blood pressure rise to the boiling point. He reached into his gallabiyah and pulled out his knife with a ten-inch blade. Charles leaned over and said in my ear, "Give him the money and let's get out of here fast." That broke my focus and total concentration on the stall owner. For the first time in several minutes, I took my eyes off the man. I looked at Charles and then behind Charles. I saw Arab men ten rows deep forming a tight semi-circle around us. I calculated about one hundred frantic Arabs with fists in the air yelling, shoving, and lending loud support to their friend. The buildings, stalls, and Arabs trapped Charles and me in a dangerously tiny space. I looked over most of their heads and saw two policemen with machine guns slung over shoulders at the far end of the block. They looked our way, pointed at us, and laughed. The cops budged not an inch from their spot to help.

I silently gave the stall owner one Egyptian pound, the currency note equivalent to twenty watermelons and two overnights at Cairo Youth Hostel. The Arab stall owner held the money high overhead in one hand for all to see and his knife just as high in his other hand. He shrilled a loud victory sound and pumped both fists with currency and knife in the air. Other Arabs shrilled a response while pumping fists and knives in the air. Everybody dropped fists and knives to their sides. The stall owner quickly jabbed the one pound Egyptian note high in the air for all to see and screamed, "Sa–id" ["said" = "glad" (happy/yes)]. They jabbed their knives high into the air and screamed, "La americana" [= "no American" (down/bad Americans)]. He led half-dozen wild cheers of his "sa-id" and their "la americana" with his Egyptian money and their knives alternating positions in the air. When the two cops meandered down the street with fingers on triggers of machine guns, the mob suddenly broke ranks and went laughing to their stalls. Charles and I closely trailed the two cops for the two blocks to the exit of the Old City bazaar.

For days afterwards I silently trembled on rubbery legs whenever I contemplated the potentially lethal mix of negative Arab pride and cultural differences. There was a danger zone when the pride of the Arabic male crosshatched and intersected different cultures. Pride was also potentially lethal within the Egyptian culture from one Arab to another. That was exactly the case in Alexandria.

I met a rich Egyptian nicknamed Nicki in Alexandria. Nicki was so rich that he isolated and insulated himself from a horrible poverty at the root of many Egyptian problems. He was in the import-export business. His mother had strong connections with the government, and those were the bases for the real wealth of the family. Mother lived in Paris, France, and she owned a shop, warehouse, apartment in the city plus the country estate. Nicki owned shops, apartments, warehouses in Alexandria, Cairo, and Luxor. The family house was the large estate in Cairo. The family also owned summer villas on the Mediterranean Sea in Alexandria and the French Riviera. Both Mother and Nicki were very well educated. Both fluently spoke five languages. Both were on the very top of the Egyptian society.

Nicki decided one hot day to swim in the Mediterranean Sea. He wanted to go from his apartment in Alexandria to family villa outside the city. He packed a picnic lunch, and he loaded three friends and me into his refurbished '57 Chevy convertible. It was stop-and-go traffic in the city, but it didn't bother us. We had the top of the Chevy down, and the music cranked up. The Chevy's sound system blared some good sounds, and we sang along while playing air guitars. We thoroughly enjoyed each other's company.

Nicki turned his car slowly into a narrow alley for the short cut through the traffic. There was only one foot of space from the sides of the car to the buildings on each side of the alley. He progressed carefully down the one block to the end of the alley. His car almost made it to the end when a car with an Arab driver turned into the alley from the opposite direction. Nicki stopped his car with his front bumper gently touching the front bumper of the Arab man's car. I looked behind the Chevy and saw five cars plus two trucks in the alley. All bumpers touched, and all eight vehicles faced the one car with the Arab man from the opposite direction. The Arab driver of the one car only had to go backwards the length of one small car for all the vehicles to exit the alley. The driver of the one car rolled up his windows, locked his doors, and shut off the motor.

Pandemonium broke out instantly. The Arab driver of the one car waited serenely as everybody else honked horns and shouted vulgarities. Nicki was furious. Sounds echoed from buildings and magnified the racket. The excruciating noise continued non-stop for almost fifteen minutes. The driver of the one car had no intention of reversing his car.

Suddenly Nicki got very calm. He and the Arab driver of the one car looked at each other silently for a few minutes. Nicki reached under the front seat and pulled out a gun. He couldn't open the door because the buildings were too close. Nicki stood on his driver's seat and faced the other seven vehicles in our line. He raised his gun and called for silence. Everybody shut up immediately. Nicki stepped over the front windshield onto the hood of his car. He walked onto the hood of the one car and slowly wedged himself between building and the driver's door. Nicki tapped gently on the driver's window with the barrel of his gun. The Arab man rolled the window down a few inches. Nicki talked quietly with the man for several seconds. Nicki squeezed himself back onto the hood of the man's car. He walked across both hoods and climbed over his windshield into his driver's seat. By the time Nicki returned his gun under the seat and shifted his car into gear, the Arab man started and backed the one car out of the alley into the street. Nicki exited the alley.

Later in the evening, I asked Nicki what he said to the other Arab driver. Nicki spoke softly, "I told him if he did not reverse his car by the time I returned to my convertible, I would shoot him dead." Nicki was most serious. We talked about the incident from the perspective of his Arab culture. Nicki explained that the pride of the man made him refuse to reverse his car. The main issue was not one car versus eight vehicles, nor backwards a few feet versus almost 150 feet. The confrontation was a clash over personal honor. The reversal of the car admitted publicly that the honor of the Arab in the one car was inferior to the honor of each Arab in the line of cars. That was the crux of the problem.

Only a call to a superior expression of honor satisfied Arab pride, and as a result, budged the Arab in the single car. The call to praise Allah in public prayer was the highest expression of personal honor. Pride demanded that the Arab sit in the one car until a time to praise Allah in the higher expression of honor. The next official time to pray in a mosque was sundown. Nicki felt that the Arab prepared himself to wait in the one car for eight hours. At sundown the reversed car of the Arab allowed him to go pray at the mosque with pride and honor intact. When Nicki promised to "shoot him dead," the best choice of the Arab shifted from a death with little honor in the alley to a life with the great honor of praising Allah with great pride in the mosque later. The Arab hit the reverse.

I asked Nicki if refusal to back the car out of the alley warranted a death shot. Nicki said, "I was definitely ready to shoot out his front windshield...If that didn't move him, I would probably have shot him in the leg and reversed the car myself...But if I only wounded him, I'd worry about the insult to his pride forcing him to get his own gun...It could get really bloody afterwards if I only shot him in the leg." Such were the thoughts on Arabic male pride from one of the richest and most-educated men in Egypt.

Probably the most bizarre episode for me involving Arabic male pride happened in Luxor, about 420 miles south of Cairo. Luxor was the ancient Egyptian City of Thebes in the Bible. It was the location of the Karnak Temple, the Valley of the Kings, and the Valley of the Queens. Archaeologists discovered 120 tombs of pharaohs in the Valley of the Kings. Tourists entered about 62 of the ancient tombs carved into the mountain. Sites of tombs included Moses' antagonist Pharaoh Rameses II, his father Pharaoh Seti I, King Tut or Pharaoh Tutankhamen. It was the history of ancient pharaohs in the Valley of the Kings that led to my friendship with Gamil. Gamil was the very good friend who rescued me from certain disaster stemming from a serious confrontation with the pride of the Arab male.

The name Gamil meant "beautiful" in the Egyptian language. Gamil was truly a beautiful individual who kept his Arabic male pride totally under control. He loved the ancient history of his ancestors. He owned a gift shop and sold quality souvenirs to the tourists. His job gave him the opportunities to share his vast knowledge of ancient Egyptian history. Gamil read hieroglyphics, Coptic Egyptian, Latin, and Greek. He was the local expert on the ancient history of Karnak Temple and Valley of the Kings. He spoke fluently English, French, German, Italian, Spanish, Arabic Egyptian, and four varieties of the Arabic language. Gamil was most educated and most humble. It was our mutual love for ancient Egyptian history that established and underpinned our friendship.

I met Gamil on my first evening in Luxor at a small cafe. The cafe was a popular gathering place for the locals. The small cafe had ten wooden tables in two rows of five on a rectangular slab of concrete. Six large poles supported a pavilion type of roof over the tables, and there were no walls around the dining area. The enclosed kitchen was at the end of the concrete slab, and it had an elongated window with drop-down wooden shutter. The open shutter meant the owner was ready to cook and serve excellent food priced cheaply. A closed shutter with an adjacent open door meant help yourself to the coffee in the kitchen. The owner/cook, however, was off the clock and ready to enjoy the company of his friends. A closed shutter and a closed door meant stay as long as you like in the open dining area, but the owner/cook was home with his family.

I found the small cafe at sundown. The view from the cafe was magnificent. The Nile River was in the foreground. Karnak Temple was on the opposite bank adjacent to the Nile River. On the horizon was the flat-topped mountain that contained the Valley of the Kings. I strategically placed myself at the center table in the row closest to the Nile River. I had a front row seat to watch the sunset over the Sahara Desert.

The sun dropped behind the Valley of the Kings in the distance. The diminishing sun fired the sky with brilliant shades of orange and splashed colors onto a blue sky. The daily natural display of glorious beauty truly lifted my soul and spirit to God. Sunsets in Egypt were for me a special time for prayer to thank God for life and to praise the wisdom of God. Sunsets in Luxor were a pure joy.

As I watched my first sunset in Luxor, I glanced left towards the kitchen and saw ten people praying east towards Mecca. I looked to my right. Gamil silently sat and looked west into the sunset. The rays from the sun bathed his face in a red glow enhancing his peaceful composure. We sat two tables from each other silently enjoying the sunset. We sipped little cups of coffee separately. We immersed minds individually in our own thoughts. When the last vestiges of the sunlight left the day, Gamil turned and invited me to sit at his table for a cup of coffee. His first question was, "What historical site did you visit today?" We talked well into the night and shared thoughts on the ancient ones. Our daily evening routine was to share sunsets in silence at different tables and conversations about ancient history at his table. We communicated into the wee hours of the morning. We became good friends based on a mutual dignity and a mutual respect for the ancient Egyptians and for modern individuality.

I noticed several things about Gamil during our conversations. He had excellent communication skills, and he listened very well. People of Luxor responded to him with love and respect. Men and women stopped at his table to receive his words of wisdom and to answer his concerned questions about their families. Gamil had a beautiful smile for everyone especially for the little people. Children approached his table to get hugs and to listen until the owner/cook shooed them away. Gamil was a very good Muslim, but he prayed the evening prayer early. Official worship of Allah never interfered with his enjoyment of the sunsets. Gamil dressed in West European clothes instead of the traditional gallabiyahs, turban, and sandals. He favored khaki slacks and light colored shirts with collar and buttons. He only needed a leather hat to give his garb a complete look of the modern archaeologist. Gamil spoke quietly, and he never raised his voice. When a conversation turned to ancient Egyptian history, he spoke barely above a reverent whisper. Gamil was polite to everyone regardless of personal wealth, status, power, age. Everyone seemed to recognize Gamil as a very good man.

Gamil's best friend was the Chief of Police in Luxor. They grew up together and valued greatly the length of their friendship. Their families lived next door to each other. Their fathers were also best friends. Both boys had many positive benefits in their lives from two close-knit families. Nothing seemed capable of breaking their lifelong friendship. When the Police Chief stole Gamil's girlfriend to marry at an early age, they remained close friends. Gamil eventually married the sister of the ex-girlfriend, and their families were more closely united. When both men had sons, they named their #1 sons after their respective fathers. They named their #2 sons after each other.

However, I noticed that neither sat at the other's table. In fact, the tables were as far away from each other as they could get and remain in the same cafe. Gamil's table, as you faced the Nile River, was front row far right. The Police Chief's table was back row far left next to the kitchen. The positions of the tables were exactly opposite. The two friends stood together to talk politely, but they never sat at the other's table. It was very odd because it meant two noticeably unusual things in the Arab society. The two Arab men stood to drink coffee, and the two close friends never shared a meal together at their favorite cafe.

Gamil had the best table. His table had the best view of the Nile River and the ancient monuments. It also had a perpetual breeze especially during the heat of the day. It was the most peaceful table because it was farthest from the noise, congestion, and heat of the kitchen. However, the Police Chief's table was squarely in the middle of every commotion. The Chief of Police loved to play chess, and the position of his table guaranteed an audience. People ordered food at the window next to his table, and they watched him play a game of chess while the owner/cook prepared food. The Police Chief reveled in the attention and the noise. On the other hand, the constant racket continually broke the concentration of the serious challengers to his chess supremacy.

I questioned Gamil about the tables. He chuckled softly, but his eyes looked sad. He explained that his table was the Police Chief's table until two years prior. The two best friends drank coffee, ate meals, and laughed together at the table. Life was good. They also played serious games of chess against all challengers at the table. However, they never played chess against each other at the table.

Both men loved to play chess. They learned the game at a very early age from their respective fathers. Some of their best memories from childhood were games of chess played against each other in the shadows of Karnak Temple and the Valley of the Kings. They were the two best chess players in Luxor. They continually proved it on the board by winning against all challengers. As adults, neither challenged the other to a game of chess. Both knew the potential complications from Arabic male pride and lost honor. However, the leading families of the region challenged both the friends to enter the same chess tournament on a special national holiday. It was simply too much pressure on the individual Arabic male pride. They entered with heavy hearts to uphold the honor of their fathers' names.

The Police Chief lost only one game of chess in ten years. He had an incredible win/loss record considering the fact that he played at least one game of chess everyday after work. The Chief of Police lost his one game of chess to Gamil. The loss was in the final game of the chess tournament before a huge crowd. The site of the lost honor was the table in question.

Since that dark night two years prior, Arab male pride dominated their friendship in public. The chess game damaged their friendship, but did not destroy it completely. Nevertheless, consequences from the game of chess intertwined with Arabic male pride were extreme. The best table in the cafe passed with the victory from the Chief of Police to Gamil. The Police Chief never sat at the table with Gamil. It took one month for the Chief of Police to return to the cafe. It was another three months before the Police Chief played any games of chess at his new table farthest from the site of his disgraced honor. Gamil played zero games of chess for two years. Gamil sadly and deeply missed the shared public meals and coffee at the best table with his best friend. Whenever Gamil asked the Chief of Police to sit and eat, the Police Chief excused himself politely, proclaimed very important police work in his most official voice, and always left the cafe immediately. The compromise for friendship was to stand and drink coffee in public.

I also loved to play chess. I learned the game from my father at a very early age just like the two best friends in Egypt. Chess was one of the few things that kept Dad and me together during the Vietnam War. We were on the opposite ends of the spectrum concerning the Vietnam War. Chess was the thing that bridged the generation gap in our love relationship. When we could not even communicate with each other around the dinner table without arguing the politics of the war, we played chess. We played in silence and with our best efforts. We played with dignity, respect, love for each other. We played to win. May Dad rest in the peace of Jesus knowing that I never threw a game of chess to a weaker opponent... except the last game we played together when he was weak from dying of cancer.

When the Chief of Police walked stiffly and proudly to Gamil's table to challenge me to a game of chess, I immediately went into my la-la-la routine touching my head, lips, heart. The two best friends laughed at their table for the first time in two years. It was indeed a special moment and spiritual food for thought. Gamil and I thought deeply that maybe, just maybe, there was a way to get around Arab male pride to bring two best friends back together in public. Gamil and I spent hours analyzing the different scenarios in the acceptance of the chess challenge.

Gamil repeatedly arrived at the same basic perceptions. The Chief of Police publicly challenged me to a game of chess because he saw Gamil and me sharing a lot of time and energy. He noticed our strengthened friendship, and he extended the public challenge at Gamil's table to consciously or subconsciously offer renewed public friendship to Gamil. If I accepted the challenge and he won the game of chess, the Police Chief beat Gamil's new friend and Gamil by Arab social laws of extension. A victory by the Chief of Police renewed his individual pride and public honor. Ultimately the result refreshed the public friendship between the two best friends.

I made Gamil totally aware that I always played chess to win out of respect for my Dad. Gamil reasoned that he and I play three public games of chess in the space between acceptance of the challenge and the big game with the Police Chief. If I won one game out of the three, it meant that I was a worthy and honorable opponent for the big game. More importantly, it meant that both Gamil and the Chief of Police were even at one loss in ten years. If the Chief of Police subsequently lost to me in the big game, the Police Chief had two losses to Gamil's one. But the friends both lost to the same person. The local social etiquette plus Arabic male pride required that the two best friends commiserate their losses together in public. The two friends were in the same boat together. Gamil hoped that the Police Chief took the opportunity to renew their public friendship through the mutual public wailing about their losses at chess to the outsider.

Of course if I won two out of three games with Gamil and then the big game, the Police Chief and Gamil were totally equal with two losses each. Equality meant honor and pride restored to the Police Chief along with their public friendship. The best case scenario for their renewed friendship was for me to win two games against Gamil and to loose the big game versus the Police Chief. In that case, the dust settled on one loss for the Chief of Police in ten years and two losses for Gamil with all honor and Arabic pride restored to the Chief of Police. Gamil thought about all the angles again, and he felt good concerning the real opportunity to renew the public friendship with his best friend. So, I accepted the challenge of the Police Chief to play one game of chess. Our hopes and our hidden agendas were that friendships prevailed over the male pride of Arabs.

I warmed up with the three games of chess against Gamil. We played at Gamil's table under close scrutiny by the Police Chief and about a dozen of his friends. They encircled us, stood in silence, and drank little cups of coffee. I think that Gamil threw the first game to me just to make sure the plan was on track. Gamil was an excellent chess player, and he was most clever in throwing the victory to me. Game #1 passed the inspection. We were hopefully on our way to reestablishing their public friendship.

Game #2 drew about thirty people to the silent circle, and game #3 had almost seventy people. The front rows whispered each move to the rows behind them. The chess savvy spectators, except for the Chief of Police, began oohing and aahing after every good move. Games #2 and #3 were excellent chess. I won both the games and established true credentials for the big game on Saturday night.

I arrived at the small cafe on time for the big game, and I barely recognized the metamorphosis of the cafe. The owner/cook had the shuttered window down and the door open for coffee. He moved two chairs and "The Table" to the center of the concrete slab. All other chairs and tables were off the concrete in the surrounding dirt. The chess set on The Table was expensive and unique. Both the kings resembled Pharaoh Rameses II. The queens looked like Cleopatra. Approximately 300 Arab men stood around The Table. All wore their fanciest turbans and gallabiyahs. All became silent upon my arrival.

I went to The Table to meet Gamil. We shook hands and bowed to each other. Gamil wore a beautiful gold-trimmed gallabiyah with a matching turban. It was the only time that I saw Gamil dressed in something other than his archaeologist outfit. Gamil looked totally Arab. All waited in silence for the Police Chief who was fashionably late. I heard the roar from the crowd before I saw the Chief of Police.

He wore a magnificent Police Chief uniform with two shiny gold epaulets. A dozen medals and ribbons, his awards for valor, hung on the front of his impeccable uniform. We shook hands and bowed to each other. He turned east towards Mecca to pray to Allah. All bowed heads in a respectful silence until he finished his prayer for a victory in battle. I attempted to join the high drama by theatrically turning west and mumbling the Our Father. It was like the worst of the Crusades all over again.

Gamil, the official Master of Ceremonies, introduced us in Arabic Egyptian. When he eloquently introduced the Chief of Police as the true champion of the town and the primary upholder of town honor, a long roar of approval went up to Allah. When Gamil introduced the challenger to the chess supremacy of the Police Chief, I stood alone in a polite but pregnant silence. The Police Chief and I shook hands again and bowed to each other again. The time for theatrics ended as we sat in complete silence at The Table for the opening move of The Game. It was time to get it on.

I won the chess game. As a result, all hell broke loose. When the Chief of Police tilted his king and laid it gently on the chessboard in the international sign accepting the checkmate and the defeat, the crowd roared disapproval. Arab men ripped open fancy gallabiyahs and threw turbans on the ground to stomp on them. It looked like a massive chess groupie temper tantrum.

My eyes locked onto the eyes of the Police Chief. We both knew that it was an excellent game of chess. Neither player made a single mistake. It was very close to a perfect game of chess. There was a basic honor in best efforts and to hell with the pride from winning or losing games. We both understood that fact as we looked into each other's eyes. We sat calmly in the middle of the outrageous rancor. We had a mutual respect for each other and for the nearly perfect game of chess. I understood why Gamil called him best friend. Then for just a few seconds, I thought that I saw a slight grin and a most mischievous twinkle in his eyes. Even more oddly, I thought that I saw him silently mouth the words, "Thank you."

The Chief of Police slowly raised himself from the chair, and the crowd was instantly silent. He stood proudly at his full stature in his Chief of Police uniform and extended his hand. I stood and accepted his handshake. He bowed his head with dignity from the shoulders and released his tight grip. I bowed with respect from the waist and almost touched my forehead on the chess set and The Table. He turned, and the crowd parted like the Red Sea for Moses. All silently watched while his First Lieutenant opened a back door of the police car and snapped to attention with the regimental salute. The First Lieutenant drove very slowly from the cafe with flashing lights and blaring siren.

Gamil touched me lightly on the arm and motioned to follow him. We discreetly eased through the silent crowd that focused totally on the retreating police car. We exited the cafe in the opposite direction. As soon as we cleared the backside of the kitchen, Gamil retrieved a stashed gallabiyah. He told me to quickly put it on. He also put a kaffiyeh, a shoulder length Arab headdress, on my head to hide my long hair. He said to follow him without talking to anybody. If anyone stopped us, let him answer all the questions. He practically sprinted down a long dark alley with me in tow. I immediately understood the hurry when I heard the silent crowd at the cafe erupt into a raging lynch mob. Thanks to his foresight, Gamil and I had disguises and a one-block head start.

Gamil wove us through the darkest alleys of Luxor. I trusted him implicitly and followed him like a shadow. Many police sirens wailed in motion through dark streets around us. The shouts localized at the cafe began to fade. We eventually reached an abandoned dock on the Nile River. He motioned for silence as we jumped into a skiff with the pilot waiting at the oars. Gamil talked in Coptic Egyptian with a low voice. The pilot haggled in harsh conspiratorial tones. Money changed hands. The pilot haggled some more, and more money changed hands. Finally, we headed for the other side of the Nile River. Angry shouts and the police sirens faded as the distance from the shore grew. I silently watched the flashing lights from the many police cars moving in systematic and methodical search patterns.

We reached the west bank of the Nile River, historically named the Land of the Dead. Gamil and I walked into a rural village with few lights filtering into deserted dirt streets. We entered an abandoned three-room adobe house with dirt floors and no electricity. Gamil lit the oil lantern and adjusted the glow to a small halo of light. The only other items in the room were a small straw mat, bucket of water with a drinking gourd, and a small bowl of fresh fruit. We sat together on the straw mat with our backs against the wall and silently drank cool water from the same gourd. There was barely enough light to see Gamil's face puckered and contorted into lines of thought and worry. I felt weariness replace the adrenaline in my body. I thought only that I was very tired of Arab pride.

Gamil finally succeeded in his task to suss out the experience to his satisfaction. Gamil chuckled softly, and his face relaxed into a million-dollar smile. His first words were, "Thank you, my friend, for restoring my public friendship with my best friend...It was excellent game of chess." We sat in the semi-darkness, and his soft-spoken words came to me full of strength and courage. Gamil explained the strange events of the night from the perspective of Arabs in relation to individual pride and personal honor.

We were in the vacant family home of the Police Chief's father. It was the only safe house on both sides of the Nile River within the jurisdiction of the Police Chief to hide from the search. My backpack was in the other room, and Gamil already paid my bill at the Youth Hostel. I was to stay in the house alone until dawn. Plans included the visible and public help of Gamil throughout the night in the Police Chief's search for me. Dawn meant a slow train south from Luxor to Aswan down by the Egyptian border with Sudan. I had all night to think about it, but a train out of town sounded good to me.

Gamil had not sold me out, and the Chief of Police had not sold us out. Gamil and the Police Chief were indeed best friends. The Chief of Police was in the loop of information after Gamil's second loss to me in chess. Gamil contacted the Police Chief privately. The two friends met and buried their pride under their friendship. They redid the original plan, and from that point on the Police Chief and Gamil were in cahoots.

It was a brilliant plan based on the total cooperation and trust of the best friends. The plan manipulated the pride of the local Arabs. Gamil apologized for not clueing me into the new information before we were on the run. But success depended on an excellent game of chess that demanded a rematch from the audience for the sake of the loser's honor. The pressures were already intense, and Gamil withheld the revised plan to ease the extra pressure on me to play well. Make no mistake about the two friends wanting to win games of chess against me. The best friends practiced sophisticated chess moves privately together in preparation for Gamil's third game and the Police Chief's big game. There was no doubt that they went for the wins with their best efforts.

The police search was ostensibly to find and protect me from the mob. It was a search with certain areas declared strictly off-limits at specific times so that Gamil and I were safe in the alleys to the River. The mob included several trusted family members of the two friends pumping up the crowd for a couple of hours to demand a rematch. It sounded to me like they did very good work.

The double commotion increased the status/stature of the Police Chief. Real pride and true honors were in such important police work as finding and protecting the tourist from the raging mob, not in the measly game of chess. The Chief of Police was simply too busy with his very important police work to honor a rematch in chess. Even Gamil, the Police Chief's best friend, helped him publicly try to keep his city record honorable and perfect with no injuries to any tourist. Nevertheless, if anyone had the time to stop and count, the exact number of chess losses on The Table in the past ten years was three for Gamil and only two for the Chief of Police. To reemphasize the true point of honor, a call would come in the morning from Cairo requesting the valuable assistance of the Police Chief in very special police work for a few days in the capitol of the nation.

When the Chief of Police returned from his very important police trip to Cairo, there was the final episode of the new and revised plan to accomplish successfully. Gamil and the Chief of Police planned to challenge each other for the sake of family honor to one last public game of chess on The Table for The Table. The best friends already choreographed a stalemate. With the tie in the game of chess, the owner/cook, a distant cousin of both families, solemnly declared both honorable Arab men entitled to The Table in his cafe. All personal honor and individual pride remained publicly intact. Then the honor and pride of owner/cook demanded that the two best friends enjoy a public meal together at The Table to publicly support the decision of the owner/cook. The final result restored and renewed the public friendship of the two best friends.

Gamil finished the explanation of the events from the perspective of Arab male pride. He left me alone in the midnight hour to ponder the truth of his statements. My reoccurring thought during the wee hours of the morning was that the story was most bizarre. Ironically I chuckled and then laughed so loudly that I worried about blowing my cover at the safe house. When the dust settled at dawn, I was on a slow train headed south to the temple of Abu Simbel at the Egyptian border with Sudan.

These events happened in July 1973. On October 6, 1973, the Egyptian President Anwar Sadat ordered the Egyptian troops into the Sinai Peninsula to surprise attack and fight the Israeli troops. It was the beginning of the Yom Kippur War with Israel. It was also a fourth armed conflict between Arab countries and Israel. Egyptian troops pushed into the Sinai Peninsula that Egypt lost to Israel in a previous Six-Day War in June 1967. Israel eventually won the Yom Kippur War militarily, but President Sadat won a moral and psychological victory for the Egyptian people.

The Egyptian military attack on the Israeli troops in the occupied territories of the Sinai Peninsula restored and renewed the honor and pride of the Egyptian nation. The restoration of national honor and pride allowed President Anwar Sadat to negotiate peace with Israel. President Anwar Sadat, Prime Minister Menachem Begin of Israel, President Jimmy Carter of the U.S.A. signed "Camp David Accords" in September 1978. Camp David was the groundwork for Egypt and Israel to sign the Peace Treaty on March 26, 1979. As part of the Peace Treaty, Israel gradually withdrew from the Sinai Peninsula. President Sadat got back in peace what Egypt had lost in war. The peace restored and renewed the national honor and national pride of Egypt. President Anwar Sadat and Prime Minister Menachem Begin shared the Noble Peace Prize in 1978 for courage at Camp David that resulted in the Peace Treaty. President Jimmy Carter won the Noble Peace Prize in 2002 for peace efforts starting with the Camp David Accords. Egypt alone signed the Peace Treaty in 1979 without the support of other Arab nations. Other Arab countries continued to fight Israel, and they had the support of Arab extremists in Egypt.

On October 6, 1981, the Egyptian Arab extremists assassinated President Anwar Sadat. It was the eight-year anniversary of the Yom Kippur War and 2½ years after the signing of the Peace Treaty with Israel. Muslim fundamentalists and religious fanatics in the Egyptian army assassinated President Anwar Sadat in Cairo during a military parade commemorating the moral and psychological victory of the Yom Kippur War ("Sadat," "Yom Kippur War," <u>Microsoft Encarta '98 Encyclopedia.</u>). The Arab extremists immediately declared that their successful assassination of President Anwar Sadat restored their personal honor and their individual pride.

B. APPLIED THEOLOGY – PRAYERS OF PETITION

People, the stories of the street life in Egypt have applications to prayers of petitions. If the Teen wants to elevate prayer-life above a kindergarten level, the Teen may utilize the full range for theology of prayer developed from ancient times to elevate spirituality. Prayer is the communication with God in a personal relationship based on the humility of the individual (Catechism, n.2558-9). All negative pride destroys the love relationship with God. Prayers of petition have the potential to restore love relationships with God and neighbor.

When Teenagers read stories about the negative pride of Arab males, Teens may easily think and feel a spiritual "thumbs down" for entire Arabic cultures. This Teen quick-fix conclusion may include a spiritual prejudice against the Arabic way of praying and relating to God. Before Teenagers judge too harshly, Teens need to remember the thoughts from Jesus expressed through Saint Luke's Gospel. Before a Teen removes a speck in a brother's eye, the Teen needs to remove the plank/log in his or her own eye so that the Teen sees clearly and avoids hypocrisy (Lk.6:41-2). Teens need to unload the negative pride in their daily lives before Teens criticize absurdities of the uncontrolled Arab pride. Stories of the negative Israeli pride or stories of negative U.S. pride could easily replace stories of negative Arab pride. It is simply easier to see the negative side of ego and pride when the culture is so different from your own. A negative male pride clearly looks spiritually absurd to the outsider. But the thoughts remain true that negative pride destroys the love relationship with God/neighbor and the wisdom in prayer restores the love relationship with God/neighbor.

If Teenagers understand the concept of prayer as the personal union with God, the ancient wisdom enhances Teenage prayers of petitions especially in dealing with the mystery of the One True God. Uncontrolled human pride is the ancient problem in salvation history. The original sin of Adam and Eve was a "civil disobedience" based on individual pride. Original sin destroyed original holiness. Negative pride destroyed positive humility. The ego dominated the balanced existence. Jesus restored the original holiness and relationship with God the Father through his humility and his perfect obedience to the Father's will especially during his Passion and death on the cross. Teenage prayer taps into the ancient wisdom of Jesus. Prayer is the result of the conversion of the heart and mind (Mt.6:1-15; Catechism, n.2808-09, 1427, 1430). Prayer restores union and relationship with the One True God of Antiquity. Prayer restores original holiness and positive humility in the individual. To delete the ancient wisdom from prayers of petitions is to open the door for a negative pride to again destroy the restoration of original holiness and original virtue.

a. Concept of Time

Ancient wisdom cautions modern Teenagers about the concept of time in relation to prayers of petitions. Many Teenagers have a fast-food mentality that produces a fast-food spirituality. They want instant gratification for all desires. When this concept filters into the pragmatic theology of prayer, Teens want and sometimes demand instant answers to their prayers of petitions. The premium virtue of patience is not a vital part of the daily spiritual vocabulary of some Teenagers. Teens pray now to God with a list of petitions, and Teens want positive answers now from God. God's time is not necessarily Teen's time. This is sometimes a difficult lesson for Teens to learn. God answers Teen prayers of petitions, but not automatically at the time of Teenage demands. In addition, God sometimes answers the petitions differently from the exact way envisioned by Teens. A Teen cannot manipulate God, and neither can a Teenager manipulate his or her petitions onto the top of the cosmic answer sheet for the first answers. God's time and God's answers to prayers of petitions are not automatically the Teen's time and the Teen's answers. Wisdom from ancient times suggested that God's time usually required the development of coping skills. From the theological perspective, this means the virtue of patience.

The author of the Second Letter of Peter in the New Testament wrote in about 100-125 A.D. and stated, "But do not ignore this one fact, beloved, that with the Lord one day is like a thousand years, and a thousand years are like one day" (3:8). This tidbit of wisdom from 2,000 years ago means that divine time is always mysterious to humanity. God's time is basically incalculable with given equations: 1 day = 1,000 years; 1,000 years = 1 day (Brown, The New Jerome Biblical Commentary, p.1021).

Most biblical scholars suggest that the author of 2Peter used the Psalm 90:4 for the reference point to God's time. Psalm 90 according to its ancient title or superscription was "A Prayer of Moses, the man of God." Biblical scholars have no modern proof that Moses actually composed Psalm 90. But the facts remain that it is the only psalm out of 150 psalms ascribed to Moses and that it was already ancient prayer to the author of 2Peter. Moses lived in 1300 B.C. about 3,300 years ago. Psalm 90:4 stated with direct reference to God and time, "For a thousand years in your sight are like yesterday when it is past, or like a watch in the night." The Hebrew military divided every night into three sentry periods or "watches" of four hours (N.A.B., Ps.90, fn.90,4; Jgs.7, fn.7,19). The ancient comparison is 1,000 years of God's time equal one yesterday or 1,000 years of God's time equal a few hours in the Hebrew sentry's night. The author of 2Peter surely deferred to the more ancient authority and agreed with more ancient wisdom concerning the concept of God's time.

Both the passages of ancient wisdom from 2,000 and perhaps 3,300 years ago suggest that God does not measure time with the human watch or the human timetable. God exists independent from the man-made concepts of time and from the constraints of space. Ancient biblical wisdom is a direct caution to all modern Teenagers about boxing God into Teen understanding of time. God's time is not Teen's time. Teenagers may hope that a loving God answers their prayers of petitions immediately. Nevertheless, many problems from discouragement and presumption develop when Teens demand the

Almighty God to fit Teenage clocks and calendars. From humanity's dawn of time to the present age, time remains a gift of God. Men and women traditionally use time to know God, to repent, to gain wisdom, to enjoy the love of God and each other.

This ancient wisdom about God's time not equaling humanity's time developed in salvation history within a "school of hard knocks." For example, the Hebrew people were slaves in Egypt for almost 430 years (Gen.15:13; Ex.12:40; Acts7:6; Gal.3:17). Jacob had twelve sons, the start of the twelve tribes of Israel. The #11 son was Joseph whose brothers sold him into slavery. Joseph rose in power from the slavery in Egypt to the prime minister of Egypt. He became the #2 man in pharaoh's court and the most influential man next to pharaoh himself. Eventually Joseph brought his Dad, Jacob, eleven brothers with their families to Egypt to live the good life (Gen.37-50). All things were fine until the pharaoh died and the new pharaoh enslaved the Hebrew people (Ex.1).

Biblical scholars think that Joseph went to Egypt about 1720B.C. Moses led the Hebrew people out of Egypt about 1290B.C. during the Exodus from Pharaoh Rameses II (Anderson, <u>Understanding the Old Testament</u>, p.45-52). That was 430 years for many generations of Hebrews to pray for their freedom from Egyptian slavery. Hebrew prayers of petitions were not necessarily for the freedom to do their own thing. Prayers were for the freedom to worship the One True God of Abraham, Isaac, Jacob without the onus of local false gods in a foreign society/culture (Ex.3:7-12). Those were pretty good prayers of petitions by many individuals for a long time. God took about 430 of mankind's years to answer those prayers. Many Hebrew people lived their entire lives with the one constant prayer of petition for the freedom to worship God. God's time is not mankind's time.

Modern Teens are not the first people to grapple with concepts of time in relation to prayers of petitions. Human demands on God for instant answers to prayers relative to concepts of man-made time sometimes cloud, confuse, and complicate simple prayers of petition. It is a wonder that any two humans tell the same time together, but it is a shame that humans demand instant answers from God for their prayers of petitions within understandable frameworks of mankind's time. Let me give Teenagers a few examples of the complexity of man-made time in relation to humanity's communication with God. Please, understand that the important bottom line is Teen prayer and not man-made concepts of time superimposed on God's answer to prayers of petitions.

Humanity's concept of time evolved from the dawn of time to the present with God and his creation as constant mysterious factors. Humanity cooperated all over the world and throughout its secular history to develop a concept of time. Many compromises among the different peoples and cultures form the basis of thought about time. Time is the period and the dimension representing the succession of actions or events. Time is the fundamental quantity of the physical world in the category with "length" and "mass" as three universal concepts ("Time," <u>Microsoft Encarta '98 Encyclopedia.</u>). Regardless of different cultures and languages, time and mathematics crisscross international boundaries as accepted fact and truth, until tested and proved false.

Humanity measures time in a single place with great accuracy and precision with modern technology. Nevertheless, time is not a physical constant. Both motion and gravity effect time by dilating or expanding time. By 1917 Albert Einstein theorized and formulated the effects of motion and gravity on time in his theory of relativity. Einstein's theory of relativity proved true in the 1960s and 1970s with scientific experiments involving high-speed aircraft and outer space programs (Ibid.).

With the introduction of the atomic clock in 1955, scientists round the world agreed to redefine the measurement of the "second" as the scientific standard of time. The atomic clock "is tuned to the resonant frequency of the transition energy between two energy states of the cesium-133 atom" (Ibid.). The "second" went from 1/86,400 of the mean solar day to a measurement of electromagnetic wavelengths based on "9,192,631,770 periods of the radiation corresponding to the transition between two hyperfine levels of cesium-133" (Ibid., "Second," <u>Encarta</u>). Whew, that complicates the simple prayer of petition in relation to demanding God's answers in a second and to understanding instant answers. Humanity barely understands and communicates the scientific second, but humans demand answers from God to their petitions in a time that people barely understand. God's time is not mankind's time.

Need for such precision and accuracy in a "second" of scientific standard of time evolved innocently in the Industrial Revolution. In 1883 scientists invented and introduced "standard time" basically to avoid hassles in the railroad time schedules due to each community using its own local solar time. The international scientific and political agreement divided the earth into 24 time zones with all the clocks set to the same time within each time zone. The base position was the zero line of longitude, which passed through the Royal Greenwich Observatory in Greenwich, England. That international agreement based the worldwide coordination of time on solar time and a human custom of dividing time into a 24-hour day ("Time," <u>Encarta</u>).

However, the people in ancient times had no atomic clocks. The ancient peoples based time and calendars on natural phenomenon. Ancient Babylonians used the cycles of the moon for their calendars. Ancient Egyptians were the first people to replace a lunar calendar with a calendar based on the sun and a solar year. The inaccuracy of the calendars magnified until calendars disagreed with the actual season experienced by the people for planting and harvesting crops.

The international leaders agreed on periodic adjustments because a solar year contained 365 days and a lunar year contained 354 days.

In 45B.C. Julius Caesar established the purely solar calendar for the coordination of the governments in all lands conquered by the Romans. Caesar's solar calendar had 365 days and the leap year every fourth year for the periodic adjustments. A Julian year was 11 minutes and 14 seconds longer than a solar year. The discrepancy accumulated until the church holidays fell outside the appropriate seasons. In 1582 Pope Gregory XIII instituted a Gregorian calendar and dropped 10 days to adjust the calendar to the actual time and seasons. When Great Britain adopted the Gregorian calendar in 1752, the international agreement dropped 11 days in another time correction. The day after September 2, 1752 became September 14, 1752 ("Calendar," Encarta).

The Gregorian calendar used today is a basic Christian calendar. It uses the birth of Jesus Christ as a starting date. "B.C." designates dates "before Christ," and "A.D." designates dates in the Christian era with "anno domini," which means "in the year of our Lord." But ancient nations determined historical time and political chronology in relation to the life of the king or a central event. The ancient people reckoned time by so many years after the birth of the king's #1 son, or so many years after the king won a very important battle. Jesus Christ is the central figure in the Gregorian calendar. Nevertheless, the chronology of Sacred Scripture is sometimes uncertain because the writers of Sacred Scripture used the various local chronologies at different times and in the dissimilar systems ("Chronology," Encarta). God's time is not mankind's time.

Our modern technology emphasizes precision and accuracy in humanity's concept of time. However, there is always the element of the mystery in God's creation involved in man-made time. Part of the mystery involves the fact that the motion of the earth on its axis is not regular. The variations in the rate of rotation amount to 30 seconds during the last 200 years. In addition, our earth slows at the rate of about 1/1000 of a second every 100 years ("Time," Encarta). These irregular variations present mystery in the future time just as there is mystery in the past time. God's time is not mankind's time.

There is also philosophical and theological mystery in present time even with the sophistication of the advanced technology. Some areas of the world today use different religious calendars based on the worship of God. The Western world and parts of Asia use the Gregorian calendar based on the solar year with the birth of Jesus Christ as the starting point. Jewish people do not believe that Jesus was the Christ, the Messiah, the Anointed One, and the country of Israel uses the Jewish religious calendar. It is lunisolar, based on lunar months of 29 days alternating with 30 days. Jewish calendars intercalate an extra month every three years. The starting point of Hebrew chronology is the year 3761B.C., which is the Jewish date for the creation of the world described in Hebrew Scriptures ("Calendar," Encarta). The established age of the earth is about 4.6 billion years based on scientific radiometric dating that measures the radioactive elements in rocks ("Geologic Time," Encarta). The man-made time expressed in the religious calendar is sometimes incongruous with the scientific reality. God's time is not mankind's time.

Almost all the Muslim countries today use the Islamic religious calendar. It is a lunar calendar with 354 days in the common lunar year, which is 11¼ days shorter than a solar year. The starting point of the Islamic calendar is in 622 A.D. on the day after Muhammad's flight from Mecca to Medina. Microsoft Encarta '98 Encyclopedia states:

> The Islamic date corresponding to a date in the Gregorian calendar can be computed by the following rule, with a maximum error of one day: multiply 970,224 by the Islamic year, divide by 6 decimal places, and add 621.5774. The figure to the left of the decimal point is the year AD, and the decimal fraction multiplied by 365 is the day of the year.
>
> "Calendar"

The man-made time expressed in a religious calendar is sometimes incongruous with scientific reality. God's time is not mankind's time.

God must raise his eyebrows when he observes people reacting to humanity's concept of time. With one hand of the clock, humanity uses time to simplify and unify for trade, business, convenience, and communication. On the other hand of the same clock, humanity uses time to complicate and divide in the name of the politically correct worship of God. God really chuckled when modern man invented and developed "standard time" to coordinate railroad time schedules to a uniform solar time. As a result, every man, woman, and child throughout the world knows that trains, planes, buses seldom travel on time! Demands that God answer prayers of petition on mankind's time approach the absurd. God's time is not mankind's time.

Nevertheless, there are five ongoing considerations from both ancient and modern wisdom for the Teen concerned with prayers of petitions in relation to time: (1) God's time is not mankind's time; (2) man's time and woman's time is barely mankind's time; (3) as far as biblical scholars know, all U.S.A. Teens mark their existence with a time based on Jesus Christ who never owned a fast donkey, never owned a fancy house, never had a good paying job, never traveled more than 200 miles from home, and always loved everybody; (4) all Teens are at the mercy of the mysterious God who loves Teenagers without regard to time; (5) God's time is not Teen's time.

b. Tweak Teen Prayers of Petitions

There is no real need for Teens to bog down in the man-made concept of time or to get stuck in the speed of God's answers to the prayers of petitions. There is, however, a real need for the Teen to petition God for the premium virtue of patience. Otherwise, fast-food mentality dominates the Teenager's spirituality. The Teenager may experience frustration and discouragement because God seems too slow to answer Teen prayers of petitions. The extreme and improper reaction is for the Teen to stop all prayers of petitions when the Teen does not get his or her way immediately. This spiritual meltdown is the negative reaction of a spoiled spiritual brat and a spiritual snob. The spiritual highlight of a brat and a snob is the thought that God kowtows to the whims and the fantasies of the individual Teenager. The negative reaction has too much individual pride and not enough humility and patience for a good solid love relationship with God. God is neither a personal magician of the Teen, nor a supercharged lucky charm of the Teen, nor a spiritual rabbit's foot of the Teenager. God is the Most Holy One of Antiquity who calls the modern Teen into a love relationship that requires Teen patience.

When Jesus Christ did miracles and instant answers to individual prayers of petitions, he quickly said that the instantaneous healing was for the honor/glory of God the Father (Jn.11: 32-44) and for the reconciliation of the love relationship with God the Father (Mk.2: 2-12). When he taught us about prayers, Jesus Christ never described prayers of petitions as psychological crutches for spiritual pains or spiritual boo-boos. Prayer is the result of the individual's choice to have union and relationship with God. Although manipulation and domination sometimes enter our human relationships, does the Teen really want these two negative factors in a relationship with God and in prayers of petitions to God? If a Teen wants to elevate spirituality off a kindergarten level, the Teen must better utilize the gifts from God to think and feel more deeply. Prayers bring the gifts from God back to God with dignity and respect for God.

Teens are very good at asking for stuff. Teens practice and fine tune prayers of petitions. On Teen lists are prayers for good health, power, money, status, better grades, boyfriends, girlfriends, athletic talents, popularity, etc. Teens regularly petition God for more stuff to make life easier. There is nothing wrong with these Teen prayers of petitions. There is no need to trash mouth any petition brought by a Teen in prayer to the Most Holy and All Powerful God.

When the disciples asked Jesus to teach them to pray, he gave the "Our Father" to them and to modern Teens. The Our Father is "the summary of the whole gospel" of Jesus because he teaches his disciples and Teens through it to pray, to live a Christian life, to act in a Christian way (Catechism, n. 2761-64). Saint Luke's version of the Our Father contains five petitions (Lk.11: 2-4), and Saint Matthew's version presents seven petitions (Mt.6:9-13). Both versions have the petition, "Give us this day our daily bread." Theologians and biblical scholars interpret the "bread" as all material goods and all spiritual blessings (Catechism, n. 2830). According to biblical scholars, the modifying word "daily" (in original texts "epiousios") is a rare Greek word. Four main English translations are "tomorrow's, daily, needful, or future" (Jerome, p. 645). In its most literal theological sense, the word "daily" from the Greek "epi-ousios" means "super-essential," and the word refers directly to the super-essential bread, the Bread of Life, the Holy Eucharist (Catechism, n. 2837).

Jesus taught his disciples and by extension modern Teenagers to pray multiple prayers of petitions. Jesus taught Teens to petition God the Father for our daily bread including all material goods, all spiritual blessings, and the opportunity for the Catholic Teenagers to experience/receive a Holy Communion with God each day. Jesus continually encouraged his disciples and modern Teenagers to pray, to petition God the Father, to ask and receive, to seek and find, to knock and open (Mt.7:7-11; Lk.18:1-8; Mk.11:23-4; Jn.15:7). Holy Scripture gives Teens a green light to petition Almighty God for stuff. When a Teen chooses to pray, he or she follows the lead of Jesus from 2,000 years ago.

Any prayer from the Teen is better than no prayer from the Teen. Every Teen is on a spiritual journey, and all Teens are at different spots in their faith journey. The Teen more advanced on the spiritual journey may encourage other Teenagers to pray. However, negative spiritual criticism of peers sometimes destroys the will of a Teenager to exist in holiness. Quantity and quality of Teen prayers rest with a Teen's initial decision to pray and not with the judgments forced on Teens from peers or other people. The fundamental decision to pray in union with God and to establish a relationship with God spins out of the fundamental freedom to choose between the good God and the evil force.

No person has the right to condemn or trash mouth the prayers of Teenagers who try in good conscience to pray. Only God and the individual Teen are in a position to judge the quantity and quality of his or her prayers. It is the internal challenge of self to foster a holy relationship with God through prayer. Only the individual Teen and God truly judge the Teen's efforts to establish union and relationship with the Most Holy God. Nevertheless, each Teenager has the ability and potential to improve individual prayer-life and spirituality. Teen prayers of petitions spiral a Teen's faith journey upward towards the high heaven like smoke from a friendly campfire. It is the individual choice of the Teenager to elevate prayer-life and spirituality above a kindergarten level with prayers of petitions. It is the choice of the Teen to grow in individual spirituality.

All prayers of petition express awareness of the relationship with God (Catechism, n. 2629). When Teens petition God, they recognize that God is the Creator and Teens are the created. God the Creator has more power than creatures. Teenagers petition God for his help because Teenagers cannot fix everything by themselves with only personal power. In a first petition Teenagers need to ask forgiveness based on acceptance of a responsibility for personal sins. Asking forgiveness for offenses against the laws of God is a prerequisite for pure and righteous prayers of petitions because a petitioner bases requests on trust of God and humility before God. Petitioning God for forgiveness is essential for both a personal prayer and the public prayer of the Eucharistic liturgy (Ibid., n. 2631).

One way to elevate prayer-life and to grow in spirituality is to shift the focus of prayers of petitions. All Teens may choose to "tweak" their prayers of petitions. The Teen may choose to broaden petitions from self and the nuclear family to other Teens in real need. Focus shifts from prayers of petitions to prayers of intercessions. Prayers of intercessions are special prayers of petitions (Ibid., n.2634-6). The prayer of intercession petitions God on behalf of another because the petitioner looks "not to your own interests, but to the interests of others" (Phil.2:4). Jesus Christ prayed and consistently interceded with God the Father on behalf of humanity and especially the sinners (Rom.8:34; 1Jn.2:1; 1Tim.2:5-8; Heb.7:25; Acts7:60; Lk.23:28,34).

When a Teenager shifts the focus from self to others, prayers of petitions shift to prayers of intercessions. Teenagers pray as Jesus prayed to intercede for others with God the Father. The typical love triangle in human relationships sometimes fills Teenage years with confusion, reflections of love, jostled positions in love relationships. However, heartfelt prayers of intercessions fill a Teenager with value and righteousness because the spiritual relationship is a love triangle created with God, others, self. Teen prayers of intercessions become premium prayers of petitions because the self diminishes in humility before God as the petitions for others strengthen personal holiness. Consequently, a Teenager elevates individual spirituality above the kindergarten level of gimme this for me and that for my family.

When the Teenage prayers of petitions shift focus to prayers of intercessions for others in real need, the new list of Teen requests to Almighty God may include:
(1) Prayers for little people with flies in their eyes,
(2) Prayers for Teens brutalized by dads because of one misplaced word in a sentence,
(3) Prayers for poor families living on streets in third world countries,
(4) Prayers for the people who teach health education to people with flies on meat racks,
(5) Prayers for the freedom and human rights of Teens in all cultures,
(6) Prayers for a release from negative pride,
(7) Prayers for common sense in human relationships,
(8) Prayers for more humility in all people,
(9) Prayers for peace among Teens,

(10) Prayers for love between Teens in different cultures,
(11) Prayers for increased communication skills among Teens,
(12) Prayers for Teens in Mideast who will lead countries in future,
(13) Prayers for emotionally depressed Teens,
(14) Prayers for physically gimped-up Teens,
(15) Prayers for mentally retarded Teens,
(16) Prayers for blind Teens.

Jesus said in the Gospel of John, "This is my commandment, that you love one another as I have loved you. No one has greater love than this, to lay down one's life for one's friends" (15:12-13). If a Teen "lays down" prayers of petitions for self in his/her spiritual life, the sacrifice of love in the exchange for prayers of intercessions for others will elevate the personal holiness and spirituality of the Teen. Sacrifices of self-petitions for the intercessions of others are within the choices of all Teenagers. However, some of the more difficult love choices of Teens are to expand the concept of "one's friends" and to choose a life of sacrifice for these new others. The result of these decisions has the potential to further elevate the holiness and spirituality of the Teen.

The tweak or shift of focus from prayers of petitions to prayers of intercessions is a way for the Teen to elevate prayer-life and to grow in spirituality. However, there is no need for the Teen to eliminate totally the prayers of petitions for self and the nuclear family. Jesus Christ instructed Teens to petition God the Father for all daily things. Nevertheless, another way to tweak and shift the focus in prayers of petitions to enhance the elevation of prayer-life is the Teen inclusion of petitions for specific virtues. When the Teenager prays for self, the Teen may refocus on spiritual virtues instead of only increases in material possessions like power, status, and money.

Most Teens need more virtue and less vice in their lives. Why not petition God the Father for the gifts of his virtues (Catechism, n. 1803)? Why not ask and receive three theological virtues of faith, hope/trust, charity/love (Ibid., n. 1814, 1817, 1822)? Why not seek and find seven gifts of God the Holy Spirit: wisdom, understanding, counsel, fortitude, knowledge, piety, fear of the Lord (Ibid., n.1831; Isa.11:1-3)? Why not knock and open twelve fruits of God the Holy Spirit: charity, joy, peace, patience, kindness, goodness, generosity, gentleness, faithfulness, modesty, self-control, chastity (Catechism, n.1832; Gal.5: 22-3)? Why not petition Almighty God for the gifts of his four cardinal virtues: prudence, justice, fortitude, temperance (Catechism, n.1805; Wis.8: 7)? Why not petition the God of All Love for truth and grace (Catechism, n.234, 2500-3,1996 -97)? It seems that all Teens could use more of these thirty free gifts from God in their daily lives. If the Teen petitions God for any one of these gifts, God will fill the Teen with the holiness from his gift. As a result, the positive actions of the Teen show living proof that God answers Teen prayers of petitions. These free gifts from God become thirty special ways to elevate prayer-life and to grow in spirituality.

Theologians define virtues as good habits and firm dispositions that allow people to do good actions and to give the best of self (Ibid. n.1803). Saint Thomas Aquinas (1225-74) stated "On the Subject of Virtue" in his Summa Theologica that "...virtue is a perfect habit, by which it never happens that anything but good is done; and so virtue must needs be in that power which completes a good act" (I–II, Q. 56, a.5). Also "On the Virtues, As To Their Essence" in his Summa, Saint Thomas Aquinas responded that "...virtue implies a perfection of power, and therefore the virtue of a thing is fixed by the peak of its power... the peak of any power must needs be good, for all evil implies defect" (I–II, Q.55, a.3).

All virtues are free gifts from God, and God answers generously the Teen's requests for virtues in prayers of petitions. However, the Teen must choose to ask God for virtues within the love relationship established in prayer. God will not fail to give his virtue to the Teen who asks for it. A primary key to open the heart to virtue is the free choice of the Teenager to pray.

Fortitude is the excellent virtue to help Teenagers through daily hassles. Catechism of the Catholic Church defines fortitude as:

> ...the moral virtue that ensures firmness in difficulties and constancy in the pursuit of the good. It strengthens the resolve to resist temptations and to overcome obstacles in the moral life. The virtue of fortitude enables one to conquer fear...and to face trials and persecutions.   n.1808

Saint Thomas Aquinas influenced the modern thoughts of the Catholic Church over 700 years ago with his definitions of fortitude in his Summa Theologica:

> ...and fortitude, a disposition whereby the soul is strengthened for that which is in accord with reason, against any assaults of the passions, or the toil involved by any operations.   I–II, Q.61, a.4
>
> ...when the passions withdraw us from following the dictate of reason, e.g., through fear of danger or toil, and then man needs to be strengthened for that which reason dictates, lest he turn back, and to this end there is fortitude. I–II, Q.61, a.2

When the Teen refocuses prayers of petitions to include spiritual virtues for self, fortitude is the ancient virtue for the modern Teen. Heavy peer pressures exert negative influences on modern Teens to do bad actions. Fortitude is the premium virtue to offset all negative peer pressures. Fortitude is the virtue to strengthen and beef-up the spirituality of the Teen with the choices for positive responses in daily life. The virtue of fortitude is the gift of God to help modern Teens through serious problems, mundane living, and boredom in daily life. The Teen with the virtue of fortitude experiences the whole gambit of human emotions and passions but continues to choose prayer and worship of God. Fortitude is the ancient virtue worthy of the petitions from the modern Teen to God for the self. Positive Teen choices to pray modified by the spiritual "fort attitude" of God are strong enough to combat negative peer pressures.

Fortitude is a well-known virtue in ancient salvation history. It is a virtue "praised under other names in many passages of Scripture" (Catechism, n.1805). Traditional names for fortitude in the different translations of the Bible are strength, might, courage (Ps.118:14; Ex. 15:2; Isa.12:2). Holy Scripture contains the virtue of fortitude in the written lists of the premium virtues from 2,000 and 3,000 years ago (Wis.8:7; Isa.11:1-2). Isaiah 11:1-3 lists fortitude/strength/might as the characteristics of the Messiah and as the Gifts of God the Holy Spirit (Catechism, n.712, 1831).

In the Our Father, the scriptural interpretation of "lead us not into temptation" is the petition for fortitude/strength (Mt. 6:13; Lk.11: 4; Jerome, p. 645; Catechism, n.2846-9). Saint Paul stated that God never tests the individual (the Teenager) beyond fortitude/strength (1Cor.10:13). Saint Paul also said that God gives individuals (Teens) fortitude/strength to guard the person against the evil one (2Thes.3: 3). Martyrs gave supreme witness to the truth of faith by enduring death "through an act of fortitude" (Catechism, n. 2473).

The Catholic Christians throughout 2,000 years of sacramental history received fortitude/strength as a Gift of the Holy Spirit in the Sacrament of Confirmation. In continuation of this ancient Sacrament of Confirmation, modern Teens receive the virtue of fortitude/courage when the Catholic Bishop extends his hands and prays to the Most Holy and the "All-powerful God, Father of our Lord Jesus Christ" to give Teens "the spirit of right judgment and courage" (Ibid., n.1299).

It is the ancient spiritual strength and spiritual courage that the modern Teenager asks and receives from God through prayers of petitions for the virtue of fortitude. The modern Teen joins excellent historical company when the Teen receives fortitude to get through serious crunch times. Moses and the historical Jesus Christ are two examples of people with tremendous fortitude just to basically exist with the pressures from their daily lives. Both men needed fortitude to accomplish their individual missions from God.

c. *Daily Need of Moses for Virtue of Fortitude*

Isolate for a good example of daily fortitude the first meeting with Pharaoh Rameses II (c.1290-1224 B.C.) versus Moses, spokesperson of Yahweh (Ex.5:1-9). Moses needed spiritual strength and spiritual courage to face-off against Pharaoh Rameses II, one of the more powerful men in recorded Egyptian history. Moses knew exactly the difficulty of the major confrontation with the Pharaoh. Moses knew that Pharaoh Rameses II thought that the pharaoh was a god. God's ancient and premium virtue of fortitude gave Moses spiritual strength and spiritual courage to demand capitulation from Pharaoh Rameses II to the will of Yahweh.

When Pharaoh Seti I (c.1305-1290B.C.), the father of Pharaoh Rameses II, decided to control the Hebrew population, he ordered the murder of all newborn Hebrew boys. Pharaoh Seti I commanded that his people throw every newborn Hebrew male into the Nile River (Ex.1:22). The mother of Moses was most clever when she obeyed the letter of Pharaoh's law and saved the baby Moses. Mommy put Moses in a special papyrus basket plastered with bitumen and pitch so that the basket floated. She "threw" Moses into the Nile River at the place where the daughter of Pharaoh Seti I took her bath. The princess, the sister of the boy Rameses II, found the crybaby Moses, took pity on him, adopted him as her own son (Ex.2:1-10). Moses "died" to the harsh daily Hebrew slavery because his natural Mom "threw" him into the Nile River just as Pharaoh Seti I ordered.

Consequently, little Moses and little Rameses grew-up together as princes in the palace of Pharaoh Seti I. Moses received the best education as an Egyptian prince in the highest caste of the existing system. The One True God thwarted the evil plan of Pharaoh Seti I for the destruction of the Hebrew boys. The historic destiny of Moses became a vital part of the divine intervention into the salvation history of humanity ("Moses," <u>Encyclopaedia Judaica</u>, Vol.12, p.372).

The problem for the adult Moses was that he knew the thought patterns of the adult Pharaoh Rameses II of the XIX Dynasty of the Egyptian Pharaohs. During his early Egyptian training, Moses was "instructed in all the wisdom of the Egyptians and was powerful in his words and deeds" (Acts 7:22). Moses knew that Pharaoh Rameses II thought basically just like almost 200 Egyptian pharaohs during the 1,640 years before the kingship of Rameses II (http://www.touregypt.net/kings.htm). The pharaoh thought he was a god.

Both men were well versed in Egyptian mythology. Pharaohs of ancient Egypt were a serious part of the religion. The kings formed a bridge between the gods and the ordinary people. Egyptian people in antiquity believed that pharaohs transformed into gods, and the transformation ritual legitimized the government. According to their mythology, every man had a spiritual double, called a "ka." The royal transformation ritual united the pharaoh's ka with his physical person. The new pharaoh entered the temple before the assumption of his throne, and his priests performed the transformation ritual. People waited outside the temple until the pharaoh exited the temple as a god. The people accepted pharaoh as the newest god, and the word of pharaoh was the new law of the land [http://www.touregypt.net/gods1.htm.(p.3 of 8)].

Both men knew Egyptian mythology. Nevertheless, both men understood Egyptian mythology differently. Moses chose to believe with his whole mind, heart, soul in the One True God of Abraham, Isaac, Jacob. Moses understood that the Egyptian stories were myth. Pharaoh Rameses II chose to believe with his whole mind, heart, soul in Egyptian mythology. Pharaoh understood that he was a god. Egyptian mythology was daily theology for Pharaoh Rameses II. The two men diametrically opposed the spiritual and religious thoughts of the other. Moses needed the virtue of fortitude to exist in the world of Pharaoh Rameses II, one of the more powerful human individuals to ever live.

Moses also understood that Egyptian mythological concepts of afterlife pressured Pharaoh Rameses II to grant a safe first meeting for Moses. The pharaoh allowed and guaranteed the safety of Moses because Moses was the official representative of the God Yahweh. Yahweh was unknown to Pharaoh Rameses II (Ex.5:1-2). However, most major gods and major goddesses in Egypt had five names. For example, the Egyptian "creator of all things" was Re, Amun, Ptah, Khnum, or Aten depending on the current popular cult in use [http://www.touregypt.net/gods1.htm(p.1)]. Viewed from the perspective of pharaoh, the name "Yahweh" might describe a major Egyptian god with a different name unknown to pharaoh.

Pharaoh took no chances on the irritation of a fellow god with an unfamiliar name. Pharaoh thought that he was a god based on the Egyptian mythology, which the Egyptians considered theology. The Pharaoh's success in the afterlife depended on no complaints from the gods and the goddesses. Moses and Pharaoh Rameses II both knew that pharaoh's potential insult to a brother god by mistreatment of the god's official representative was a gamble of pharaoh's cozy immortality. Moses knew that he was safe for his first meeting with Pharaoh Rameses II. But a guarantee of safety was only good at their first meeting, and there was no safe guarantee for any second meeting.

Moses simply did not know the reactions of Pharaoh Rameses II to their first meeting. Would Pharaoh decide that Yahweh was a very minor god with little temporal power, and as a result, enslave Moses with all the rest of the Hebrew people? Would Pharaoh deduce that Yahweh was no god, and then destroy Moses? Would Pharaoh think that neither Moses nor Yahweh threatened Pharaoh's afterlife, and therefore ignore Moses? All reactions of pharaoh depended on his answer to the most basic and the most important question, "Exactly how strong was the God Yahweh?"

Moses needed fortitude expressed as the spiritual strength and spiritual courage to stand before mighty Pharaoh Rameses II with those questions in the forefronts of both their minds. The Pharaoh granted the first meeting based on basic Egyptian mythology. But all subsequent meetings and reactions focused directly on Pharaoh's interpretation of the Egyptian mythological concept of the afterlife.

All pharaohs believed that death brought a final judgment in the Court of Osiris. When the pharaoh died, his journeys through dark regions of the afterlife ended with one final test in the Court of Osiris. Osiris, great god of the dead, sat on a throne surrounded by 42 gods and goddesses. They watched the final test to determine if pharaoh was a good pharaoh or a bad pharaoh during his earthly life. The test was the weighing of the heart of pharaoh on scales of justice against the feather of truth (Budge, The Egyptian Book of the Dead, pp.255-63, 11-17, 90, 308-9).

Egyptian hieroglyphics of the Court of Osiris and the manuscript illuminations of The Egyptian Book of the Dead pictured Osiris sitting to the right on the throne in a courtroom (see also expanded picture, "Illuminated Manuscripts," Encarta). Isis, the wife of Osiris and the mother goddess of all pharaohs, stood behind the throne of Osiris. A huge balance with two scales stood in the center of a judgment hall. The balance was the T-bar of justice, and it had two ropes of equal length and weight tied to the ends of the crossbar. Two flat pans or scales with equal weight and size hung attached and balanced at the lower ends of the ropes. Pharaoh stood with Anubis, the god of the dead, to the left of the scales of justice. Picture scripts represented Anubis with the body of a man and the head of a jackal. Thoth, the god of wisdom and learning, stood to the right of the scales. Thoth's hieroglyph had the body of a man and the head of the ibis. At the foot of the T-bar of justice sat Ammit, the Devourer. Ammit had the head of a crocodile, the forequarters of a lion, the hindquarters of a hippopotamus (Egyptian Book, p. 257).

The ibis-headed Thoth, who was official scribe of the afterworld, declared the scales on the balance at equilibrium. The jackal-headed Anubis put pharaoh's heart on the left pan and the feather of truth on the right pan. If the scales of justice stayed level, it meant that the pharaoh's heart was equal to the feather of truth. The pharaoh was a good pharaoh. Osiris welcomed pharaoh into the presence of the gods for all eternity and into the Field of Reeds where the grain grew 12 feet high. However, if pharaoh's heart went down and the feather of truth went up on the scales of justice, it meant that the heart of the pharaoh was heavier than the truth. Pharaoh was a bad pharaoh. Ammit, the Devourer, immediately ate pharaoh's heart and doomed pharaoh to wander aimlessly in the thick darkness for all eternity. On the other hand, the best case scenario was for pharaoh's heart to go up on the T-bar of justice and the feather of truth to go down. That meant pharaoh's heart was lighter than all truth. Pharaoh was a very good pharaoh.

Consequently, the great company of the 42-tribunal gods passed the judgment in agreement with the ibis-headed Thoth. All the gods found the good pharaoh with no evil against the gods while pharaoh was upon the earth. The gods recommended pharaoh for the meat offerings, the admittance into the presence of Osiris, and an abiding habitation in the Fields of Offerings.

Horus, the falcon-headed god with the body of a man, was the son of Osiris. All pharaohs were the earthly embodiment of Horus, and Horus spoke on behalf of a good pharaoh. After Horus officially introduced the pharaoh to Osiris, Horus requested that Osiris let the good pharaoh into the presence of Osiris for all eternity. Horus also asked Osiris to grant the good pharaoh cakes and ale. Osiris, the great god of the dead, welcomed the good pharaoh into the glory of the company of gods and goddesses for all eternity.

Both Moses and Pharaoh Rameses II knew Egyptian mythology. Pharaoh Rameses II thought that he was a god on earth. However, Pharaoh Rameses II knew the consequences of any gripes from any god or goddess. Ammit, the Devourer, waited with crocodile jaws for the weighing of Pharaoh's heart on the scales of justice against the feather of truth. It was cakes and beer in the company of the gods for all eternity or aimless wanderings alone in thick darkness for all eternity. Pharaoh Rameses II had to give Moses the first meeting because no pharaoh risked his personal immortality on a potential insult and disrespect to the official representative of a god with the unfamiliar name. Pharaoh was most careful with his eternity, and so a test of strength was necessary.

The strength of Yahweh was unknown to Pharaoh Rameses II. Rameses planned to test the fortitude of Yahweh through Moses, the spokesperson of Yahweh. Moses knew an epic battle brewed in the hardness of the Pharaoh's heart (Ex.7:3-5). Moses, who could barely string a sentence together, spoke for Yahweh in the face-off against a most powerful Pharaoh Rameses II (Ex.4:10-16; 6:12, 30). Moses was in the middle of the power struggle between Pharaoh Rameses II and Yahweh, the One True God of Abraham, Isaac, Jacob. Faith in Yahweh's fortitude was the only real weapon of Moses. Moses stood before Pharaoh Rameses II armed only with a deep faith in the strength of Yahweh the One True God. God did not fail Moses. Moses confronted Pharaoh Rameses II with the fortitude of the One True Almighty God. Pharaoh Rameses II learned the strength of Yahweh in the ten plagues. The fortitude of Yahweh included the destruction of Pharaoh's proud charioteers and the death of proud Rameses' first-born son, the little pharaoh.

Moses had the premium virtue of God's fortitude in his daily life exemplified repeatedly as the spiritual strength and spiritual courage to cope with his anxieties and hassles. Moses talked "face to face" with the One True Almighty God of Abraham, Isaac, Jacob (Num.12:

6-7; Ex.33:11; Deut.34:10). That took fortitude! The Hebrew slaves made the bricks for Pharaoh Rameses II to build the temples and monuments in which Pharaoh Rameses II worshiped himself and his fellow gods. Moses faced-off Pharaoh Rameses II and demanded an Exodus from Pharaoh for the Hebrew people to worship Yahweh. That took fortitude!!!

d. *Daily Need of Jesus for Virtue of Fortitude*

There is only One True Almighty God. God's gift of fortitude to Moses is God's gift of fortitude to modern Teens. About 1,280 years after Moses, the historical Jesus said to ask and to receive. About 2,000 years after the historical Jesus, it is the choice of the modern Teen to ask for fortitude and to receive the spiritual strength and the spiritual courage to cope with daily anxieties and hassles.

Until the time of the historical Jesus, Moses had no equal on the earth in might/strength/fortitude (Deut.34:11-2). The historical Jesus was the Son of God and the Son of Man. Jesus is the mystical and the holy union of divinity and humanity in salvation history. However, Jesus Christ also needed fortitude/strength when his public ministry challenged the Jewish hierarchy of the Temple to change. Jesus needed fortitude/courage when he challenged the Roman authorities with his concept of the kingdom of God.

Jesus in his humanity asked and received from God the Father the virtue of fortitude/strength to cope with the anxieties and hassles of his sufferings. Before his arrest and passion, Jesus prayed in the Garden of Gethsemane for God the Father to take away his cup of suffering. Jesus added to his prayer "...'yet, not my will but yours be done'. Then an angel from heaven appeared to him and gave him strength" (Lk. 22: 42-3). Jesus suffered real pain out of obedience to the will of God the Father and out of love for God and neighbor. The historical Jesus is the most excellent example of a person with the virtue of fortitude.

The historical Jesus existed against the backdrop of the history of Rome. There was no escape from Roman History and the Roman presence. Jesus walked and talked in a world of the Roman Empire. Ultimately, Jesus suffered and died under Roman law after a Roman trial. The Roman procurator/governor, Pontius Pilate, pronounced a death sentence on him. Roman soldiers flogged Jesus and crowned him with thorns. The Roman executioners hammered the nails into Jesus under the watchful eyes of the Roman centurion. The Roman presence confronted Jesus with the daily need for the premium and the pragmatic virtue of fortitude.

A good method to get a feel for the world of the historical Jesus is to study and to think about the ancient Roman way of life. Study and thoughts about the Roman way of life shed understanding on the tremendous need of Jesus for fortitude in his face-off against the everyday Roman system. The Roman way of life was a system that dominated all daily life throughout the Roman Empire including the Palestine area. Reflection on the Roman way of life focuses on the study of the Roman military machine. The Roman army perpetuated the entire Roman system for many centuries through domination, intimidation, brute strength in the military conquest and occupation. To understand the daily need of Jesus for the virtue of fortitude is to understand the dominant Roman mentality exhibited in the whole makeup of the Roman military machine.

1.0 Roman Military Machine

The Roman mentality dominated all the cultures and confronted all spiritualities. Starting with Julius Caesar, early Roman Emperors deified themselves, and Roman citizens were into emperor worship. The Christian way of life was in major conflict with the Roman way of life. There was the real need for fortitude in all early Christians and especially in Jesus, the leader of the Christian way of life. Jesus had the fortitude/spiritual strength to continue his nonviolent ways based on love of God in the face of the Roman way of life supported and enforced by the very violent Roman army.

The Roman military power was the epitome of physical strength dominating life with death as the ultimate penalty for disobedience to the will of the Roman Emperor. Jesus was the epitome of spiritual strength, the premium virtue of fortitude, dominating death with the life of Resurrection as the ultimate reward for obedience to the will of God the Father. There was a dichotomy 2,000 years ago between physical and spiritual strengths. The people saw the signs of Roman physical strength around them in their daily lives. The people learned the signs of spiritual strength in the faith and the sufferings of Jesus. The Roman Empire is dead except as a historical fact. The historical Jesus is alive in the Holy Eucharist and in the minds and the hearts of billions of Christian people.

Nevertheless, there was no messing with the Roman military machine of 2,000 years ago during the time of the historical Jesus. The Roman army was the best for centuries. The Roman military machine lost a few battles, but they lost zero wars against people of other cultures. The Roman army was the dominant force especially during the times of Julius Caesar (b.101B.C. -assassinated Dictator 44B.C.), Augustus Caesar (Emperor 27B.C. -14A.D.), Tiberius Caesar (Emperor 14 37A.D.). The only semblances of any lost wars were the Roman Civil Wars in 49-46B.C. and in 44-27B.C. when the Roman military fought against themselves. Pax Romana, the Roman Peace, existed because the Roman army was undefeated in all major wars for hundreds of years. The Roman sword enforced the Pax Romana.

The powerful Roman army dominated all the cultures around the Mediterranean Sea including the homeland of the historical Jesus.

Many Hebrew people in Palestine waited for the promised Messiah to militarily release the Hebrew people from Roman military power. The historical Jesus found himself sandwiched between the military expectations of Hebrew people and the military reality of the Roman army. The feared Roman army and its whole interlocked system of existence confronted Jesus and his kingdom ministry. The historical Jesus needed fortitude to face-off against the Roman system, one of the more powerful systems to exist in human history.

1.1 Roman Legion and Roman Centurion

The Roman legion underpinned the most feared military force during the time of the historical Jesus. The Roman legion had about 5,000 "heavy infantrymen" divided into ten cohorts with 500 men in each cohort. The centurion commanded about 100 men. There were five centurions in each cohort and 50-60 centurions in each Roman legion. A centurion was the backbone of the Roman army because the centurion had direct contact and disciplined control over his 100 legionnaires during each battle.

The Roman centurion in war and peace gave both life and death orders to his 100 legionnaires. Total obedience and discipline were mandatory. Legionnaires felt the "vine-rod," the familiar emblem of a centurion's power, on their backs for the slightest insubordination. Tacitus (b. 55?A.D. – d. after 117A.D.), a Roman historian, commented:

> The centurion Lucilius also met his end. Camp humorists had surnamed him 'Fetch-Another,' from his habit, as one cane broke over a private's back, of calling at the top of his voice for a second, and ultimately a third.
>
> <u>Annals</u>, Book I.XXIII

Any equal warfare usually swayed to a Roman success on the commands of the centurions implementing battle plans for Roman legions. When a legion formed with Roman citizens, the consuls and the Roman military tribunes chose the centurions based on merit. Polybius (b.200?B.C. – d.118?B.C.), a Greek historian living in Rome, stated that Roman military leaders throughout the years customarily wanted:

> ...the centurions not so much to be venturesome and daredevils as to be natural leaders, of a steady and sedate spirit. They do not desire them so much to be men who will initiate attacks and open the battle, but men who will hold their ground when worsted and hard-pressed and be ready to die at their posts.   <u>Histories</u>, VI.XIV.9

Numbers within a legion changed depending on a job description of the legion. If doing police work as a garrison army, the number of legionnaires sometimes decreased below 5,000 men. If stationed in a potential war zone, the numbers of the legion increased with added cavalry and auxiliary troops. Legions sometimes beefed up numbers to 6,000 men: basic heavy infantrymen in cohorts; cavalrymen with 120 horses; archers and slingers (both accurate to 600 feet) in light infantry; men for the 55 "ballistae" (the hurling machines mounted on mule-drawn carriages with 11 men per ballista for the loading, firing, hurling missiles); men for the 10 onagri or "wild asses" (ready-armed catapults for discharging stones transported on ox-drawn carriages); men with "wolves" (special grappling hooks for siege tactics); men for the "single plankers" (small boats joined together with long cables and covered with boards for instant bridges); extra men with extra supply trains for self-sustaining legion (Lewis, Roman Civilization, Vol. II, p.499-500).

1.2 Military Training, Discipline, Battle Tactics

The Roman legionnaires fought for the honor and glory of Rome, but the basis of success for the Roman military system was "military training, discipline in their camps, and practice in warfare" (Ibid., p. 497). Recruits learned the "military step" and marched twenty miles together in five hours carrying sixty pounds of gear. Soldiers learned to leap and swim to gain advantages over the enemy. Soldiers drilled every day in the morning and afternoon with every type of weapon. Soldiers especially learned to attack the sides, feet, and head of the enemy with both the point and the edge of the sword. The men in the basic infantry exercised at least three times per month by marching "ten miles with the military step, wearing armor and equipped with all weapons...compelled to ascend and descend sloping and steep places" (Ibid., p.498). Josephus (37A.D.-c.101A.D.), a Jewish historian, stated that Roman "...military exercises differ not at all from the real use of their arms... nor would he be mistaken that should call those their exercises unbloody battles, and their battles bloody exercises" [Wars of the Jews, Book 3.5.1 (73, 75)].

Discipline in a Roman camp of legionnaires was most strict. The nightly guard duty, for example, was a serious routine. The tribune in charge gave the "tessera," a little tablet with written signs, to each man assigned to picket duty (Polybius, Histories, VI.35.1-36.9). Four legionnaires accompanied by some friends as witnesses made the nightly rounds of the guard stations. If a legionnaire found any guard asleep or away from his post, he called his friends to witness the fact and proceeded without collecting the tessera from the guard station. At dawn, the four legionnaires gave all the tesserae from the nightly rounds to the tribune. If there were fewer tesserae than the number of guard stations, the tribune confronted the night patrol and the men on picket duty. Polybius stated that the investigations resulted in the following procedures and penalties:

> A court-martial composed of all the tribunes at once meets to try him, and if he is found guilty he is punished by the bastinado (fustuarium). This is inflicted as follows: The tribune takes a cudgel and just touches the condemned man with it, after which all in the camp beat or stone him, in most cases dispatching him in the camp itself. But even those who manage to escape are not saved thereby: impossible! for they are not allowed to return to their homes, and none of the family would dare to receive such a man in his house. So that those who have once fallen into this misfortune are utterly ruined...Thus, owing to the extreme severity and inevitableness of the penalty, the night watches of the Roman army are most scrupulously kept...The bastinado is also inflicted on those who steal anything from the camp; on those who give false evidence; on young men who have abused their persons; and finally on anyone who has been punished thrice for the same fault...If the same thing ever happens to large bodies, and if entire maniples desert their posts when exceedingly hard pressed, the officers refrain from inflicting the bastinado or the death penalty on all, but find a solution of the difficulty which is both salutary and terror-striking.The tribune assembles the legion, and brings up those guilty of leaving the ranks, reproaches them sharply, and finally chooses by lot sometimes five, sometimes eight, sometimes twenty of the offenders, so adjusting the number thus chosen that they form as near as possible the tenth part of those guilty of cowardice. Those on whom the lot falls are bastinadoed mercilessly in the manner above described; the rest receive rations of barley instead of wheat and are ordered to encamp outside the camp on an unprotected spot...and as the public disgrace of receiving barley rations falls on all alike, this practice is that best calculated both to inspire fear and to correct the mischief.
> Histories, VI. 37.1-9; 38.1-4

The military training and discipline maximized the available battle tactics for the Roman Army. Dio Cassius (c.150-235 A.D.), a Roman historian, described the Roman battle formation called the "testudo" (the tortoise) used by Mark Antony in 36 B.C. Barbarians ambushed the legionnaires of Mark Antony and showered the legionnaires with their arrows. Dio Cassius described the "tortoise" as a versatile battle formation with battle tactics based on total discipline:

...they suddenly formed the testudo by joining their shields, and rested their left knees on the ground. The barbarians, who had never seen anything of the kind before, thought that they had fallen from their wounds and needed only one finishing blow; so they threw aside their bows, leaped from their horses, and drawing their daggers, came up close to put an end to them. At this the Romans sprang to their feet, extended their battle-line at the word of command, and confronting the foe face to face, fell upon them, each one upon the man nearest him, and cut down great numbers, since they were contending in full armour against unprotected men, men prepared against men off their guard, heavy infantry against archers, Romans against barbarians...This testudo and the way in which it was formed are as follows. The baggage animals, the light-armed troops, and the cavalry are placed in the centre of the army. The heavy-armed troops who use the oblong, curved, and cylindrical shields are drawn up around the outside, making a rectangular figure; and, facing outward and holding their arms at the ready, they enclose the rest. The others, who have flat shields, form a compact body in the centre and raise their shields over the heads of all the others, so that nothing but shields can be seen in every part of the phalanx alike and all the men by the density of the formation are under shelter from missiles. Indeed, it is so marvellously strong that men can walk upon it, and whenever they come to a narrow ravine, even horses and vehicles can be driven over it. Such is the plan of this formation, and for this reason it has received the name testudo, with reference both to its strength and to the excellent shelter it affords. They use it in two ways: either they approach some fort to assault it, often even enabling men to scale the very walls, or sometimes, when they are surrounded by archers, they all crouch together-even the horses being taught to kneel or lie down- and thereby cause the foe to think that they are exhausted; then, when the enemy draws near, they suddenly rise and throw them into consternation.   History, XLIX. 29.2-30.4

1.3 Gladius, Sword of the Roman Legionnaire

Military equipment of the Roman soldiers perfectly complimented the military training and discipline. Romans equipped their army with the very best equipment and supplies from all their conquered lands. For example, the sword of the Roman infantryman for hundreds of years was the "gladius Hispanus," the Spanish sword. The gladius was a short sword with a long history of violence in the hands of the Roman legionnaires. The gladius was only 20-inches long (50 cm.)

with very sharp edges and a sharp point on a broad blade. It was a cut-and-thrust sword, and it meshed tightly with the battle tactics of all Roman legionnaires.

Livy (59B.C. -17A.D.), a Roman historian, reported situations that combined the training and the discipline of the Roman army with the power and terror of the gladius. Livy wrote 142 books about the past and present glory of Rome. Livy published his books in c.26B.C. to 14A.D. during the reign of Augustus Caesar and in the lifetime of the historical Jesus. Perhaps his books were the intellectual talk of the town when Jesus walked the earth. The Romans loved them, and all conquered peoples hated them for the very same reason: the books reminded people of the Roman domination. Typical of Livy and his power to incite reactions pro and con to the Roman way of life were his gladius stories.

For example, in 361B.C. the Gauls matched the Romans evenly in a battle over the possession of a bridge. A physically huge Gaul stepped onto the empty bridge, and he challenged the Roman army to send out their bravest man to fight one-on-one. The huge size of the Gaul silenced the Roman legionnaires for a long time. Finally, a legionnaire asked the General for the honor to fight for Rome and his family. Livy described the outcome of the challenge from the Roman point of view:

> The young man's friends then armed him; he assumed the shield of a foot-soldier, and to his side he buckled a Spanish sword, convenient for close fighting...the Gaul...thrust his tongue out in derision...the Gaul, whose huge bulk towered above the other, advanced his shield with the left arm, to parry the attack of his oncoming enemy, and delivered a slashing stroke with his sword, that made a mighty clatter but did no harm. The Roman, with the point of his weapon raised, struck up his adversary's shield with a blow from his own against its lower edge; and slipping in between the man's sword and his body, so close that no part of his own person was exposed, he gave one thrust and then immediately another, and gashing the groin and belly of his enemy brought him headlong to the ground, where he lay stretched out over a monstrous space.
> History of Rome (Ab Urbe Condita), Book VII, X.5-6, 9-11

Livy also reported a situation in the Roman battle in 200B.C. with the Macedonians. Both sides fought on equal terms for hours. The Macedonian leader brought the bodies of his dead warriors into his camp for funeral honors. Livy stated:

> Nothing is so uncertain or so unpredictable as the mental reaction of a crowd. What he thought would make them

more ready to enter any conflict caused, instead, reluctance and fear; for men who had seen the wounds dealt by javelins and arrows and occasionally by lances, since they were used to fighting with the Greeks and Illyrians, when they had seen bodies chopped to pieces by the Spanish sword, arms torn away, shoulders and all, or heads separated from bodies, with the necks completely severed, or vitals laid open, and the other fearful wounds, realized in a general panic with what weapons and what men they had to fight. Fear seized the king as well, who had never met the Romans in ordered combat.
History of Rome (Ab Urbe Condita), Book XXXI. xxxiv.3-6

Some historians called the gladius "unsurpassed among ancient weapons" (Cary, History of Rome, p.158). A gladius in the hands of the Roman army conquered the Mediterranean world, but the Roman short sword was also most impressive as a manufactured article. A gladius was a steel sword. Craftsmen started with iron ore, timber, and quality water. They heated the iron ore in furnaces by burning charcoal. Smiths intensified the heat with foot bellows to the 2,795°F (≈1,535°C) needed for the chemical transformation from iron ore to a molten metal (www.Britannica.com/Technology in the Ancient World/ The Mastery of Iron). Artisans lacked the valved bellows for complete smelting until the invention in the fourth century A.D. So, craftsmen for the Roman army worked with a small spongy ball of iron, called a bloom. They hammered the bloom into bars of wrought iron. Master craftsmen reheated the bars of iron between the layers of charcoal to carburize the surface of the iron, and consequently produced a coat of steel. "Gladiarius" ("swordmaker") at individual forges repeatedly heated, hammered, tempered the casehardened iron to make a high quality sword blade (Frank, Economic Survey, Vol. V, p.186-7). The gladius with a steel blade was ready-made for the hand of a Roman legionnaire. Both the gladius and the Roman legionnaire were lethal.

1.4 Perks of Legionnaire, Wealth of Victorious Caesar

The Roman legionnaires were Roman citizens who served in the army infantry for 20 years. The elite Praetorian Guards, "who did double duty as the emperor's guards and his orderlies" (Cary, History of Rome, p. 481), were also exclusively Roman citizens, and they served for 16 years. The Roman cavalry and the infantry auxiliaries of the legions recruited and included the conquered peoples. After 20 years of exemplary service in the auxiliary legions, the honorable discharges of former enemies of Rome included Roman citizenship (Roman Civilization, Vol. II, p.521-6).

All the honorably discharged veterans received the temporary "Certificate of Discharge." Eventually the more permanent bronze

"Military Diploma" guaranteed their rights. The principal reward of all veterans for service in the Roman army was the grant of land in the military colony. After military reforms of Augustus Caesar in 6 A.D., the veteran normally received the discharge bonus in cash and only occasionally received land (Ibid., p.28). Rights of the Roman veteran included the legal Roman marriage, forbidden during active military service, and the subsequent legal enfranchisement of the soldier's children (Ibid., p.521). The veterans also enjoyed some exemptions from taxes, billeting troops, housing government officials, compulsory public services (Ibid., Vol. I, p.392).

Roman legionnaires shared by their rank and at the discretion of the triumphant general the captured booty and the spoils of war from conquered civilizations. After his military triumph in 61B.C., Pompey distributed a bonus of 71,000,000 denarii to the legionnaires for six years of service. Pompey gave the centurions twenty times as much as the ordinary legionnaires and the tribunes six times as much as the centurions. Each higher officer received nearly 800,000 denarii, which was the approximate equivalent of $160,000 (Economic Survey, Vol.I, p. 324-5).

Teens, please, note the basic difficulty of converting the value of money in antiquity to the equivalence of modern money. The value of a troy ounce of gold fluctuates daily on modern international stock markets. A further complication is the fact that the Roman denarius was a silver coin based on a gold standard. For the sake of scholarly convenience and academic communications, economic historians often utilize a conversion ratio of 1 denarius = 20 cents (U.S.) for the value of money during the time of Jesus (Frank, Economic History, p.335-7, 502-5).

Jesus told the parable about sending workers into the vineyard at the different times of the day for the same wage (Mt.20:1-16). The biblical scholars, theologians, historians supported by literal Greek translations assume that the "usual daily wage" in Palestine equaled one denarius or approximately 20 cents per day (NOAB/NRSV, Mt. 20.9n.; fn. v). In 6A.D. Augustus Caesar fixed the rate of pay for the ordinary legionnaire at 225 denarii per year minus the deductions for equipment and food. It was approximately 12-15 cents per day, but some historians estimated that the Roman soldiers lived comfortably with perks on five sevenths of their military pay (Roman Civilization, Vol. II, p.512-4).

In 301A.D. Diocletian (Emperor 284-305A.D.) issued an edict with a list of maximum prices to control the high cost of living. He based prices on one pound of gold refined in bars or coins and valued at 50,000 denarii. Some of the noteworthy items with the equivalent in modern money from the conversion ratios follow:

Wheat	bushel	75 cents...
Soldiers' shoes	pair	33 "

Woman's shoes	pair	26 " ...
Wool	pound	22 " ...
Purple wool	pound	$217.40 ...
Manual labor, per day		11 cents + food
Bricklayers...carpenters...		22 cents + food...
Teachers, per pupil, per month		22 cents + food
Teachers in arithmetic		33 cents + food
Teachers in Greek or geometry		87 cents + food...

The wage itself had, however, remained about stationary, since eleven cents and food would be about the equivalent of the old time wage of a denarius per day.

Frank, <u>Economic History</u>, p. 503-5

It is important for Teenagers to remember: (1) all the monetary conversions from antiquity are approximations; (2) money in antiquity had more purchasing power than today; (3) there were the incredible gaps between the rich and the poor in the time of Jesus.

When Jesus Christ continually busted out the rich, he challenged directly the values of the rich Hebrews and the wealthy Romans. The words of Jesus confronted the Roman riches and the basic power of the Roman military system reinforcing the Roman way of life. Jesus offered the Beatitudes as spiritual reality (Mt.5:1-12; Lk.6:20-25), and they were a real solace to marginalized, downtrodden, conquered peoples in their physical, spiritual, psychological existence. Money and power were the basics in the Roman way of life. The people in conquered cultures emulated the Roman riches and the power from wealth. The message of Jesus Christ to love God above all things including above money and power was a direct confrontation to the basic Roman way of life. Romans dominated and manipulated the people in conquered cultures. Jesus needed fortitude to confront the excesses and abuses of a Roman way of life based on money/power and reinforced by the gladius in the hands of Roman legionnaires. Let me give more examples of the Roman mentality that Jesus faced with nonviolence and with fortitude.

Julius Caesar was "the ugliest example in Roman history of provincial looting for personal gain" (<u>Economic Survey</u>, Vol.I, p.325). Julius Caesar imposed a tribute/tax of 10,000,000 denarii ($\cong$$2M) on conquered Gaul in 63B.C. as part of provincial dues worth 40,000,000 denarii ($\cong$$8M). Hated "tax farmers" collected another 10,000,000 denarii ($\cong$$2M) especially from customs dues at the harbors and from the taxes on monopolies in public forests, fishing, salt, etc. (Ibid., p. 324). However, in 61B.C. Julius Caesar was so heavily in debt that he had to borrow money from Crassus, the richest man in Rome "whose real estate alone was reputed to be worth 50,000,000 denarii" (Cary, <u>History of Rome</u>, p.454).

Plutarch (b.46?A.D.-120A.D.), a Greek biographer and essayist, described the situation in his <u>The Parallel Lives</u>:

> ...Caesar received Spain as his province, and since he found it hard to arrange matters with his creditors, who obstructed his departure and were clamorous, he had recourse to Crassus, the richest of the Romans...And it was only after Crassus had met the demands of the most importunate and inexorable of these creditors and given surety for eight hundred and thirty talents, that Caesar could go out to his province.
> Plutarch's Lives: Caesar, Vol. VII, XI.I-II, L.C.L. #99 p.467-9

A "talent" was the Greek monetary unit worth 6,000 drachmas, and a drachma was the Greek silver coin valued at one Roman denarius (except in Egypt, where the equation was 4 drachmas = 1 denarius). Consequently, Julius Caesar borrowed about 4,980,000 denarii ($\cong$$1,000,000) to pay the worst of his debt. Julius Caesar went to Spain broke.

Nevertheless, from 59–50 B.C. Julius Caesar became immensely wealthy in Gaul. The lowest figures from ancient historians stated that Caesar killed 400,000 Gauls and enslaved even more captives. If sold at the low price of 250 denarii per slave, Caesar generated 100,000,000 denarii ($\cong$$20,000,000) to pay his debts and bonuses of his legionnaires. Caesar also sold captured gold, and the price of gold fell by 1/6 (Economic Survey, Vol.I, p.325).

However, Plutarch estimated the wealth of Caesar much higher:

> For although it was not full ten years that he waged war in Gaul, he took by storm more than eight hundred cities, subdued three hundred nations, and fought pitched battles at different times with three million men, of whom he slew one million in hand to hand fighting and took as many more prisoners.
> Plutarch's Lives: Caesar, Vol. VII, XV.V, L.C.L., #99, p.479

The one million prisoners sold into slavery each for 250 denarii equaled 250,000,000 denarii ($\cong$$50,000,000), and do not forget the sold gold! Julius Caesar probably gave his officers and legionnaires bonuses equal to Pompey's distribution of military bonuses that were 800,000 denarii ($\cong$$160,000) to all higher officers (Economic Survey, Vol.I, p. 325-6). Based on his manipulation of the Roman legionnaire with the lethal gladius, Julius Caesar became very rich from Roman victories in wars.

After Julius Caesar defeated Pompey during the Civil War in 49-46 B.C., Caesar returned to Rome and displayed more of his great wealth. He celebrated five triumphs in one parade in 46 B.C., and the proceeds from the spoils of war carried into Rome in the triumphal parade were more than 600 million sesterces (Hadas, Rome, p.80). The ratio for the conversion was 4 sesterces = 1 denarius. Julius

Caesar flaunted 150,000,000 denarii (≅$30,000,000) from the sale of war booty and heavy requisitions on the conquered peoples. But the greatest expense remained the list of the dead Roman legionnaires on both sides of the Civil War.

1.5 Power Dispute and Roman Empire at Time of Jesus

With Julius Caesar in total and undivided command of all Roman legionnaires and a vast Roman treasury, the subsequent dictatorship of Julius Caesar ended the Roman Republic. However, M. Brutus and C. Cassius led 60 to 80 conspirators in a futile attempt to restore the Roman Republic (Cary, History of Rome, p.416). In 44B.C. on the Ides of March (15th), 20 identifiable conspirators assassinated the defenseless Caesar in the Senate chamber by stabbing him 23 times with daggers (Plutarch, Lives: Caesar, Vol. VII, LXVI.XIV, L.C.L.,#99, p.599; Roman Civilization, Vol. I, p.289). Elimination of the Dictator Julius Caesar did not return the good old days of a Roman Republic. The death of Julius Caesar brought 17 years of more Roman Civil War between his heir, Octavius, and his #1 general, Mark Antony.

Julius Caesar left his immense fortune to Octavius, who was his grandnephew, his adopted son, only eighteen years old. Octavius changed his name to Octavian Caesar "to steal the sympathies of Caesar's old soldiers from Antony by the magic of his new name" (Cary, History of Rome, p.425). Octavian fought and defeated the more experienced Mark Antony, the best general of Julius Caesar. Octavian won the Roman Civil War in 27B.C. He again changed his name to Augustus Caesar to rule as the first emperor of the Roman Empire until his death in 14A.D.

The decisive encounter of the Civil War was on September 2, 31 B.C. at the Battle of Actium in western ancient Greece on the Ionian Sea. Octavian had 45 Roman legions and almost 600 warships at his disposal. Antony had 30 Roman legions and 500 warships. The ally of Mark Antony was Cleopatra with her 60 Egyptian vessels. The warships of Antony had approximately equal tonnage to the warships of Octavian. The 75 Roman legions at Actium never fought one huge land battle with the winner-take-all. The combatants fought on the sea when Antony tried a retreat with his fleet to regroup his troops in Asia Minor. Octavian had the best advantage and the consequent victory because his high admiral was Agrippa, "the greatest naval tactician in Roman history" (Ibid., p.444).

Mark Antony brought aboard the canvas sails for his ships with intentions of sailing the typically brisk breezes of a summer afternoon on the Ionian Sea. His strategy was contrary to normal procedures in ancient naval warfare that left the flammable sails on the shore and powered the warships with slave oarsmen (Ibid., p.445; Cook, Cambridge Ancient History, Vol. X, p.236-7). Antony's fleet obeyed his order to hoist sails badly. A fiasco ensued when the squadron of

Cleopatra broke free in her escape to Alexandria and the flagship of Antony sailed in her wake for all to see. The instantaneous charges of Antony's intentional desertion of his army were valid excuses for deserting him. His fleet capitulated to Octavian immediately, and the most proud Roman legionnaires of the deceased Julius Caesar and General Mark Antony surrendered in one week without a land battle (Cary, History of Rome, p.439, 445). Mark Antony and Cleopatra committed double suicide in Egypt in the winter of 31-30B.C.

With the opposition dead, Octavian celebrated his triumph in 27 B.C. with the name change to Augustus (the holy, the divine) Caesar. He ended 20 years of Roman Civil Wars, 17 years of his own war + 3 years of the war from his adoptive father, Julius Caesar. Augustus Caesar totally controlled the 75 Roman legions of veterans, the vast Roman treasury including all the wealth of Egypt, the new Roman Empire, worship of a deified Julius Caesar, worship of a deified self (Ibid., p.475, 479-80, 512, 516).

Augustus Caesar experienced forty years of unopposed power. The time of his reign included the birth of the Baby Jesus. Augustus Caesar based his Pax Romana, his Roman Peace, on the gladius of the powerful Roman legionnaire:

> By virtue of this extended 'imperium' he controlled the entire armed forces of the state...Every Roman soldier continued to take the oath of allegiance to him and to look to him for his material rewards... Augustus never surrendered the power of the sword; in the last resort he could, de facto, exercise the power of life and death over all the inhabitants of the Roman empire...The permanent master of the legions had the last word on every question of peace and war.
> Cary, History of Rome, p.479

When Augustus Caesar died in 14A.D., his handpicked heir and stepson, Tiberius Caesar, inherited all wealth and all Roman power as Emperor #2. Tiberius Caesar ruled an estimated 70–100,000,000 inhabitants in the Roman Empire within the 4,000 mile border (Ibid., p.507). He ruled from 14-37A.D., and the time of his reign included the death and Resurrection of Jesus. Tiberius Caesar inherited from Augustus Caesar the 25 Roman legions plus the auxiliaries in a new army downsized from the 75 legions in the Civil War. The Emperor Tiberius Caesar ruled with the power of the gladius in the hands of 300,000 Roman legionnaires (Cambridge Ancient History, Vol. X, p. 223, 228-9).

The Roman centurions were ready to die at their posts following orders of Caesar's generals. Roman legionnaires had the military training and discipline to follow orders with no questions asked. The Roman soldiers very seldom risked the loss of potentially lucrative war booty and the veteran benefits for disobeying a direct order. The punishment for the cowardice in the disobedience of orders was the bastinado, a certain death penalty. The Roman governor/procurator had authority by the extension of the imperium of Caesar. When the governor of Caesar ordered the Roman centurions and the Roman legionnaires to crucify someone like Jesus, they crucified him with gusto and without expressed qualms. There was no moral hesitation in Roman legionnaires to follow orders.

The sight of Roman legionnaires executing a condemned person with a crucifixion was most horrible. Roman legionnaires designed, staged, implemented all crucifixions for the maximum effect of terror and intimidation. The living saw the crucified and knew for a fact that they did not want death from crucifixion. Roman legionnaires got the desired effect when the people avoided treason against the Roman Empire due to fear of crucifixion as the capital punishment.

Slaves especially knew the sad history of Roman legionnaires crucifying people. In the last of the great slave revolts, Spartacus led gladiators against the Roman legionnaires for two years (73-71B.C.). The Roman legionnaires killed more than 100,000 slaves during the revolt. After a Roman victory in the final battle, Roman legionnaires crucified 6,000 slaves on a main road to Rome (Roman Civilization, Vol. I, p.231). Captured slaves "...were exhibited on crosses set up like telegraph posts along the whole length of the Via Appia" (Cary, Roman History, p.365). It was not a pretty sight, and there were no more slave revolutions.

It was in the everyday presence of the Roman legionnaire with the gladius and against this backdrop of Roman History that Jesus faced the tortures of his Passion. Internal and external components in the mystique of the Roman legionnaire and in the domination of the Roman system combined to activate the mockery and torture for Jesus. Jesus needed the virtue of fortitude to cope with the hassles and anxieties in the daily reality of his public ministry and Passion.

2.0 Extreme Sufferings of Jesus from Roman Violence

A main hassle of the Roman authority in Palestine with Jesus was the message of Jesus about the kingdom of God. Any attempt to establish the unauthorized kingdom within the Roman Empire or to incite a riot was sedition. Roman penalty for sedition of the foreigner was crucifixion as the capital punishment. The written inscription in Hebrew (Aramaic), Latin, Greek on the cross of Jesus declared the charge and the reason for his death penalty: "The King of the Jews" (Mk.15: 26; Jn.19:19-20; Lk.23:38; Mt.27: 37). A Roman crucifixion meant negative contact with Roman legionnaires and serious need for the positive virtue of fortitude.

A main hassle of the Jewish hierarchy in the temple with Jesus was the message of Jesus about the worship of God. The standing orders of the high priest and the well-established priestly caste were for the temple guards to prevent specific people from entering the Jerusalem temple. The temple guards blocked the sick, poor, dying, lame, less desirable others from worshipping Yahweh in the temple precincts. The temple hierarchy through temple guards marginalized and disenfranchised whole segments of Jewish society from worship of God in the holiest shrine of Judaism. The preservation of temple purity seemed the top priority. The rationale was the law of divine retribution with the interpretation that God rewarded the good and punished the bad. If specific people looked like the sinners divinely punished with sickness, poverty, etc., the temple hierarchy judged those people unworthy to enter the temple and pray to God.

The public ministry of Jesus was on a collision course with the power of the temple hierarchy. Jesus healed the sick and forgave sinners. He brought people to God and God to people. Jesus spent time, energy, and love on the people traditionally marginalized and disenfranchised by the temple hierarchy. Jesus returned isolated and lonely people into the community for the worship of God.

The hierarchy of the temple thought that Jesus was impure. He was too close to sinners. The temple hierarchy judged that Jesus committed blasphemy by his claim to forgive sins (Jn.5:16-8). The Jewish penalty for blasphemy was stoning to death outside the walls of the city (Lev.24:16). The temple hierarchy had no power under the Roman law to implement the death penalty, and they deferred to Pontius Pilate, Roman imperial governor. Any conviction by Pontius Pilate meant negative contact with Roman legionnaires and serious need for the positive virtue of fortitude.

Jesus chose to focus on the will and the love of God the Father. The will of God the Father was for Jesus the Son to set the example of self-sacrifice at the hands of the Roman legionnaires in total trust of God the Father. A constant self-sacrifice is never easy. It was not easy for Jesus, and a constant self-sacrifice is not easy for modern Teenagers. Acceptance of self-sacrifice with total trust in the One Holy God necessitates the virtue of fortitude. Ultimately, Teens trust in the holiness of God. But fortitude equals spiritual strength and spiritual courage. Jesus utilized fortitude to cope with the cross of Roman legionnaires. Teenagers may utilize fortitude to cope with their daily personal crosses. Teens get fortitude by asking God the Father for it in prayers of petitions just like Jesus did in the Garden of Gethsemane before his arrest.

If Teens know the truth about the extreme sufferings of Jesus, all Teens are most capable of love for Jesus. However, no Teen needs to make any mistake about the Roman crucifixion. It was a serious business, and the crucified experienced serious pain on the way to violent death. Jesus with the virtue of fortitude coped with the pain, but the pain was as real as the Roman legionnaires inflicting it.

Let us examine two specific tortures, the scourging at the pillar and the crowning with thorns, to isolate the physical misery of Jesus during his Passion. It was the usual practice for Roman legionnaires to scourge the condemned before the actual crucifixion. However, the crowning with thorns was totally unique to Jesus. Jesus is the only crucified man also crowned with thorns in all of written history (Barbet, Doctor, p.37, 156, 164). Until modern archaeologists find new discoveries of ancient evidence, Jesus has a horrible monopoly on the tortures of scourging and crucifixion combined with the crown of thorns.

About 2,000 years ago the historical Jesus suffered tortures that included scourging at the pillar and the crowning with thorns. Jesus died from a Roman crucifixion on the cross, and the Christ rose out of death from a Roman crucifixion on the cross. Joseph of Arimathea asked Pilate, the Roman governor of the imperial province of Judea (26-36A.D.), for permission to take down the crucified body of Jesus from the cross and bury the corpse (Mk.15:42-7; Mt.27:57-61; Lk.23: 50-6; Jn.19:38-42). The usual routine was for the dead body to stay on the cross until the birds of prey and wild beasts ate it. If the family asked to decently bury the crucified body, Roman law permitted the release of the corpse for burial "without hindrance or a demand for payment" (Doctor, p.51). The corpse prematurely unnailed from the cross depended entirely on the judgment of the ruling Roman judge. Sometimes the judge refused the authorization and that increased the punishment and humiliation for the family of the crucified (Ibid.).

When asked for the authorization to bury the corpse of Jesus, Pilate questioned the Roman centurion in charge of the execution squad about the death of Jesus. The thrust of the Roman spear into the side of the crucified was the centurion's insurance for the death of the condemned. The centurion in charge assured Pilate that the Roman legionnaire speared Jesus according to the execution policy. Jesus was dead.

The Jewish purity laws stated that orthodox Jews bury the dead "hung on a tree" before sundown (Deut.21:22-3). Both the third commandment from Yahweh to Moses and the Jewish Sabbath laws required zero work from sundown on Friday to sundown on Saturday (Ex.20:8-11; Jer.17:21-2). The major Jewish holiday of the Passover began at sundown on the day of Jesus' death. Pilate did not want to rile the Jewish people over their religious laws about purity and work on the Sabbath. Pontius Pilate gave his burial permission for the corpse of Jesus.

With the fast approach of sundown for the Passover Sabbath, Joseph of Arimathea with others unnailed Jesus from the cross, and they transported Jesus to the tomb. They laid the corpse of Jesus wrapped in a burial shroud in the tomb. Joseph of Arimathea sealed the tomb with a large round stone until later. The plan was to return on Sunday at the end of the Sabbath to correctly prepare the corpse for permanent burial with oils and perfumes. Before they returned,

Jesus rose from the dead. The disciples found the Holy Shroud of Jesus in the empty tomb (Jn.19:40; 20:5-7).

2.1 The Holy Shroud of Turin

My inquiry into the two tortures of Jesus from the scourging and crowning with thorns developed into extensive research, intensive soul-searching, and much personal prayer. The research led me to the Shroud of Turin. The Shroud at the Catholic Cathedral in Turin, Italy, is the ancient burial sheet of a crucified man with the imprints apparently from a scourging and a crown of thorns. The Shroud of Turin is not an article of faith for the Roman Catholic Church at the beginning of the third millennium. However, countless millions of people choose to believe that the Shroud of Turin is the burial sheet of Jesus Christ.

On May 24, 1998, Pope John Paul II visited the Holy Shroud of Turin during the public exposition at the Cathedral. The Holy Father stated in his public address:

> The Shroud is a challenge to our intelligence. It first of all requires of every person, particularly the researcher, that he humbly grasp the profound message it sends to his reason and his life...Since it is not a matter of faith, the Church has no specific competence to pronounce on these questions. She entrusts to scientists the task of continuing to investigate, so that satisfactory answers may be found to the questions connected with this Sheet...according to tradition, wrapped the body of our Redeemer after he had been taken down from the cross...For the believer, what counts above all is that the Shroud is a mirror of the Gospel ...The image of human suffering is reflected in the Shroud.It reminds modern man, often distracted by prosperity and technological achievements, of the tragic situation of his many brothers and sisters...Before the Shroud, how can we not think of the millions of people who die of hunger, of the horrors committed in the many wars that soak nations in blood, of the brutal exploitation of women and children...The Shroud is also an image of God's love as well as of human sin...the Shroud invites us all to impress upon our spirit the face of God's love, to remove from it the tremendous reality of sin...The Shroud is an image of silence...offers a moving confirmation of the fact that the merciful omnipotence of our God is not restrained by any power of evil, but knows instead how to make the very power of evil contribute to good...The Shroud shows us Jesus at the moment of his greatest helplessness and reminds us that in the abasement of that death lies the salvation of the whole world. The Shroud thus

becomes an invitation to face every experience, including that of suffering and extreme helplessness, with the attitude of those who believe that God's merciful love overcomes every poverty, every limitation, every temptation to despair. May the Spirit of God, who dwells in our hearts, instill in everyone the desire and generosity necessary for accepting the Shroud's message and for making it the decisive inspiration of our lives.

http://sindone.torino.chiesacattolica.it/en/past/papagp.htm

My research, soul-searching, prayer led to thoughts and feelings that the face on the Shroud is the face of Jesus. The face of Jesus is the face of God according to nuances of truth throughout 2,000 years of Catholic theology. In my opinion, the face on the Holy Shroud is a face dead to torture and alive to God the Holy Spirit.

I suggest that all Teenagers look and decide for themselves at www.sindone.org, which is the official Catholic Web site for the Holy Shroud at the Catholic Church in Turin, Italy. Another excellent Web site is www.shroud.com, maintained by Mr. Barrie Schwortz, Official Documenting Photographer for the Shroud of Turin Research Project (STURP). In 1978, the STURP team spent 120 hours in extensive hands-on scientific examination of the Shroud under the supervision of the Cardinal in Turin. Barrie Schwortz maintains on his Web site some of the 2,700 original photographs and other materials that he collected in four years of analysis for the STURP project. Please, Teenagers, check out both Web sites to see what you think and feel about the Shroud. Is the image the face of Jesus?

Teens, please, also consider the following hypothesis by Mr. Ian Wilson, a scholar from Oxford University and the author of <u>The Blood and the Shroud: New Evidence That the World's Most Sacred Relic Is Real</u>:

> ...I specifically suggested that the image came to be formed by some such nuclear-type blinding flash from the body... In the darkness of the Jerusalem tomb the dead body of Jesus lay, unwashed, covered in blood, on a stone slab. Suddenly there is a burst of mysterious power from it. In that instant the blood dematerialises, dissolved perhaps by the flash, while its image and that of the body becomes indelibly fused onto the cloth, preserving for posterity a literal 'snapshot' of the Resurrection. p.233-4

2.2 The Scourging at the Pillar

The Shroud of Turin reveals the horrors of the tortures from the crucifixion. The injuries of the Shroud man included marks from the ancient scourging:

> ...more than a hundred dumb-bell-shaped markings...found to measure some one and a half inches (3.7 cm) long [pl.15a]...reasonably interpreted as from a whipping, the apparent instrument having been a two- or three-thonged whip that had dumb-bell-shaped metal pellets at the tip of each thong [pl.15b].
> Ibid., p.32

Jewish law limited the number of strokes in a flogging to forty, because more lashes degraded the neighbor (Deut.25:3). Pharisees in the time of Jesus developed the equation of "forty less one" or 39 strokes to insure against a miscount (2Cor.11:24). Roman law had no written limit to the number of strokes on a flogged criminal. When the Roman scourging preceded the crucifixion, the only pragmatic limits for the flogging were:
(1) the executioners delivered strokes until they lost strength/stamina to administer the lashes;
(2) the condemned had enough energy and enough strength to carry the crossbeam of cross through the city to the crucifixion site outside the city gates;
(3) the condemned stayed alive until the death sentence of Roman governor ended in the actual crucifixion.

The Shroud man received over 100 contusions from the strokes of the flogging. After examination of the Shroud, Doctor Pierre Barbet counted perhaps 120 contused wounds and concluded, "This means, if there were two thongs, that Our Lord received about sixty strokes apart from those which have left no mark" (Doctor, p.3). The Roman legionnaires as executioners of Jesus almost overdid the scourging at the pillar. Jesus was physically and dangerously weak from the flogging, and the Roman soldiers were afraid of his death during the carrying of the cross (Brown, Death of Messiah, Vol. 2, p.914-5). Jesus collapsed from loss of blood and exhaustion under the weight of the 125-lb. crossbeam (Doctor, p.48-9). The Roman legionnaires "seized a man, Simon of Cyrene, who was coming from the country, and they laid the cross on him, and made him carry it behind Jesus" (Lk.23:26).

The whip, which inflicted the scourging wounds on the man of the Shroud, was probably the flagrum (diminutive flagellum). Roman owners punished slaves with the flagrum, and the gladiators fought battles to the death with it. A flagrum was a whip with a solid straight wooden handle for the grip with one or both hands. The two or three leather thongs attached to the end of the handle. The executioners usually made the thongs from the sturdy ox's hide, and they knotted bones, sharp metals, or pellets of leaden dumbbells into the loose ends of the leather thongs. A Roman flagrum sometimes "terminated by hooks, in which case it was aptly denominated a scorpion" (Smith, Dictionary of Greek and Roman Antiquities, p.179-180).

Archaeologists found an intact flagrum at Herculanaeum, which was the Roman city buried with Pompeii in 79A.D. during the Mount Vesuvius volcano in Italy. The flagrum had the dumbbell tips just like the whip that did so much damage and created so much pain for the man of the Shroud. Ian Wilson suggested from both the historical and archaeological perspectives that "the Shroud's whipping injuries undeniably correspond to the type of implement that the Romans would have used for Jesus's scourging as described in the Christian gospels" (Blood and Shroud, p.42).

2.3 The Crowning with Thorns

Although the historians and writers from antiquity documented crucifixions with the preliminary scourging at a pillar, Jesus' crown of thorns was an entirely different story. Specific knowledge of details from Jesus' crown of thorns rests in the deep silence of antiquity. Until the modern archaeologists perhaps uncover new data from the ancient sites, five primary sources exist from ancient Christianity for crowning the head of Jesus with thorns:

(1) Christian Oral Traditions of Twelve Apostles (Matthias replaced Judas Iscariot in Acts1:26) in circa 30-100A.D. with the responses of the popular piety and imagination for the Passion of Jesus ultimately written into the Gospels and eventually developed into Christian art (Death of Messiah, Vol. 2, p.1346);

(2) the Gospel of Mark, Chapter 15 verse 17, written in circa 60s A.D. before Roman army's destruction of the Jerusalem Temple in 70A.D. (Jerome, p.596);

(3) the Gospel of Matthew, Chapter 27 verse 29, written in circa 80-90A.D. (Ibid., p.631);

(4) the Gospel of John, Chapter 19 verse 2, written in circa 90-100 A.D. (Ibid., p.949).

(5) Holy Shroud of Turin assuming with individual faith that it is the same Holy Shroud of Jesus at his death and Resurrection in circa 30-33A.D. (Death of Messiah, Vol. 2, p.1376).

Teens may note several fine points about this list in a scholastic discussion concerning Jesus' crown of thorns. The Gospel of Luke had no report of the dramatic thorny crown in the oldest manuscripts (Ibid., Vol.1, p.865, fn.6). Also, there was the "Gospel of Peter" that early Christian writers mentioned before 200A.D. It was not included in the Church canon and the subsequent New Testament of the Bible because of nonuse in the Church liturgy. Perhaps it was a popular passion play (Ibid., Vol.2, p.1317-49). French archaeologists in Egypt in 1886-87 discovered a partial 7th-9th century copy of a noncanonical "Gospel of Peter," and a fragmentary parchment in Greek mentioned "a thorny crown." However, there remains zero extant non-Christian source from antiquity with the mention of Jesus crowned with thorns. Consequently, if the Holy Shroud of Turin is the actual burial sheet of

Jesus, the Holy Shroud remains the oldest and the most sacred relic with the evidence of the brutality from the tortures of Jesus including the crowning with thorns by the Roman legionnaires.

When the modern biblical scholars try to determine the details about Jesus' crown of thorns, they immediately run into a brick wall of temporal ignorance. The evangelists of the Gospels mentioned the crown of thorns in stressing a royal mockery of Jesus, but they gave no specific details for the size of the thorns, the thorn plant, or the style of the crown. The historical facts about the crown of thorns in the original preaching of the Twelve Apostles were lost in antiquity after the Resurrection of Jesus. Time made biblical scholars ignorant of historical details in the crown of thorns as the eyewitnesses died. Nevertheless, the written and oral traditions combined without exact historical details to make the crown of thorns a symbol in Christian thought and art for the pain and the misery of Jesus in his Passion. Therefore, predominance of torture or of mockery in understandings of pious Christians decided the length of thorns, type of crown, and number of thorns.

When modern biblical scholars investigate the extent of physical pain for Jesus from the crown of thorns, they delve into the botanical types of thorn plants to determine the length of thorns in the crown. A lack of a precise description in Holy Scriptures limits the scriptural knowledge and the best efforts of scholars to discover specific truth about the crown of thorns. The inability to understand definitive truths about the historical crown of thorns reduces the biblical scholars to educated guesses. Scholastic guesstimates for the length of thorns in the crown of Jesus range from ½ to 4 inches.

Modern botanists seem cautious to use a scientific perspective in retrospect and to deduce truthful conclusions about past thorn plants with the resultant size of thorns. However, caution is probably a wise choice since the evangelists are silent with crown details and since humanity has a record of wasting flora and fauna over the past 2,000 years. It is the basic presumption that knowledge of the thorn plant is still in humanity's database and that a similar thorn exists today as it did 2,000 years ago. Nevertheless, the eligible plants in Palestine from 2,000 years ago diversify the theories of the biblical scholars (Ibid., Vol.1, p.866-7). The botanical experts split opinions, but they consistently suggest three plants to support the theories of biblical scholars: (1) Zizyphus spina-christi, (2) Paliurus spina-christi, (3) the Gundelia turentfortii. Consequently, the best averages for the length of the thorns in Jesus' crown produced from these three plants range from ¾ to 1½ inches (2-4 cm.). Since modern botanists simply do not have enough details for the ancient thorn plant, the length of the thorn in Jesus' crown depends on the choice of the biblical scholar for a favorite mature plant. In a modern Teen reality, all thorns hurt.

Teenagers, please, understand that no generic theory about the exact length of the thorns refutes the immense pain of Jesus and the amount of lost blood from the crowning by the execution squad of the Roman legionnaires. It was no fun for Jesus or the ones who loved him. The thorns were long enough for Jesus to need the premium virtue of fortitude to deal with the real pain.

After the biblical scholars decide on a range for the length of the thorns, they face some historical complications about the type of the crown and the number of thorns. Was the crown a wreath like the laurels worn by the Caesars, or was the crown a cap like the crowns worn by oriental monarchs in the Middle East? The number of thorns in Jesus' crown depends on the analysis of the style of crown. There is only the deep silence from the evangelists.

Without the definitive statement from the Gospels, the historical problems magnify because there are more than 700 sacred relics of thorns varying in size throughout the world. Authorities agree that all are not authentic, but all are objects of devotion. Some thorns are traceable, and it seems that pious people often divided the thorn and consequently multiplied them (Thurston, "Crown of Thorns," Catholic Encyclopaedia, p. 541). There is also medieval evidence that devout people "touched" the real crown of thorns with their thorn and as a result had a new object of pious devotion to venerate (de Mely, Exuviae Sacrae Constantinopolitanae, Vol. III, p.362).

Some biblical scholars think from the historical perspective that many pilgrims venerated the original crown of thorns in Jerusalem for hundreds of years after the Resurrection of Jesus. Saint Helena, the mother of Emperor Constantine the Great, visited Jerusalem in c.325 A.D., and according to legend she discovered the true cross and the crown of Jesus. The original crown of thorns apparently transferred to the Byzantine emperors in 1063. In 1238 Emperor Baldwin II of Constantinople (Istanbul, Turkey) ceded the crown to St. Louis IX, King of France. It was in Venice, Italy as the security for a sizable loan to Baldwin. When St. Louis got the crown out of hock, he built the Sainte-Chapelle in Paris to house the crown of thorns. After the French Revolution the crown of thorns went to the Cathedral of Notre Dame in 1806.

That crown now consists of only a circlet of rushes (stems/stalks) in the reliquary at Notre Dame Cathedral in Paris, France. There are not any thorns in the circlet of rushes venerated as Jesus' crown of thorns. Some authorities think that the Roman legionnaires in the execution squad twisted the original crown with 60 or 70 thorns into a caplet or a helmet. The circlet of rushes held the cap together (http://www.newadvent.org/Cath. Encyclopedia, "Crown of Thorns"). St. Louis and his successors distributed authentic thorns until nothing remained except the circlet of rushes at the Notre Dame Cathedral.

If the Shroud of Turin is the Holy Shroud of Jesus, it is not only a snapshot of the Resurrection but also a blueprint of the Crucifixion. The Shroud of Turin as an ancient relic supports the combination of the headband and the cap-of-thorns theories. There are more than thirty blood flows from spike punctures on the frontal and the dorsal images of the head (http://www.shroud.com/meacham2.htm). All the blood flows from the wounds on the back of the head stop at a curve very noticeable on the negative picture of the Shroud. Some experts deduced that plaited bands held together a cap or helmet of possibly 70 thorns on branches (Wilson, Shroud, p.33-4; Barbet, Doctor, p.84-7). Thorns pierced both arteries and veins. The Shroud face has a large venous blood flow, the "3" rivulet on the forehead above the left eyebrow. There is an arterial blood flow on the face from a puncture of the right temple. Experts agree that the massive loss of blood from the head wounds tremendously weakened the man of the Shroud.

There is no disagreement among the theologians and the biblical scholars that there was excruciating pain and extensive lost blood from possibly 60-70 thorns of 1½ inches in length stuck in the head of Jesus. The serious pain left no room for the lack of the virtue of fortitude. If there are doubts that the Holy Shroud of Turin was the burial Shroud of Jesus, there is no doubt left to the imagination that excessive scourging at the pillar and horrible crowning with thorns became deadly painful tortures for the Shroud man. Careful scrutiny of the scourging at the pillar and the crowning with thorns divulges that the mockery of Jesus from the Roman legionnaires deteriorated into extreme physical torture. The additional psychological suffering of Jesus disintegrated into real physical pain.

The most innocent Jesus had the virtue of fortitude to exist with spiritual strength and spiritual courage throughout his scourging at the pillar and his crowning with thorns. Jesus suffered because of his choice to obey and love God the Father above all things including great physical pain. As a result, the salvation in the re-establishment of a personal love relationship with the Most Holy God of Antiquity exists in the reality of the modern Teenager.

It is that same ancient virtue of fortitude that Teens may petition from the One True Holy God in prayer. The most innocent Jesus got through his Passion/death to his Resurrection with the real virtue of fortitude. Moses got through his face-off with Pharaoh Rameses II to the Exodus with the real virtue of fortitude. Teens get through their daily hassles and negative peer pressures to a holy life with the real virtue of fortitude. Prayer of petition to God for the virtue of fortitude is a prayer to the owner of a cosmic library filled with all knowledge, all truth, all virtue, all power. God answered prayers of petitions from Jesus for the virtue of fortitude. God answered prayers of petitions from Moses for the virtue of fortitude. God answers the prayers of petitions from the modern Teen for the virtue of fortitude, spiritual strength, spiritual courage. There is nothing wrong with asking for "stuff" in daily prayers of petitions. However, to elevate prayer-life and raise spirituality above a kindergarten level Teenagers need to consider asking for the premium virtue of fortitude with dignity and respect for the True and Holy God of All Power and All Love.

C. PLEASE, CONSIDER THE FOLLOWING:

(1) Do a three-minute mediation with eyes closed, racket blocked out, thoughts/feelings concentrated on the focal point: God, please, give me fortitude/spiritual strength/spiritual courage to do your will...

(2) Create a mental list of needs, wants, virtues and petition the Most Holy God of All Knowledge and All Power...(for the ancient and the modern virtue of fortitude, good health, patience, humility, moderate power, moderate popularity, moderate status, kind friends, better grades, boyfriends, girlfriends, athletic talents, daily bread, freedom, goodness, forgiveness, gratitude, trust, love, faith, value, common sense in relationships, righteousness, peace, intercessions for little people with flies in eyes, enough money, holiness, intercessions for blind Teens, intercessions for abused Teens, kindness, gentleness, spiritual courage, spiritual strength, modesty, self-control, better job for Dad, joy, cure for Grandma's cancer, understanding, trade "old banger" for a new car, wisdom, Mom to stop hurting, good and loyal friends, more laughter, etc.)...

(3) Compose a homemade prayer of petition to Almighty God which you can think and feel several times throughout the day...remember it's between you and your God...

(4) Try loving God and all neighbors to the point that personal petitions always include intercessions for other people and requests for virtues...

CHAPTER 5

CHANGE...GOOD BULLY
THEOLOGY OF HOLY TRINITY, GRACE, HOLY EUCHARIST

A. GOOD BULLY

The students at Linden Lodge School for the Blind feared and hated Bully. Bully was dangerous especially on the days with bright sunshine. Bully closed his bad left eye tightly and opened wide his good right eye to "see" through glasses with thick lens. He focused on people to thump and hurt for the sake of a laugh. He did not care about the other students. When the dust settled on Bully's negative behavior and dangerous action, his stock phrase to the Headmaster always rang true, "What's it matter—nobody loves me—and besides, I should be dead."

We had faculty and staff meetings concerning Bully. Consensus was always that Bully would never change until he felt love. As much as the faculty and staff tried to generate love for Bully, Bully reigned in terror, and the students responded with hatred. All changed when Bully fell in love and became the Good Bully. However, the change due to love was not the most idealistic plan of anyone.

Mr. McMillan and I scheduled blocks of time off campus to work mobility with small groups of students and to let the students practice changing money at the local shops. It was a fun learning experience for the students. We posted notices for the field trips about a week before the events. All students displayed best behaviors with hopes of going to their favorite shops during a school day. Bully never went shopping. However, the faculty and staff usually got a halfhearted effort out of Bully to act halfway right for a few days.

The downfall of Bully was always the sunshine that gave him the advantage of sight. Bully tried to behave decently, but the sunshine brought out the big, old, fat, mean Bully in him. When Bully felt the sunshine, he slowly polished his big thick glasses while meditating on his next escapade. Trouble happened when he got a wicked grin on his fat face and replaced his ultra clean glasses on his fat head. Bully always closed down his bad left eye, opened wide his good right eye, and moved his head quickly from side to side. He cocked his head to the left and locked his good right eye in a totally focused radar vision on his next victim. Invariably, Bully's vicious left elbow knocked a blind student into the deep end of the swimming pool, or he played "airplane." Both got the bad Bully kicked off the list for the travel squad of shoppers.

There was always the march to the Headmaster's office. Then, a harangue from the Headmaster until he ran out of steam. The Bad Bully always sat quietly in the big leather chair reserved for guests.

The Headmaster ended with a question, "Why do you always act like a big bully?" Bully ended with a deep sigh and his answer, "What's it matter—nobody loves me—and besides, I should be dead." It was always the same old routine until the week of cloudy weather before the coveted field trip.

The combination of no sunshine and a new guinea-pig medicine had Bully virtually comatose for a week. He only pepped up to beg Mr. McMillan and me for the umpteenth millionth time to let him work on his mobility and go shopping at his favorite candy store. If trouble tempted him, we simply asked, "Bully, do you want to shop at the candy store on Friday?" Bully instantly shaped up and replied, "Oh, yes Sirs, oh yes, I want to shop at the candy store on Friday, I'll be a good Bully." And Bully was a good Bully while temptation for trouble passed. As a result, there was peace on the campus.

The Friday for mobility arrived with clouds, a forecast of rain, no gripes from the faculty or the staff about Bully's behavior for a week. Mr. McMillan and I checked the heavens a zillion times for inspiration and any semblance of a blue sky. The time for the decision was at 1:00pm. Bully stood patiently and silently in front of us dressed in his best clothes, and he had his white cane. Mr. McMillan looked at me, and I looked at him. We shrugged our shoulders, raised eyebrows, and threw hands despairingly and silently into the air. We sighed in stereo with the resignation that it was time for Bully to work mobility and to practice changing money. I said silent prayers of petitions that all might survive the experience.

Bully rarely went with other students to work on mobility around the surrounding neighborhood, but on those limited occasions, Bully always tapped with his white cane ahead of the other students. He liked to arrive at the corners first and listen by himself to the different sounds. When all students arrived at the same corner, Mr. McMillan and I requested silence. All listened for potential dangers from the flow and direction of traffic. Mr. McMillan and I chose one student to make the decision for the group to safely cross the street. We silently crossed each street as a group. Then Mr. McMillan and I released the group to progress individually and noisily to the next corner for a repeat of the procedure.

The shops were to the right at the front gate of Linden Lodge for ½ block, again a right turn, and then straight down the hill for the four blocks to a stoplight at a very busy street. Our usual routine worked for 1½ blocks. Unfortunately, for the collective blood pressure of all Bully's teachers, the sun began to shine in block #2 from the holes in the clouds for a few precious seconds. By block #3, the sun played a serious game of peek-a-boo behind the clouds. Both Mr. McMillan and I broke into cold nervous sweats. Potential dangers from buses, cars, trucks, too many people were at the stoplight at the end of the extra long block #4. It was prime territory for a bad Bully with the full radiant sunshine for an ally. Mr. McMillan and I thought most horrible scenarios of a bad Bully giving the old elbow to his innocent victim and knocking the person off the curb just to hear squeals of braking tires and the sounds of honking horns. Mr. McMillan motioned at the start of block #4 for me to tighten the shadow on Bully.

With the little bit of sunshine, the instantly happy Bully practically sprinted to the stoplight at the end of the long block #4. When Bully stopped at the curb of the busy street, he was totally unaware that I was beside him. There were sounds galore. Bully stood motionless and straight as an arrow. He opened both eyes wide and stared into black space with outlines of bright light. Bully had a huge grin on his face. He looked as if he connived and snuck his way into a personal heaven to overdose on sights and sounds. He listened happily. Cars screeched to a halt with each change of the stoplight. Small trucks and big lorries gunned engines. Busses roared past us. Underground cars (the subway) on overhead rails click-clacked down the tracks. People everywhere yelled, laughed, and talked with many different accents. Oh, life was good for Bully!

With all the commotion, Bully was totally unaware that a "Bobby" (policeman) sat on a horse at the corner of the curb to his left within reach of his white cane. The Bobby was ready to ride to the center of the busy intersection and direct traffic manually if the congestion worsened. The Bobby looked down from his horse at Bully with his white cane and then at me. We nodded silently and respectfully to each other. Mr. McMillan trailed the safe arrival of the students to the corner, and all stood along the curb facing the traffic. Students stretched out shoulder to shoulder from the corner along the curb to the right. The pecking order from left to right at the curb was Bobby on his horse, Bully, myself, Mr. McMillan, Colin Browne, Libby Lou, and the rest of the class. All the blind students listened intently and silently to the incredible mixture of sounds.

Before long the horse snorted and shifted his weight. The Bobby adjusted himself in the saddle, and the leather creaked. Bully's radar ears instantly picked up the sounds. Bully snapped his head left and demanded, "What's that sound?" I looked at the Bobby and then at Mr. McMillan. They looked at me, and we shrugged our shoulders. I said, "What sound, Bully?" The horse obliged on cue and snorted loudly. He shifted weight to his other feet, and the Bobby made the suitable adjustment in the creaking leather saddle. Bully immediately did a left face, pointed directly at the horse, yelled excitedly, "That sound!" I told Bully that the sound came from a big brown horse with the Bobby sitting in the saddle. Bully whispered in awe, "A hoorrse." Even with all the sounds, Bully's whisper reached Colin Browne, who passed the word to Libby Lou, who passed the word down the line of students. The pure excitement ratcheted up a notch.

Then the sunshine came out from behind the clouds. Bully saw the horse. His mouth dropped open. He was speechless. It was the most beautiful sight that Bully had ever seen in his blind life. Bully half whispered excitedly to me, "Please, Sir, may I pet the horse?" I glanced silently at the Bobby on the horse and questioned him with my raised eyebrows. The Bobby nodded a silent "yes." I answered Bully, "Why don't you ask the Bobby?" After Bully summoned all the fortitude in the world, he boldly blasted his request with his very best Queen's English in his deepest voice, "Beg your pardon, Sir, I beg your pardon." However, the enormity of his request got to him, and it collapsed his confidence. A barely audible Bully hesitated but bravely continued in his meekest and mildest voice, "Sir, may I, please, pet your horse?" The Bobby said in his official tone, "Yes, Lad, you may carefully pet the horse." There were fading echoes, "Bully is going to pet the horse, Bully is going to pet the horse," as energized students passed the word down the electrified line.

Bully reached his hand out and tentatively found the horse. He petted the horse on the front right flank. The animal calmly turned his head and looked down at Bully. In the flash of a heartbeat, the horse gave Bully a big slobber kiss. The wet lick started at Bully's chin and went up his right cheek onto his ear and across the top of his head. The slobber kiss almost knocked off Bully's thick glasses. Bully threw his arms high into the air and proclaimed to the whole world, "This horse loves me!" Bully hugged and petted the horse. Mr. McMillan and I looked silently at each other, and we raised our eyebrows. Bully was so happy.

Finally, Bully took a step backwards and looked up at the Bobby with a big smile. Bully asked very politely, "Beg your pardon, Sir, beg your pardon, but some of these blind students have never seen a big beautiful horse, and I was wondering, Sir, if they might, please, pet your beautiful horse?" After Bully received the proper permission, he turned to the other students. Bully said in his most important and his deepest voice, "Now listen up, Students, if you want to pet this horse, queue up next to me, and you can pet this horse one at a time, but it might get dangerous, so I'll stand here and protect you, because this horse and I are friends, and this horse loves me!" I looked silently at Mr. McMillan, and he looked at me. Again, we raised our eyebrows.

Bully was sky-high and a very good Bully for the rest of the field trip. In fact, he bought three Snickers bars and three Cokes to share with Colin Browne and Libby Lou without utilizing the peace tokens as bribes. He held the doors open for the lady students without trying to trip them with his white cane. When the clouds allowed sunshine, he described the size and numbers of cars to the young men without trying to booty bop them into traffic. He stood frequently next to Mr. McMillan and me to "help survey the troops" and anticipate potential trouble. Bully bought ice cream for me and chips (french fries) for Mr. McMillan without taste-testing them first. Moreover, if we wanted to take a break, Bully offered to "keep an eye on things." Bully was a good Bully and full of kind gestures for all. When we returned to the school, Bully asked politely for permission to go to the Braille library to do research on horses.

The Headmaster, Mr. McMillan, and I powwowed to brainstorm Bully and the horse. We eventually devised the "Good Bully Plan." We received appropriate permission for Bully to work at the police horse stables on Saturdays. Bully started his job at exactly 8:00am each Saturday, and he worked to exactly high noon. Bully traveled to and from the stables by himself. He rode the Underground and two busses to his job, and he reversed the pattern from work to school. Bully entered and exited vehicles by himself. He changed money and made transfers as needed. Bully woke up at 5:00am to allow enough time to meet the train and bus schedules. Bully was totally unaware that Mr. McMillan or I trailed him to keep an eye on things. We never interfered no matter how tough things got for Bully. His work was the perfect combination of freedom and responsibility on the weekends. Bully drew his individuality from his work with the police horses at the police stables. He was a Good Bully because of his love for horses.

Bully's job at the police stables was not easy. Bully mucked out the stalls. Good Bully shoveled horse manure out of individual stalls. Bully never complained because his work was so necessary for the horses. The police stables formed a square, and stalls boxed in the exercise courtyard. The half-doors of twenty stalls faced inwards into the open-aired inner courtyard. Bully was "the Lad" responsible for the five stalls and the four horses along one side of the square.

Bully first cleaned the empty stall at the end of his row. He then walked horse #1 by the reins from the dirty stall to the clean empty stall. He returned to muck out the dirty but now empty stall. Bully shoveled the horse manure into a bucket, and then he muscled the heavy bucket to the disposal trench. He raked the old straw on the floor of the stall into piles. Bully used a pitchfork to throw old straw into a wheelbarrow, and he hauled it to the dump. Bully next hosed down the stall walls and floor. While the stall dried, Bully freshened the horse's water trough and filled both grain and hay feeders. He finished the cleaning process by strewing fresh straw onto the floor of the stable. Bully collected horse #1, and he walked the horse back to the newly cleaned stall. Bully then repeated the procedure with horses #2, #3, #4.

Remember that Bully was blind from birth. Bully calculated and memorized his steps and his angles from each stall to the different task areas. He received no special treatment, and he did the same work on the same rigid schedule as sighted Lads. The meticulous Sergeant-in-Charge of Stables scrutinized all work of the Lads. Bully had only four hours until the noon inspection. Bully was a volunteer and worked for zero money. His only incentive was the contact with his horses. If his stalls passed a detailed scrutiny of the Sergeant's inspection, his reward was a ten-minute ride on one of his horses. He sat on his horse while the horse walked around the exercise path of the inner courtyard. Bully was one of the Lads at the police stables as long as Bully arrived on time and his work passed inspection in the allotted time. In the final analysis, Bully loved his horses, and his horses loved Bully.

Bully's #1 horse was the same horse that the Bobby rode at the stoplight by the school. The #1 horse was Bully's first love. Now Bully had three other horses to love. Mucking out their stalls was truly a physical labor of spiritual love for Bully. He returned to school totally exhausted from his job. Bully slept with a big smile on his face, and the Saturday night watchman slept as much as he wanted.

Bully chose to change into a Good Bully, and there was peace on campus. Bully developed a weekly routine that geared everything towards Saturday at the stables. For example, Bully collected little sugar cubes during the week so that he could give special treats to each of his horses. The sugar cubes were the "one lump or two" that went into the traditional English afternoon tea. Bully usually had four lumps in his tea, but Good Bully sacrificed his lumps for his horses. He even traded his french fries for sugar cubes. By the weekend, Bully had his stash of sugar cubes just right for each of his horses.

The Good Bully chose to avoid trouble so as not to jeopardize Saturdays at the stables. His greatest temptations for trouble came with the combinations of sunshine and new guinea-pig medicines. The combinations made him ping off the walls, but Mr. McMillan and I helped him through his troubled spots. If trouble tempted him, we simply asked, "Bully, do you want to shovel horse shit at the stables on Saturday?" Bully immediately shaped-up and replied, "Oh yes, Sirs, oh yes, I want to shovel horse shit on Saturday, I'll be a good Bully." And Bully was a Good Bully while the temptations for trouble passed. As a result, there was peace on campus.

Everything was hunky-dory until the Friday night power failure. Good Bully had a bad week because dosages of the new corrective medicine were out of whack. The quasi Good Bully made it to Friday with just a few minor injuries and hurt feelings for the other students. Before going to bed Bully again went over his mental checklist for his Saturday preparations. He had his clothes ready on his chair. His little piles of money for the Underground and the busses were on the corner of his desk. His "Wellingtons" (knee-high rubber boots) were with his clothes by the chair. His backpack contained the precious sugar cubes for special treats for his horses, his sandwich for lunch, his water bottle, and two Snickers bars for quick energy. His white cane leaned on his backpack. His thick glasses were next to his little piles of money. He set an electric alarm clock with Braille numbers to ring at 5:00am. He was ready for Saturday. It was time to sleep and dream about riding handsome steeds and racing the wild wind.

Unfortunately for Bully, the new medicine conked him out. Bully was usually a light sleeper as a defensive mechanism against boys trying to get their revenge for his bad Bully days. The meanest thing, which the boys did to each other, was the rearrangement of furniture in familiar surroundings. Normal precautions of counting steps and holding hands out to find potential dangers did not exist on automatic pilot in familiar territory. Bully snored in false security while two boys on campus for the weekend rearranged his bedroom furniture in a stealthy commando run. Bully slept through a violent midnight storm with the high winds and torrential rains that knocked out the electrical power to his alarm clock.

Bully slept until he heard the neighborhood church bells toll six times. He snapped awake and knew instantly that he was one hour late. As he jumped out of bed, he tried to calculate in his foggy mind the alternate times for the trains and busses. He immediately tripped over his Wellingtons strategically positioned to cause maximum pain. He dove headfirst towards his repositioned desk, and his awkward swim through the thin air failed to regain his balance. He banged his head on the corner of his desk and gave himself a throbbing knot on the forehead. The violent collision spewed his thick glasses and his little piles of money everywhere. Bully crawled on hands and knees reaching quickly in all directions and searching desperately for all his stuff. He tried frantically to calculate the sum of fares in his aching head. All the repossessed coins felt the same, and he repeatedly jumbled his calculations. Meanwhile, time ticked away unceasingly without sympathy. The feeling of nausea from the impending doom overcome Bully. However, the brave little Bully struggled forward because he loved his horses.

Things got worse. When Bully tapped his white cane quickly past the Caretaker's Cottage at the front gate, he almost heard the snores from Mr. McMillan because of another failed electric alarm clock. Bully had no emergency back-up troops trailing him to the stables. Bully was alone. When he rushed downhill in the four blocks to the busy stoplight, he lost count of his steps, and the sidewalk raised by tree roots in block #2 ambushed him. Bully sprawled brutally to the ground. He quickly recovered and simply ignored the blood flowing from his left knee out of the new hole in his torn jeans. The brave little Bully limped forward because he loved his horses.

Total disaster hit Bully in block #3. The storm dropped a large tree limb across the sidewalk, and it bushwhacked the limping Bully. He crashed spread eagle onto the ground. When Bully slowly raised himself from the mud, he stood wobbly with another lump pounding on his forehead and with blood dripping from nose and mouth. His fall broke his thick glasses. The left eyeglass over his bad left eye was undamaged. The eyeglass over his good right eye had designs of spiderwebs. His glasses were useless if any sunshine appeared. Bully stood weaving back and forth with a white cane in each hand because the fall broke his cane into two short pieces. Neither piece of cane touched the ground. However, the brave little Bully struggled forward because he loved his horses.

Bully finally arrived at the police stables at 8:51am. Bully found the Sergeant-in-Charge of Stables standing and carefully watching the morning routine from the middle of the exercise courtyard. Bully tried to explain his tardiness, but he became thoroughly flustered and tongue-tied. The morning agony and frustration prevented him from stringing a sentence together. Emotions from the morning tensions flooded into his total incoherent speech. The Sergeant, a stickler for routine and proper procedure, halted Bully's inadequate attempt at the explanation. The Sergeant-in-Charge of Stables said in his most authoritative voice, "Lad, you are fifty-one minutes late, so we do not need you today." The Sergeant stunned Bully into silence. Finally Bully feebly tried to protest, "But, but the horses and, and the stalls." The Sergeant cut off Bully's sentence and said emphatically, "You were late, so I assigned another Lad to muck out your stalls; you are my best Lad at mucking out the stables, but I do not need you if you are not responsible enough to arrive on time; so run along, Lad, we have schedules in Her Majesty's Police Force."

Bully snapped. Bully relapsed into bad Bully. He cussed and cursed the Sergeant. The Sergeant responded by dismissing Bully permanently from the stables in order to "maintain discipline in Her Majesty's Police Force." Bully went berserk. He threw his two pieces of white cane at the Sergeant and missed by a country mile. Bully charged the Sergeant in a bull run. The Sergeant casually stepped aside, and Bully fell flat on his face in the mud. Bully charged again, and the Sergeant held his ground. Bully bounced off the big stomach of the Sergeant into the mud again. Bully jumped up and swung both clenched fists trying to connect for one good blow. The Sergeant stood six feet tall, and he simply extended his arm out straight with his hand on top of Bully's head. Bully swung viciously at thin air with both fists until he wore himself out. Then Bully crumbled to the mud in real tears.

Mr. McMillan and I received the call at 9:00am to collect Bully. We borrowed a car from a friend, and we drove to the police stables. We found Bully on the bench outside the Sergeant's office. He sat silently with pieces of white cane in each hand. He realized that we were with him, and he stood up slowly. Bully said in a barely audible and very shaky voice, "I am very sorry for everything, Sirs, and I can never see my horses again." Then the brave little Bully cried silent tears that left trails in the dirt on both sides of his face.

The ride to the Linden Lodge School for the Blind was miserable. Bully slumped in the back seat crying silent tears. All our bribes to cheer him up with ice cream, french fries, Snicker bars failed. Bully quietly said, "Sirs, I don't feel so good; I just want to go home." When we arrived at the school, Bully went to his room and sat at his desk for the entire afternoon and night. Bully looked out the window at the things that he could not see. His thoughts and feelings were on his horses, and he skipped his two favorite meals. Bully truly loved his horses, and his horses loved Bully. The Good Bully for a little while was a sad Bully for a very long time.

B. APPLIED THEOLOGY — HOLY TRINITY, GRACE, HOLY EUCHARIST

People, Bully loved "his horses." His mind and heart connected with horses in a type of platonic and spiritual love. When his physical connection with the horses broke, Bully was very sad for a long time. His love for his horses was strong enough to change Bully in a short period from a living terror to a pretty good guy. When he separated from the objects of his love, Bully had only a few memories of love. His pain was too great for him to realize that he still had choices to give and receive love.

Following Bully's experiences of love and a broken heart, there remained some good-better-best questions. Would Bully choose to reestablish his love with horses? Would Bully choose to transfer his love for horses to human peers? Would Bully choose to transfer his love for horses to God? But the most asked question by the faculty, staff, students was, "Will we have the good Bully or the bad Bully on a day with bright sunshine and repaired glasses?" The choices of Bully to love or not to love had serious and major consequences for the peace and security of the everyday people around him.

It is the same case scenario with modern Teens. The individual Teen has a free choice to love or not to love. Teenage choices have serious and major consequences for the peace and security of the peers, parents, siblings, teachers, grandparents, strangers, God, and friends around the Teen. If Bully chose to revert into the bad Bully because of the frustrations and sadness of not getting his way in a love relationship with his horses, Bully blundered. Love experiences of Bully were like a bucket full of love when he had real opportunities for a barrel full of love with the everyday people around him.

If a modern Teen isolates and insulates self from love because of the frustrations and sadness in the lack of instant and prolonged gratification from the real love relationship, the Teen blunders. The modern Teen settles for a kicked over bucket full of love. However, the Teen has a very real opportunity for a full barrel of love with the everyday people around the Teen and a very real opportunity for a water tower full of love with God. Full is full, but a difference between the full bucket and the full water tower is the difference in freedom of choice. Within God's sovereignty and freedom to create, God the Father makes Teenagers with the freedom to choose. God makes Teens with the capacity to love to the fullest. God makes Teens with a genuine capability to choose love of God. In everyday reality, the Teenage choice to love God is a Teenage choice to know God and to worship God.

The Teenager utilizes mind and heart with the inner freedom to choose and establish relationship with God through love, knowledge, and worship. Teens think and feel love, knowledge, worship with a dignity and a respect for God. The efforts of Teens, not necessarily I.Q. or emotional intelligence, influence growth of a relationship with God. If a Teen tries to the best of God-given talents to love, know, worship God, positive things happen. However, make no mistake that the excellent effort is work and a battle.

Individual Teen commitment to daily increase love, knowledge, worship of God is most difficult. Teenage commitment is a constant battle against the domination by the Teen ego and a battle against the manipulation of sinister evil spirits seeking the destruction of all Teen relationships with the Most Holy God. Certainly, the Teen can quit the effort of trying to love, know, worship God and still be on a hunky-dory level of spirituality. But to quit is to stagnate. Teenage spiritual stagnation is ultimate denial of the Teen spiritual dynamics which bring to the entire world so much love, positive energy, smiles, happiness, empowerment, idealism, laughter, goodness, holiness, joy, pure worship of the Most Holy God.

Teen prayer is simply the tip for the dynamics of Teen spirituality. Prayers of thanksgiving, forgiveness, adoration, petition are truly the keys to Teen spirituality and to elevating prayer-life off a kindergarten level. However, keys open doors. Prayer is a point where the Teen meets the living and eternal God. Every Teenager has the ability to choose to pray to God during good and bad times. Every Teen may also choose to live prayer daily by better understanding the inner dynamics of Teenage prayer as the progressive growth pattern of knowing, loving, and worshiping God. Teenage spirituality originates with God expressed as the love of the Divine Presence in the Teen consciousness. Teen response is a free choice of the individual to pray and to communicate with God. Teen prayers quickly include and hopefully embody trust in God, individual fortitude, patience with self and others, individual courage, individual faith in God within the larger worshiping community, and love of the Most Holy God.

Fear is the potential and serious block to the progressive growth pattern of prayer as knowing, loving, worshiping God. "Fear vs. love" is not a flawless dualism because of nuances of truth in knowledge throughout the ages. However, fear is the umbrella for all negative combative forces, and love is the spiritual umbrella for all the good positive forces. Fear vs. love is the basic tension, which can block the living daily prayer of the Teenager as growth of knowledge, love, worship of God. A Teenager with no fear and no negative combative forces is the Teen who sees a spiritual reality with eyes of love for God. When the Teen decides to increase love of God, knowledge of God, worship of God, the Teenager deletes fear as the debilitating negative emotion. The Teenager takes a step on a spiritual journey to advance faith in God.

It does not really matter where Teens start within the realms of knowledge, love, worship of God. These three avenues interlock and intertwine with the face-to-face vision of God as the end result. All avenues to God reach points where the Teen must admit to self that the Teen just does not know. That is a real point of faith and trust in God. That is also the point of serious prayer as an open and humble communication with the Most Holy God of All Truth. It is the Teen's call to desire an advance of his or her faith journey, and it is God's call to allow understanding of knowledge, love, and worship of God. God's self-communication advances the Teenager with eyes of faith towards the vision of God. As a result, the simple tip for dynamics of Teenage spirituality is prayer, and all Teenagers definitely have the ability to crank it up.

a. Most Holy Trinity

Whenever the Christian Teenager decides to expand spiritual consciousness and knowledge of God, the Teen has no way to avoid the Mystery of the Most Holy Trinity. The Holy Trinity is the central mystery of Christianity. Three religions, which believe in monotheistic God (one and only one God), are Judaism (Jews), Christianity, and Islamism (Muslims). Christianity is the only religion that believes in the Holy Trinity. The Holy Trinity is the Mystery of God in one nature and in three Divine Persons: the Father, the Son Jesus Christ, the Holy Spirit. One True God in Christianity reveals Self in the Father, in the Son, in the Holy Spirit. There is only One God. The Christian revelation of the one nature of God is the basic essence of One God in the Divine Person of Father, and in the Divine Person of Jesus the Christ, and in the Divine Person of the Holy Spirit. Christians believe that the three Divine Persons are in the essence of the One Almighty God. The Holy Trinity is the Most Holy God in whose name Catholic Christians baptize, start and end prayers, worship in liturgy as One True God. The Holy Trinity is the undivided unity of One Almighty God. Christians adore and worship only the Most Holy Trinity. The Most Holy Trinity remains the Most Holy Mystery.

The <u>doctrine</u> of the Most Holy Trinity, as Christians understand it today, is not explicitly in the Old Testament or in the New Testament of our Bibles. Nowhere did God give the doctrine of the Holy Trinity in one swoop of divine revelation with the theology packaged neatly in words understood by all people. God is Divine Mystery, and God reveals Self in divine communications throughout salvation history. God did not, does not, and will not do our thinking and our choosing for us. The freedoms to think about God, to know God, to choose love and worship of God are in the essence and the nature of each human being. God did not give us the doctrine of the Holy Trinity in a single divine revelation, and God respects the human freedoms to think, know, and choose within human essence. Consequently, the doctrine of the Most Holy Trinity took about 400 years to hammer out and about 15 centuries to refine into the doctrine of today (McBrien, Catholicism, p.283). We still do not fully understand the doctrine of the Most Holy Trinity because God always remains a Divine Mystery. Hopefully, the knowledge and the understanding of God will advance because a few modern Teens will choose the theologian's profession and dedicate their lives to study the Christian Traditions about the Most Holy Trinity.

Let me, please, share some research and explain the sweeping generalities and statements about the long frame of time to develop the central Christian doctrine of Triune God. Teens need to keep in mind and heart five underlying pragmatic thoughts throughout this discussion of the Holy Trinity.

First, Teens hopefully understand that Christianity is as "heavy" as the Teenager wants to get into theology and as "light" as the Teen feelings of true love. Every Teenager has the gifts from God to pray, study, think about God.

Second, Teenagers hopefully realize that the revelations of God about Self are decisions of God concerning the revealed facts and the time for the distribution of the information. With help and grace from God theologians understood, interpreted, developed more fully the original revelation without denying any spiritual concepts in the initial revelation. The basic problem with the solely fundamentalist approach to the reading of Holy Scripture is denial of advancement in theology. Fundamentalist interpretations of the Bible are so strict and literal that fundamentalists imply no growth in theology beyond the first century (Brown, Biblical Exegesis & Church Doctrine, p.15-7, 146). Humans can not box the Transcendent God into first century theology.

For example, biblical scholars and theologians distinguish three different stages of inspiration from God in the formation of the four New Testament Gospels. God the Holy Spirit of Truth inspired three stages of Gospel development: (A) life and teachings of the historical Jesus; (B) the oral traditions of Apostles as they preached what they heard, saw, interpreted about Jesus; (C) the Four Gospels written by evangelists from the oral and the written pre-forms synthesized in the schools of thought by the disciples of the Apostles (Vatican II, Dei Verbum, n.19; Catechism, n.126; Acts1:1-2; Jn.14:26, 16:12-3, 2:12-22, 14:26, 7:39).

The biblical scholars and theologians concede that the historical memory of Jesus underwent many years of development through the preaching of the Apostles and the rewriting by individual evangelists. The final results were the Four Gospels that evangelists wrote not for chronological historical facts but for written accounts of the preached testimony, which offered the Church the basis for faith and morals (Brown, The Community of the Beloved Disciple, p.21, fn.26). The fundamentalist, who insists on a traveling companion of Jesus as the eyewitness writing a history book dictated word for word by God, needs to consider the very tiny box of first century theology forced upon the Transcendent God. Teenagers do not need to limit God in efforts to expand knowledge, love, worship of the Almighty God.

Third, the Teen is not alone on his or her faith journey. There are many spiritual writers and spiritual directors from the past and in the present to help the Teen. That's one of the beautiful things about the Catholic Church. There are legions of Saints who asked pertinent spiritual questions similar to modern Teen questions: (A) where did I come from/what are my origins/who am I; (B) where am I going/what is my ultimate destination; (C) what am I doing now/why am I here (Marien, Letter, p.6).

We have written answers of the Saints concerning themselves as they looked through the optics of their specific times and cultures. Teens also have modern priests, nuns, brothers, and informed laity for discussions to help guide Teenagers on their spiritual journeys. Truly Teens have brothers and sisters in faith from the past and in the present ready to help. There is no need for the modern Teen to reinvent the spiritual wheel. If a spiritual thinker from antiquity or the Middle Ages can help the modern Teen with some answers, bring on the help. If the ancient traditions of the Catholic Church and biblical interpretations of Catholic theologians can help modern Teens with answers, bring it on. Teenagers know in their hearts that old does not mean bad or automatically unacceptable. If God the Holy Spirit gave the feeling of a home full of love to the ancient lonely spiritual traveler (Ps.68:7), God can give the same feeling to a modern Teen in his or her quest for greater spirituality. If the spiritual voice of the Most Holy God of Antiquity spoke inner spiritual peace to friends who turned to God with hope in their hearts (Ps.85:8-9), the same God can give the same feeling to the modern Teen.

Fourth, Christianity is capable of encompassing all humans in all periods of time because God the Father is Creator with Holy Love, God the Son Jesus Christ is Redeemer with Holy Obedience, God the Holy Spirit is Sanctifier with Holy Grace. God creates, redeems, sanctifies every individual regardless of the culture, wealth, personal power, race, color, creed. A reason Christianity does not encompass all humanity in all times is the free will of each human to choose. Free will is sometimes a double-edged gladius. Freedom of choice can lockout God, but Jesus is always the master key.

Fifth, the hierarchy of the Catholic Church, Pope and Bishops, takes seriously the responsibility to transmit through preaching and teaching the "deposit of faith" which it received 2,000 years ago from the historical Jesus and the Apostles (Mt.28:16-20; Mk.16:15; Lk.24: 45-8; Jn.20: 21-3; Acts2:1-26; Vatican II, Lumen Gentium, n.19, 25; Dei Verbum, n.10).

The purpose of this manuscript is not to give Teenagers spiritual gasoline to throw on a spiritual fire. My intent is not to encourage the butting of heads between the Teenager and Priest/Bishop/Pope as a Teenager with spiritual age/maturity experiences choice in freedom of thoughts and feelings. The purpose of this manuscript is to help Teens choose prayer as the expression of the Teen relationship with dignity and respect for the Most Holy God. Consequently, I seek to expand recognition within the People of God for the basic truth that prayers of Teens have value in the worship of the Most Holy God.

Please, consider the following logic. I studied over 200 books and 200 Web sites to write this manuscript about the relationships of Teens with God through prayers and worship of God. To find truth and value in Teen worship of God through Teen prayer, a Teen may choose to read and to study the books/Web sites in the bibliography. Or a Teen may choose to trust my interpretations of research in the same books and Web sites. Read 200+ books or read 200+ pages of this manuscript with a certain amount of trust in my interpretations of Truth...hmmm seems like a no-brainer. If Teenagers choose to trust my interpretations of the nuances of Truth, what's wrong with Teen trust of the Catholic Church that spent 2,000+ years thinking and praying about the Truth of Jesus?

Teens sometimes nitpick rules, regulations, and interpretations of the Catholic Church at the same time in life when Teenagers often buck authority. Instead, Teens need to consider total concentration on prayers felt and thought in the conversion of the Teen heart to the worship of God. Pope, Bishop, Priest poise in the Mass (the Ritual of Prayer) "as the one who moves through the Mass into the mystery of God" (Marien, *Letter*, p.1). At a time when Teens need acceptance and freedom of choice to think and feel, the Priest and Teens may join together in the Mass to pray and worship the Most Holy God of All Love. Consequently, the Priest feeling responsibility to the 2,000 year "deposit of faith" and the Teen feeling freedom to experience a personal faith journey worship the same God.

The discussion of the Christian concept of the Most Holy Trinity hopefully includes the above five thought patterns in the minds and hearts of Teens. All thoughts and feelings about God the Most Holy Trinity revolve around Jesus existing in human reality as the Christ, the Messiah.

1.0 Divine Jesus

The Divine Jesus remains the key to developed theology about the Mystery of the Most Holy Trinity. If Jesus is divine, Jesus is God ...heavy thoughts and heavy feelings! On the other hand, if Jesus is not divine, there is no Trinity, and consequently, there is no crucified "Christ" ("Messiah"), and there is no bodily Resurrection of "Christ" from death, and there is no Christian religion (possibly just a sect of the Jewish religion), and there is no salvation from sin, and there is no distinct Person defined as God the Holy Spirit...heavier thoughts and heavier feelings!

The question of a Divine Jesus was exactly the problem 2,000 years ago for the Pharisees, Sadducees, Essenes, and Zealots. The Jewish leaders and people saw and heard about the extraordinary power in the miracles of Jesus. Such power to cure the blind, heal the lame, caste out devils, resuscitate the dead only came from God. Jewish leaders might call Jesus a holy man or a prophet or maybe a messiah (the anointed one) especially if he raised a Hebrew army and kicked out the Romans. But the man Jesus said that he forgave sins when he healed the people (Mk.2:1-12). Only God forgave sins. The man Jesus displayed the divine power when he healed, but only God forgave sins. According to Jewish authorities, the man Jesus blasphemed because he claimed to forgive sins...only God forgave sins...therefore, he must think that he is God...the man Jesus must die to end such outrageous thoughts and such confusion...the man Jesus must die to maintain the status quo of Hebrew religion handed down from Hebrew ancestors...crucify him.

To call Jesus Divine is to call Jesus God. To call Jesus God was the denial of the very identity of the Jewish religion, which was belief in one and only one God. If Jesus was God, there were two gods according to the Jewish authorities. However, two gods broke the First Commandment of Yahweh given to Moses on Mount Sinai, the command of God reverenced for almost 1,300 years before Jesus. Two gods clearly contradicted a main belief of Abraham, Isaac, and Jacob that Hebrew people venerated for almost 1,800 years before Jesus. From the optics of the Jewish authorities, there was only one answer to the problem of the man Jesus...crucify him.

Nevertheless, the problem of the man Jesus was not answered with death because Jesus the Christ rose from the dead through the ultimate power and the rule of God over everything including death. Many followers of Jesus Christ had to think and feel and pray about such mysterious stuff. Many spiritual thinkers thought, felt, prayed about the Mystery of Jesus for 400 years as the theology developed for the Mystery of the Most Holy Trinity. Many spiritual thinkers for 1,000 years thought, felt, prayed about the "proper distinctions" in the doctrine of the Most Holy Trinity. Theological discussions led to nuances in spiritual thoughts and to a synthesis of the theology in the Doctrine of the Holy Trinity: One God in Three Divine Persons, the Father, the Son, the Holy Spirit.

Teens may choose to increase spiritual knowledge by studying the Mystery of the Most Holy Trinity through optics of the Traditions and authentic interpretations of the Catholic Church. Modern Teens learn that the Doctrine of the Holy Trinity is the summary of the basic truth of Christianity: God saves people through Jesus Christ by the power of the Holy Spirit (McBrien, Encyclopedia, p.1270).

Saint Thomas Aquinas (1225-74) was most influential in defining the synthesized theological thoughts for the Holy Trinity. Thomas Aquinas wrote, "It is impossible to believe explicitly in the mystery of Christ, without faith in the Trinity, since the mystery of Christ includes that the Son of God took flesh; that He renewed the world through the grace of the Holy Spirit; and, again, that He was conceived by the Holy Spirit" (Summa Theologica, II-II, q.2, a.8). Yet, nowhere in Old or New Testaments of the Bible is a developed Church doctrine of One God in Three Divine Persons. Nevertheless, both the Old and New Testaments revealed the essential elements of the Holy Trinity as theologians searched the Sacred Scriptures in retrospect.

The method of scanning the Hebrew Scriptures for the passages with a Triune name for God in a single verse is an unsuccessful and futile attempt to prove the Holy Trinity in the Old Testament. Father McBrien states in Catholicism:

> Because the Old Testament is pre-Christian, it does not provide any trinitarian understanding of God. This is not to say that the Old Testament's understanding of God is utterly *inconsistent* with the subsequent trinitarian development of the Christian era...the personification of certain divine forces or modalities (the 'word,' the 'wisdom,' and the 'spirit' of God) ...provides perhaps a certain prelude to the Christian understanding of God as triune. p. 280

Many Old Testament verses testified to the "movements of God" throughout human salvation history, which provided theologians with essential ingredients for a Trinitarian doctrine. For example, the Old Testament pictured God as the Creator of all humans (Gen.1:27-31) and as the Father of the Hebrew people (Hos.11:1; Jer.31:1-3, 9; Ex. 4:22-3; Deut.32:6; Mal.2:10; etc.). Research provided examples for a personification of God through concepts of divine forces: the Word (Ex.20:1-26, 19:3-6; Deut.4:10, 5:1-31; 2Sam.7:4-17; Ps.89; Isa.43, 42:1-9; Jer.31:31-4; Ezek.11:14-21, 36:22-32; etc.) and the Spirit (Gn.1:2, 2:7; 1Sam.16:13; Isa.11:2-3, 61:1, 42:1, 59:21, 44:3; Ezek. 2:2, 37:1-10; Ps.104:30, 33:6; etc.) and Wisdom (Prov.8, 2:1-12, 3: 13-22, 1:7; Job 28; 1Kings3:9-14; Sir.1:4; Wis. 7:7, 22-30, 9:1-4, 17-8, 6:17-20, 1:3-4). Notice in the Hebrew Scriptures that Wisdom is a feminine noun...you go girl.

The theologians in the New Testament found the concepts of the Holy Trinity in the saving work of God who redeems human beings through Jesus, the Christ/the Messiah (Greek/Hebrew words for the "anointed one"), by the power of the Holy Spirit. The theology of the Holy Trinity developed through revelations from the oral teachings of Jesus and through inspirations from the Holy Spirit in the written New Testament. There are many expressions of the Christian Triune God concentrated in the salvation history of Jesus and in the liturgical worship of the early Church (Mt.28:19, 3:16-7; Mk.1:9-11; Lk.3:21-2, 10:21-2, 24:49; Jn.1:29-34, 14:23-6, 15:26, 6:7-11, 20:21-3; Acts1:4, 2:1-4, 32-3; Rom. 1:1-5, 8:14-7; ICor.12:4-6; 2Cor.1:20-2, 5:5, 13:13; Gal.4:6-7; Eph.1:3-22, 5:18-20; etc.).

Gospels in the New Testament state 170 times that God is the Father of Jesus Christ (Encyclopedia, p.1270). The more personal Abba, the Aramaic word for Father or Daddy, is in Holy Scriptures three times (Mk.14:36; Rom.8:15; Gal.4:6). The evangelist of the Fourth Gospel connects Jesus directly to the Word of God from the more ancient times, and as a result, states that Jesus is God:

> In the beginning was the Word, and the Word was with God, and the Word was God...And the Word became flesh and lived among us, and we have seen his glory, the glory as of a father's only son, full of grace and truth.   Jn.1:1,14

The New Testament establishes the divinity of Jesus the Son as the living image which perfectly reveals the invisible God (Phil.2:5-11; Col.1:15-7; Heb.1:3-4; Jn.1:1,18). Jesus is the Divine Presence of God's kingdom/rule (Mt.12:28; Lk.11:20).

Great concerns for the early Christian writers and the spiritual thinkers were the serious challenges to the divine relationship of God the Father, the Son, the Spirit. The objection was to the oneness and to the unity of the Trinity. The importance of establishing the divinity of Jesus Christ was that the salvation of people was at risk. Because only God forgave sins, either Jesus Christ was truly divine and our sins forgiven through his self-sacrifice on the Cross, or Jesus was a creature just like the Teen and had no special standing in essence before God to forgive sins.

There is relationship between Jesus the Divine Son and God the Father and God the Holy Spirit. However, the New Testament does not specify the terms of the Divine relationship in a clear theology of Three Divine Persons in the One Nature of God (Catholicism, p.282-7). Bible texts refer to the saving actions of God in human history: creative, redemptive, sanctifying activities of the Father, the Son, the Holy Spirit. As a result, early Church theologians in $1^{st} - 3^{rd}$ centuries thought about the Mystery of God in terms of the "economic Trinity" (Father, Son, Holy Spirit experienced in knowable salvation history, i.e. the Bible) and the "immanent Trinity" (Father, Son, Holy Spirit existed and interrelated in the inner but unknowable essence of God) (Ibid., p.283; Catechism, n.236-7, 66). Christian theologians prayed, thought, felt, and developed the distinctions of the Most Holy Trinity for literally hundreds of years.

Church leaders at the 1st ecumenical Council of Nicaea (Nicea) in 325 and at the 2nd ecumenical Council of Constantinople in 381 painstakingly synthesized Trinitarian theology. The resultant Creed was the definition, not just a description, of the Most Holy Trinity:

> We believe in one God, the Father, the Almighty, maker of heaven and earth, of all that is, seen and unseen. We believe in one Lord, Jesus Christ, the only Son of God eternally begotten of the Father, God from God, Light from Light, true God from true God, begotten, not made, one in Being with the Father. Through him all things were made...We believe in the Holy Spirit, the Lord, the giver of life, who proceeds from the Father *and the Son*. With the Father and the Son he is worshiped and glorified...
> Nicene Creed, Catechism, p.49-50

Catholics today recite the same Nicene Creed in every Sunday Mass throughout the world. All Catholics testify every Sunday that there is One God in Three Persons. Every Sunday Catholics worship and adore the Most Holy Trinity.

2.0 Difficulty with Developed Theology of Divine Mystery

Let me, please, use the italicized phrase, "*and the Son*," in the Creed as the example to show modern Teenagers the complexity and difficulty of developing theological thoughts about the Mystery of God. The theologians today experience difficulties similar to those of past theologians with the interpretations of Sacred Scripture and the development of theology about the Mystery of the Holy Trinity. The Nicene/Constantinopolitan Creed stated the belief in the Holy Spirit, "who proceeds from the Father *and the Son (filioque)*." This phrase was a description concerned with the essence of the Spirit, and the phrase was from the Western/Latin tradition of the Catholic Church. The "and" emphasized consubstantial union ("one in being" and "of one being" and "of one substance") of God the Father and God the Son (Catechism, n.242, 251, 252, 253). The Eastern/Greek tradition of the Catholic Church rejected the "and the Son/*filioque*" phrase. Bishops in the Eastern/Greek tradition emphasized that God the Holy Spirit proceeds from the Father "*through the Son (per Filium)*" (Jn.15: 26; Catechism, n.248, 245, 246). The modern Teen may rightly ask, "What difference does it make if you use the conjunction 'and' or the preposition 'through' for the description of where God the Holy Spirit comes from?"

That was exactly the heart of the theological debates before and at the Council of Nicaea in 325. Western/Latin Church theologians orientated toward the "immanent Trinity" (the inner essence of God unknowable). Eastern/Greek Church theologians orientated toward the "economic Trinity" (God knowable in salvation history, i.e. in the Bible). Christian theologians from the West and the East agreed that God exists as the Most Holy Trinity.

However, the Western theologians thought, "One Essence (one being, one substance) of God equals ($\equiv$) Father, Son, Spirit"; Eastern theologians thought, "Three Persons of God equals (≡) Father, Son, Spirit." Western theologians thought "*Filioque*" (the Spirit proceeds from the Father <u>and</u> the Son because of One Essence in God with the Father/Creator <u>and</u> the Son/Word sending the Spirit); the Eastern theologians thought "<u>*per* *Filium*</u>" (the Spirit proceeds from the Father <u>through</u> the Son because of three Persons in God with the Father as the origin sending the Son and then sending the Spirit). As a result, Eastern/Greek theologians thought that "*Filioque*" of Western/Latin theologians implied a double principle in God; and the Western/Latin theologians thought that "*per Filium*" of Eastern/Greek theologians implied a subordination of the Son to the Father (<u>Catholicism</u>, p.329).

Written phraseology concerning Jesus Christ from the Council of Nicaea in 325 was: "The only begotten generated from the Father, that is, from the being of the Father, God from God, Light from Light, true God from true God" (Ibid., p.288-9). The most basic theological interpretation was that Jesus the Son did not emanate from the <u>will</u> of the Father, like a creature, but from the <u>essence</u> of the Father.

The more conservative elements of Eastern theologians were especially unhappy with a Nicene formula of faith for the entire West and East Church. Eastern conservatives wanted a biblical literalism because they were "fundamentalists." Their deeper issue was the acknowledgment of a possibility for development of doctrine beyond biblical sources (Ibid., p.290). There was also a serious concern that the Nicene faith formula about divine equality of the Son Jesus Christ and God the Father needed to better express the divine relationship of the Holy Spirit with the Father and the Son. The Church needed more prayers and more theological reflections to better express the Mystery of the Most Holy Trinity.

The Council of Constantinople in 381 endorsed the Trinitarian theology from the Council of Nicaea (325). So Catholics today recite the Nicene (Nicaea + Constantinople) Creed at every Sunday Mass. Nevertheless, theological debate between "*Filioque*" and "*per Filium*" concerning the Holy Spirit continued after the end of the Council in 381. The debate continues today.

There were between 228 and 318 bishops from West and East at the Council of Nicaea in 325. There were no official minutes of the Council, and the later writings of some participants established the range for the number of bishops (<u>Encyclopedia</u>, p.916). There were 186 bishops at the Council of Constantinople in 381. All the bishops were from the East (36 were considered "heretical"). There were no bishops from the Western Church and no representatives for Pope Damasus I (d.384) at the Council of Constantinople.

The wording in the final form of the Creed from the Council of Constantinople stated: "We believe in the Holy Spirit, the Lord and giver of life, who proceeds from the Father." There was no "*Filioque*" and no "*per Filium*." In 8th–11th centuries, the Western/Latin Church gradually added "and the Son (*Filioque*)." The Eastern/Greek Church rejected, denied, ignored the right of the Western Church to make additions to the ancient Creed of Constantinople. Unfortunately, one word concerning God the Holy Spirit produced disagreement among the Christians, and "the introduction of the filioque into the Niceno-Constantinopolitan Creed by the Latin liturgy constitutes moreover, even today, a point of disagreement with the orthodox Churches" (Catechism, n.247, 248, 246, 245, 243; Encyclopedia, p.361, 529-30, 916, 1270-1; Catholicism, p.293-4, 316-9, 326-30).

2.1 Spiritual Process of New Testament Writers

There is much value and even salvation in the Teenage choice to grow in the knowledge of God through prayers to God the Father, thoughts and feelings about God the Son, love and worship of God the Holy Spirit. There is also a challenge for modern Teenagers to understand that theology is not frozen into the last third of the first century by thoughts of the New Testament authors. Trajectories of New Testament thoughts into development of church doctrine were complex and required much prayer to discern the truth and the will of God. According to insights of New Testament authors, the Catholic Church had the assurances of Jesus' presence and of sending the Holy Spirit of Truth to help the Church through troubled times (Mt.28: 20, 18:19-20; Jn.14:13-8, 15:26-7, 16:12-3). Nevertheless, no quote from the Bible guaranteed instant answers without growth pains to theological developments like the Trinitarian doctrine.

The authors of the New Testament were the "second-generation" Christians and not the eyewitnesses to the ministry of Jesus. Their sources were the original twelve Apostles, who were eyewitnesses with post-resurrectional appearances and the explanations of Jesus to help formulate understanding of God. The Apostles adapted the message of Jesus into the Greek language for people in large cities of the Roman Empire, and "they brought to the memories of what Jesus had said and done the transforming enlightenment of their post-resurrectional faith in Jesus" (Exegesis, p.13).

New Testament writers brought three different figures (Father, Son, Holy Spirit) "into conjunction" in the New Testament. The New Testament authors had the basic truth of the Trinity in their writings: "...truth ultimately phrased in the trinitarian dogma, since that truth was already revealed when God sent Jesus Christ and when the risen Christ communicated his Spirit" (Ibid., p.32). The "precision" of the Trinity was not in their writings. However, their texts played the crucial role in development of the New Testament trajectory. Their writings employed new terminology, embodied new insights, were the core of Trinitarian doctrine (one divine Nature and three divine Persons, co-equal but distinct) (Ibid., p.31-2). Authors of the New Testament had insights divinely inspired by the Holy Spirit about the

Trinity, but they did not have the Triune vocabulary, terminology, and the basic clarity of ideas.

The historical Jesus was the epitome and the end of the divine Revelation of God about God, but New Testament authors did not totally understand Jesus the Christ (Catechism, n.65-6). Therefore, they did not fully understand the Mystery of the Trinity. The spiritual process included the real guidance from the Holy Spirit of Jesus to understand Jesus as the Christ in relationship to the Holy Trinity. The original Apostles prayed, thought, and felt about their experiences of Jesus the Christ. The Apostles preached their interpretations of their Jesus-experiences to people in the second third of the first century. The writers of the New Testament prayed, thought, felt about their experiences of hearing the interpretations of the Apostles concerning personal Jesus-experiences. The New Testament authors wrote their interpretations to the people in the last third of the first century about the preached interpretations of Jesus-experiences of the Apostles.

The early Church Fathers of the second century prayed, thought, felt about their experiences of reading the interpretations of the New Testament authors who heard the original Apostles' interpretations of Jesus-experiences. Early Church Fathers taught their interpretations to people in the first half of the second century about the writings of New Testament authors who heard and interpreted original Apostles' interpretations of personal Jesus-experiences.

There was no interpretation of Jesus the Christ that stood frozen in time, place, specific mentality. The resurrected Jesus was a living experience of God's power in all the interpretations. The developed understanding of Jesus as the Christ from 30 – 150A.D. produced the more developed thoughts and feelings about the Most Holy Trinity. God the Holy Spirit of All Truth inspired the better understanding of Jesus as the Christ and of the Holy Trinity.

Teens, please, remember that the last name of Jesus was not Christ. The basic concept of Christ (Messiah/Anointed One) was the developed theology inspired by God the Holy Spirit in the Apostles, the Evangelists, and the early Church Fathers. Because God is Holy Mystery, the theology of Jesus the Christ still develops alongside the theology of God the Most Holy Trinity. Modern people simply do not know God completely. God the Holy Spirit did such good work in the first 100 years after the historical Jesus that modern people think the first name = Jesus and the last name = Christ.

Modern Teens pray, think, feel about their experiences of Jesus the Christ as they study interpretations of the Jesus-experiences of the Apostles, New Testament authors, and early Church Fathers. In the development of salvation history from ancient times to modern Teens, the centrality of Jesus is paramount to the study of God. The divinity and humanity of Jesus Christ, and consequently the study of the Most Holy Trinity, involved and involves faith, prayers, thoughts, feelings, trust and a whole bunch of spiritual efforts.

2.2 Problems with Fundamentalism and Holy Scripture

It is so much easier to point with a fundamentalistic or literalistic attitude to one or two verses of the Bible and to claim the doctrine of the Holy Trinity with all its developed nuances. For instance, Jesus Christ after his Resurrection directed the eleven Apostles to "make disciples of all nations, baptizing them in the name of the Father and of the Son and of the Holy Spirit" (Mt.28:19). The verse seems a straightforward Trinitarian statement from the mouth of Jesus.

However, current biblical scholars and theologians think that the evangelist wrote the Gospel of Matthew in about 85A.D., roughly 55 years after Jesus rose from the dead. And they move the statement from a direct quote of Jesus heard by the eyewitness/"earwitness" into the process of Matthew's evangelist praying, thinking, feeling the interpretation of the Apostolic preaching about Jesus-experiences. Father Brown commented directly on Matthew 28:19 in the Biblical Exegesis & Church Doctrine:

> Yet the absence of such a command in the other Gospels and the seeming ignorance of this directive among early Christians, both in terms of baptizing in the triadic formula and a mission to the Gentiles, causes critical scholars hesitation. A moderate biblical criticism, with which I would associate myself, would maintain that the Matthean text is an ecclesiastical interpretation of the mind of Jesus–an inspired interpretation but one that reached clear formulation decades after the resurrection. p.46

Biblical scholars and theologians utilized Mt.28:19 and similar New Testament quotes (Mt.3:16-7; Mk.1:9-11; Lk.3:21-2; Jn.1:32-4) as evidence for the beginning to the development of the Trinitarian doctrine. However, there is no easy proof in Sacred Scriptures from the last third of the first century for "immanent Trinity" (unknowable inner essence of Trinity = One Divine Nature) and "economic Trinity" (knowable salvation history = Three Divine Persons with co-equality and distinctions). Direction existed from Sacred Scriptures for the trajectory of theology for the Mystery of the Holy Trinity based on the prayers, thoughts, feelings of many spiritual thinkers and guided by the Holy Spirit in Apostolic memories of experiences with Jesus.

Remember, Teens, that God did not do the thinking and feeling for the scripture writers, and God will not do your thinking and your feeling for you. God has a dignity and a respect for the basic human freedom to choose. Nonetheless, as with Teens in past centuries, God blesses modern Teens with talents, and God expects spiritual efforts from Teenagers.

A fundamentalistic or literalistic disposition may also try to use Hebrew Scriptures to claim Trinitarian doctrine. For example, some fundamentalists point to creation of the world in Genesis to assert God's plurality of persons: "Then God said, 'Let *us* make humankind in *our* image, according to *our* likeness...' " (1:26). Teenagers recall the serious theological hazards in isolating single words such as the "*Filioque*" or "*per Filium*" to explain the Mystery of God. The verse in Genesis contains the added problems of age and mythical language with a distinct mythical imagery.

The origins of the world and mankind are prehistoric. Thoughts about the beginning of mankind predate mankind's ability to write. The thoughts of the ancient ones about their origins passed verbally through numberless generations, and their thoughts came to us in mythical language full of mythical images. The oldest cave art and picture "writings" on walls of the Chauvet cave in the Ardeche Valley in southern France are 32,000 years old ("Paleolithic Art," Encarta).

The ancestral history of the Hebrew people began with Abraham who lived in approximately 1,800B.C. or almost 4,000 years ago. The mythical language and images expressed orally and in the cave art and picture writings predated everything Abraham said or wrote by 28,000 years. The "new" belief in One God defined the prayers, the thoughts, and the feelings of Abraham. However, Abraham's culture was in the context of the Near East with mythology galore. Abraham inherited and passed on a "language of myth" to describe the origins of humankind.

Consequently, theologians and biblical scholars interpreted the plural "us" and "our" in Genesis 1:26 (also, Gen.3:22, 11:7; Isa.6:8) to not reference multiple persons within one God as in the Most Holy Trinity. The plurals refer to divine beings composing the heavenly court of the Almighty God (also, 1Kgs.22:19; Jb.1:6) (NOAB/NRSV, p.3 OT, fn. 1.26; Brown, New Jerome Biblical Commentary, 77:23-31, p.1288-90, 2:4.26,p.11, 2:2, p.8-9). The Hebrew Scriptures accepted the mythical imagery of a divine assembly, but the One True God Yahweh made the decisions alone (Deut.32:6-9; Isa.40:10-5, 25-6; Jb.1: 6-12, 2:1-7). The truth of Genesis 1:26 is not explicit proof for God as the Holy Trinity. The truth of the verse is that Almighty God made mankind in God's image and in God's likeness with mankind's ability to freely choose prayers for the worship of God, thoughts of obedience to God, feelings of love for God.

Fundamentalists, who interpreted the Bible with literal infallibility, may claim a Trinitarian doctrine in Genesis 1:26 and in Matthew 28: 19. However, historical and critical study of the Bible allowed no such easy way to understand the Truth of God in the Mystery of the Holy Trinity. Early believers in Jesus Christ returned to prayers, thoughts, feelings, and they concentrated on a trajectory going beyond biblical categories and yet faithful to the direction of Sacred Scriptures. That process happened to the Apostles/Disciples at the first Pentecost and to the Church Bishops at the Council of Nicaea in 325.

Apostles and Disciples went from a scared group remembering Jesus' death on the cross and Christ's Resurrection to preachers and teachers of Jesus the Christ filled with fortitude of the Third Person of the Blessed Trinity (Acts2:1-47). The Apostles and Disciples at the first Pentecost had no written New Testament to muddle over for the right answers. They lived the New Testament with their experiences alive with God the Holy Spirit. They had to pray, think, feel beyond the Hebrew Scriptures to explain their Jesus-experiences of Cross and Resurrection. Their prayers, thoughts, feelings combined with their Spirit-experiences of Pentecost in relation to Yahweh, the One True Almighty God of Abraham/Isaac/Jacob.

Church Bishops at the Council of Nicaea had the testimonies of the Apostles, the New Testament, and 325 years of Christianity to help them. However, the fortitude of the Third Person of the Blessed Trinity inspired the prayers, thoughts, feelings of the Bishops to go beyond the Old and New Testaments. They defined the doctrine of the Most Holy Trinity within the faithful direction from Holy Scriptures.

3.0 Spiritual Dynamics and Symbols of Holy Trinity

Teens, please, note that developed theological doctrine from a biblical trajectory in later years implies neither lesser faith nor lesser holiness of the Apostles and early believers in Jesus Christ because of the incomplete Christian doctrine. The developed doctrine of the Mystery of the Holy Trinity with nuances of Three Persons (Father, Son, Spirit) in One God did not automatically produce a greater faith and a holier life. Faith in the salvation of Jesus the Christ from the beginning opened people to a "deep holiness of life" (Exegesis, p. 135). It is hard to imagine a person in any age more full of faith and more holy than Mother Mary. Mary was the first and most consistent "Christian disciple" based on Luke's criterion of hearing and doing the Word of God (Ibid., p.93-4).

It is also important for Teenagers to remember that defining the doctrine of the Most Holy Trinity is ultimately about the love of God for human beings. If Jesus Christ is not "true God from true God," modern Teens do not know God in human terms. If Jesus was just a good guy or even the most perfect creature, the maximum that Jesus could tell Teenagers about the transcendent God was simply second hand info given by God to a creature like a martyred prophet.

On the other hand, if Jesus Christ is "true God from true God" as Catholic Teens proclaim in the Nicene Creed at every Sunday Mass, then Teenagers know the tremendous love of God for Teens. Father Brown stated in An Introduction to New Testament Christology:

> Only if Jesus is truly of God do we know what God is like, for in Jesus we see God translated into terms that we can understand. A God who sent a marvelous creature as our

Savior could be described as loving, but that love would have cost God nothing in a personal way. Only if Jesus is truly of God do we know that God's love was so real that it reached the point of personal self-giving. This is why the proclamation of Nicaea was and is so important–not only because it tells us about Jesus, but because it tells us about God. p.150-1

    Catholic Teenagers receive the benefits from so many serious spiritual thinkers when they make the Sign of the Cross before and after prayers. Teenagers pray with the Unity of the Most Holy Trinity, "In the name of the Father, and of the Son, and of the Holy Spirit." Credit God the Holy Spirit working through past spiritual thinkers that modern Teens accept as a way of life the Unity of One God in Three Divine Persons without really thinking about the ramifications. The Sign of the Cross with the vocalized or thought Trinitarian words is a proper and true way for Catholic Teens to pray, worship God, feel the truth about God. It is so simple an action for Jesus and so simple a formula for the Triune God that parents teach their pre-k children the sign with the words. Both the sign and the words remain with the child for a lifetime. However, it is not simple theology to understand. The Trinitarian words contain thoughts, feelings, faith, trust, prayer, and worship for almost 2000 years.

    There is much value and even salvation in the Teenage choice to grow in the knowledge of God through prayers to God the Father, thoughts and feelings about God the Son, love and worship of God the Holy Spirit. Teens may utilize highfalutin words to describe this inner dynamics of Teen spirituality and the understanding of God the Most Holy Trinity. However, Teens may also utilize simple symbols to express proper dignity and respect for the Mystery of God in the Holy Trinity. If Teens consider the three all-encompassing actions or movements or "jobs" of God in relation to mankind, Teens know and experience God the Father through creation, God the Son through redemption, God the Holy Spirit through sanctification. However, the distinct "jobs" of God intertwine and overlap within the Unity of the Most Holy Trinity.

    As a result, symbols for God the Most Holy Trinity may include the following thoughts, but these symbols are imperfect and certainly do not exhaust a list:
(1) Sign of the Cross...with Trinitarian words;
(2) rosebush...three blooms on one stalk in one root system;
(3) isosceles triangle... one figure with three equal sides and three equal interior angles;
(4) straight line...one geometric element with path of one point on one line moving outward to infinity;

(5) circle...one plane curve where every point is equally distant from a fixed point within it and the group of points are bound by a common tie to itself;
(6) ray of light...one beam of radiant light energy;
(7) rainbow...In Genesis 9:11-17 the rainbow was God's sign of the covenant with Noah. In Ezekiel 1:28 splendor of rainbows resembled God's glory and absolute majesty: "Like the bow in a cloud on a rainy day, such was the appearance of the splendor all around. This was the appearance of the likeness of the glory of the Lord."

If we expand Ezekiel's vision report from 593B.C. with the modern Teen imagination in search of a pious symbol for God the Most Holy Trinity, we may express the relationship of God and Teenager with a "Rainbow Bridge." The Rainbow Bridge has the three primary colors (gold, emerald, violet) and symbolizes God the Most Holy Trinity. A bright light of truth is equally in the essence and the elements of the rainbow before the perceived brilliant shine of the three individual but united colors. One end of the Rainbow Bridge is positive spirituality of the individual Teenager. The other end is access to God through Teen prayers of thanksgiving, adoration, forgiveness, petition as the progressive growth pattern of knowing, loving, and worshiping God. A Rainbow Bridge is God's Golden Means (helpful resources for holy existence). The Rainbow Bridge is Unity of the Divine Presence in God the Holy Trinity. The Rainbow Bridge of the Most Holy Trinity is the connection and balance through the power of God between the macrocosm of the Teen's spiritual world and the microcosm of the individual Teen's cell of spirituality. The Rainbow Bridge looks pretty and puts the Teen in a very good mood. The Rainbow Bridge is a symbol of God the Most Holy Trinity to help Teens feel special.

b. Grace

When Teenagers choose to live daily prayer through efforts to increase love, worship, knowledge of God, Teens experience a living God. The One True God is in past definitions of the Holy Trinity and in the Holy Scriptures from antiquity. The One True God is also alive today for Teens. The media usually concentrates on the spectacular and the negative with the ulterior motive to sell stuff. However, the Almighty God of All Love exists out of the headlines and in the hearts and minds of everyday Teenagers. In a spiritual journey of the Teen to God, the Teenager usually experiences the same thing that Bully experienced with his horse. Teens experience the Grace of God. For Bully, grace was in one slobber kiss from his horse. Bully instantly loved his horse and all horses.

One might say that Bully had a "root experience" like the root experience in the Hebrew Exodus from Egyptian slavery to freedom of worship for the One True God. The grace of God shook Bully and the exiting Hebrews to their spiritual roots. The direct intervention of

God into Hebrew history defined the character of the people. The grace of God in the slobber kiss of the horse defined and established the individual character of Bully. Love was the result of grace. Bully chose to change his mind and heart from a bad Bully to Good Bully because of love. Bully had a conversion of mind and heart because of love. Bully became an individual graced by God.

The concept of grace most definitely is an expression for the love of God. However, grace, like Holy Trinity, deals with the Mystery of God and with the eyes of faith. Teens know that the Mystery of God suggests as heavy or light as the Teen wants to get into theology. There is the grace of an ice skater, ballet dancer, or football receiver jumping high for a superstar catch. There is the grace in the prayers before and after meals. There exists an entirely different tone in the conversation with the definition of grace as "God's free and forgiving self-communication that enables humans to share in the trinitarian relationship of love" (Encyclopedia, p.577).

Grace (Greek, "charis"; Latin, "gratia") never had only a single meaning in Catholic theology. The concept of grace is a developed theology, like the theology of the Most Holy Trinity, with progressive understanding of the ramifications for relationship with God. In the New Testament Gospels, the word charis/grace is neither in Matthew nor in Mark, but charis is in Luke eight times and in John four times. Charis/grace occurs 101 times in the bulk of Paul's collected works to help form his theological vision. However, Stephen Duffy in The Dynamics of Grace provides clarification:

> Not that Paul provides a theology of grace or that the rest of the Christian Scriptures are ignorant of the reality Paul calls grace. Paul uses *charis* often because of its association with themes central to his thought. Grace, however, never became a focal point of explicit theological reflection until the time of Augustine (354-430)...This does not imply that all talk of grace is second-order language. p.17

In a basic understanding, grace refers to the love of God within a relationship of the Most Holy Trinity, and therefore, "to the favor God bestows upon us: the gift of divine life itself" (Catholicism, p.171). If stated holistically and simplistically, the equations become a life with grace = a life with love and a life without grace = a life with fear. The Catholic Church declares and affirms: "Grace is a *participation in the life of God*. It introduces us into the intimacy of Trinitarian life: by Baptism the Christian participates in the grace of Christ... Grace is *favor*, the *free and undeserved help* that God gives us to respond to his call to become children of God, adoptive sons, partakers of the divine nature and of eternal life" (Catechism, n.1997-6; 2Pet.1:4; Jn. 1:12-8, 17:3; Rom.8:14-7; 2Pet.1:3-4).

The two definitions in the Catechism reflect the early Christian perspectives of the writers and theologians in East and West. The Eastern/Greek Church developed a tradition of grace with emphasis on participation in divine life (2Pet.1:4) and on divine indwelling of the Holy Spirit in the human (Jn.14:23). The approach of the Eastern Church included the sharing of grace through the participation in the sacraments especially Baptism and the Holy Eucharist. In the Greek Church, death was the major consequence of sin, and theologians stressed immortality with God as the special effect of grace.

The Western/Latin Church developed a tradition of grace with emphasis on the healing effect of grace (Rom.3:23-24; Titus3:6-7) and on the resultant salvation from sin (Eph.2:4-7; Titus2:11-3). Saint Augustine greatly influenced the approach of the Latin Church, and he sparked theological debates for many centuries. The approach of the Western Church included sharing of grace through participation in the sacraments especially Baptism and Reconciliation (Penance/Confession). In the Latin Church, guilt was a major consequence of sin with death as the penalty, and theologians stressed immortality in hell with Satan as the special effect of no grace.

1.0 Eastern/Greek Church and Western/Latin Church

Sharing some notes concerning the Eastern/Greek Church and Western/Latin Church are necessary for proper understanding of the theological debates in the early life of the Catholic Church. During the time of the historical Jesus of Nazareth, Jerusalem and Palestine areas were melting pots for diverse cultures. Alexander the Great (d.323B.C.) conquered and "Hellenized" the entire Mediterranean world. He established the Greek culture (philosophy and language) as the basic intellectual force. Emperor Tiberius Caesar (d.37A.D.) inherited the Roman Empire with the Roman Army from Augustus Caesar (d.14A.D.) and Julius Caesar (d.44B.C.). The Latin culture dominated everyday life in the Jerusalem area, but the Greek culture dominated intellectual life throughout the eastern Mediterranean. Jesus of Nazareth was a Jew from Galilee, so the Hebrew culture (ancient Hebrew written scrolls and Aramaic spoken language) was most important in his daily life and in his intellectual life.

After the death, Resurrection, and ascension of Jesus Christ the original Apostles had the difficult task of orally spreading the Gospel of Jesus in the multi-cultured world. Biblical historians assume that they spoke in Latin, Greek, and Aramaic depending on the linguistic talents of the Apostles and the audiences. The writers of the New Testament wrote in Greek. Father McBrien stated: "As the young Church progressively detached itself from Judaism and entered the mainstream of Graeco-Roman civilization, it confronted the challenge of communicating the message of Jesus across diverse social, intellectual, and cultural lines" (Catholicism, p.613).

By the end of the first century, the missionary journeys of Saint Paul established the Church around the eastern and northeastern Mediterranean world. Paul went north and west from the Jerusalem area into Damascus and Antioch (modern Syria), Ephesus and Colossae (modern Turkey), Corinth and Philippi and Thessalonia (modern Greece). Paul ended his career in Rome, his only western missionary city. As a result, his Eastern/Greek bases in the eastern Mediterranean world were home for early Christianity.

In the second and third centuries, Church theologians/leaders established the major theological centers in Alexandria, Egypt and in Antioch, Syria. The two schools were "principal competing forces" in theological debates of the fourth and fifth centuries concerning the humanity/divinity of Jesus Christ and the Holy Trinity. Eastern/Greek thought patterns filled both theological centers of learning. Father McBrien commented, "During the same period theological activity in the Latin West was significantly less pronounced" (Ibid., p.617). The Western/Latin theological centers of learning formed later than the Eastern centers usually around individuals especially in North Africa, home for Augustine (d.430) of Hippo (now Annaba, Algeria), and in Rome, home for the Petrine (the Apostle Peter) trajectory.

A defining moment in the East-West Christian theology was the political and the military success of Constantine the Great (d.337), Emperor of the re-united Roman Empire. Constantine had a major impact on the Mediterranean world and Christianity in only 25 years: conquered Western Roman Empire in 312; became Christian in 312; gave Christians in West and East religious freedom and legitimacy with Edict of Milan/Constantine in 313; conquered Eastern Roman Empire in 324; called Church leaders to first Council of Nicaea in 325 (at his summer home in modern-day Turkey); moved the capitol of Roman Empire from Rome to Constantinople (now Istanbul, Turkey) in 330; received baptism in 337. Constantine's patronage, protection, and imperial favor allowed the development of the institutionalized Catholicism, the proclamation of Jesus' Gospel to all nations, and a theological order in doctrine through the Church Councils.

All the doctrinal controversies in the 4th and 5th centuries about the Holy Trinity and the mystery of Jesus' humanity/divinity occurred in a Greek-speaking East, and all the early Church Councils to solve theological problems were in the East (Ibid., p.616-7). Undercurrents of the East-West theological tensions existed from the beginning of the Christian heritage because of a legitimate variety in the Churches of the Apostles and in theological expressions of developing doctrine (see, Brown, The Churches the Apostles Left Behind). With distinct articulation of Saint Augustine on the concept of grace, there were sharp contrasts between the East-West theologies as applied to the pastoral needs of the Christian people.

1.1 East-West Schism

Unfortunately for all Christians of all times, there developed slow estrangement between the Eastern/Greek Church and Western/Latin Church. The result was the "East-West Schism" and the history of a divided Christianity. Both East and West Churches share the sorry responsibilities for the aggressive Church politics and the breach of Christian faith. The total absurdity of the Christian breach is no less absurd than individual historical straws that broke the camel's back.

For example, East-West gaps widened in the 8th century with the foolhardy attempt of the Eastern emperors to enforce "iconoclasm" (abolishing religious images and paintings) because of the warped sense of personal imperial piety. In 726 to 843, Eastern emperors destroyed religious images and brutally persecuted Christians in the East. Monks had the choice between a forced marriage or blinded then exiled (Encyclopedia, p.650).

A horrific lack of communication magnified problems between West and East. The West no longer understood the nuances of the Greek language, and leaders did not discern the differences between "veneration" and "adoration." The monks and Christians in the East recommended veneration of paintings and images to help elevate spiritual life. Westerners thought that Easterners meant the adoration of paintings and images, which was idolatry. The Eastern emperors used the theological controversy to renew persecutions of Christians until Empress Theodora restored the veneration of icons in 843.

Miscommunication got worse between West and East. Leo IX was the Pope in the West (1049-54), and Michael Cerularius (d.1058) was the patriarch of Constantinople. Pope Leo IX insisted that the Easterners, who lived in southern Italy, conform to Latin customs. In reaction Cerularius ordered the Latin churches in Constantinople to adopt the Greek customs. When they refused, he closed them down. Cerularius ordered an Eastern bishop to write a letter denouncing the Latin customs and to send the letter to the Pope. The letter arrived at the time when the Normans of the "barbarian invasions" not only defeated the army of the Pope but also captured Pope Leo IX. As a result, Humbert of Silva Candida, the cardinal-secretary of the Pope, received the letter. He mistranslated the Greek in the letter, and he exaggerated the letter's offensive tone. Humbert dispatched papal legates, including himself, to Constantinople.

Father McBrien described the disastrous results:

> To compress the story: The legates botched their diplomatic mission, dealing heavy-handedly with the patriarch. On July 16, 1054, they marched into the Church of Santa Sophia just before the afternoon liturgy and laid on the altar a bull [papal document] excommunicating Michael Cerularius, the emperor, and all their followers, and then departed,

ceremoniously shaking the dust from their feet. The general populace...rioted and could be calmed only after a public burning of the bull. <u>Catholicism</u>, p.626

However, Church historians give no exact date for the beginning of the East-West Schism. Most of the historians point to the Fourth Crusade (1202-04) as the last wedge that split Christianity into East and West. Western knights displayed a gross abuse of prideful ego and temporal power. In 1203, the Western crusaders sacked and looted the city of Constantinople. Crusaders stole and plundered the most valuable souvenirs throughout the city. Western knights did not even spare the Eastern churches (Ibid., p.627). Western crusaders stole holy objects of veneration from the Eastern Church.

1.2 Vatican II Calls For East-West Unity

The scandal of the split in Christianity exists at the beginning of the third millennium. The hope for the unity of Christianity is in the implementation of the <u>Decree on Ecumenism (Unitatis Redintegratio)</u> from Vatican II Council (1962-65). Vatican II was a truly ecumenical council with the 2,908 Bishops eligible for participation (1,089 from Europe, 489 from South America, 404 from North America, 374 from Asia, 296 from Africa, 84 from Central America, 75 from Oceania). The Decree states that a principal concern for the Vatican II Council was the "restoration of unity among all Christians" and that "division openly contradicts the will of Christ, scandalizes the world, and damages that most holy cause, the preaching of the Gospel to every creature" (n.1).

The Decree explains "certain rifts" in the time of the Apostles (1 Cor.11:18-9; Gal. 1:6-9; 1Jn.2:18-9), but "men of both sides were to blame" for the separation of the large communities of Christians from the Catholic Church (n.3). The Decree acknowledges that Churches based on Jesus Christ (i.e., Eastern Orthodox or Oriental Churches, Reformation Churches) share the same Sacred Scriptures, the same life of grace, the same faith/hope/charity, the same gifts of the Holy Spirit (n.3). A basic unity comes with overcoming "obstacles" in the doctrine, discipline, and Church structure (n.3). The way to Christian unity involves reform and renewal of the Catholic Church (n.6), and a change of heart and holiness of life (n.7). The Decree clearly states: "This change of heart and holiness of life, along with public and private prayer for the unity of Christians, should be regarded as the soul of the whole ecumenical movement, and merits the name, 'spiritual ecumenism' " (n.8).

<u>Decree on Ecumenism</u> deals directly with the East-West Schism:

> For many centuries the Churches of the East and of the West went their own ways, though a brotherly communion of

faith and sacramental life bound them together...From their very origins the Churches of the East have had a treasury from which the Church of the West has drawn largely for its liturgy, spiritual tradition and jurisprudence. Nor must we underestimate the fact that the basic dogmas of the Christian faith concerning the Trinity and the Word of God made flesh from the Virgin Mary were defined in Ecumenical Councils held in the East...the heritage handed down by the apostles was received differently and in different forms, so that from the very beginnings of the Church its development varied from region to region and also because of differing mentalities and ways of life. These reasons, plus external causes, as well as the lack of charity and mutual understanding, left the way open for divisions...These Churches, although separated from us, yet possess true sacraments, above all – by apostolic succession – the priesthood and the Eucharist, whereby they are still joined to us in closest intimacy... What has already been said about legitimate variety we are pleased to apply to differences in theological expressions of doctrine. In the study of revealed truth East and West have used different methods and approaches in understanding and confessing divine things. It is hardly surprising, then, if sometimes one tradition has come nearer to a full appreciation of some aspects of a mystery of revelation than the other, or has expressed them better. In such cases, these various theological formulations are often to be considered complementary rather than conflicting...the Council hopes that with the removal of the wall dividing the Eastern and Western Church at last there may be but one dwelling, firmly established on the cornerstone, Christ Jesus, who will make both one.
     n.14, 15, 17, 18 (See also, Catechism, No. 817-822)

   It was the hope and prayer of the Bishops at the Second Vatican Council that the Roman Catholic Church reunites with the Churches of the East and the Churches of the Reformation. Unity is not reality yet. My personal prayers of petitions include the hope that certain modern Teenagers respond to God's grace and choose a career in Theology to repair the spiritual damage by reuniting all the Christian Churches in the worship of the Most Holy God. Teenagers, will you, please, bring Christians together with your prayers and your study of Theology, thank you?
   The Eastern/Greek Church and Western/Latin Church developed very distinct traditions about the theology of God's grace because of divergent ways of life and the different mentalities. Father McBrien analyzed both early Christian perspectives:

The Greek Fathers (from Origen on) developed a doctrine of grace in keeping with the Trinitarian questions of the period. Because the Spirit is truly God, we are truly *divinized* by the presence of the Spirit, i.e., we participate in divine life...The Greek doctrine of grace is optimistic about salvation, therefore, because the Holy Spirit truly dwells within us... Western Fathers (Augustine, and others) were less interested in the intellectual and cosmic aspects of divinization and more *moralistic* in tendency. They also oriented their theology of grace toward the history of salvation and of the individual... Grace is a free gift of God and, because of sin, is necessary for salvation... Augustine's view of grace was also *sacramental* in character. He saw 'vestiges of the Trinity' throughout all of creation...He stressed the damage done to human nature by Original Sin and the radical incapacity of the human person to fulfill the will of God without God's grace.   Catholicism, p.174-5

2.0 Saint Thomas Aquinas and Modern Teens

Both the Eastern tradition of the Greek Fathers and the Western tradition of the Latin Fathers reflected truth about grace. It was Saint Thomas Aquinas (d.1274) who synthesized the spiritual concepts of grace. Saint Thomas Aquinas was a Dominican Priest who prayed, thought, felt deeply and spiritually about humans in relationship with the Mystery of the Most Holy Trinity. He developed the theology of grace, which incorporated Western (Augustine) emphasis on healing aspects of grace with Eastern emphasis on human participation in the divine life of love through the indwelling of God the Holy Spirit in men and women.

Young Aquinas made the distinctions between "uncreated grace" (inner life of the Holy Trinity) and "created grace" (change made in individual by God's life of love). Stephen Duffy analyzed Aquinas: "Grace is either uncreated, God's own self as the gracious giver, or a created gift superadded to natural human powers and rendering their acts meritorious. This created gift, moreover, perfects the essence of the soul" (Dynamics, p.127).

Saint Thomas made distinctions between "sanctifying grace" and "actual grace" (Summa Theologica, I-II,q.112, a.2; q.111, a.2; q.110, a.2). Sanctifying or habitual grace refers to the indwelling of God the Holy Spirit in a human, and it "perfects" a soul (innermost aspect or spiritual principle of man/woman) to live with God and act by God's love (Catechism, n.363, 2000). Actual grace is God's assistance or divine influence of God or the "interventions" of God to help humans perform positive actions (Ibid.). Duffy analyzed nuances in Aquinas' mature understanding of his developed theology of grace:

> Habitual grace is tacit, unobtrusive, awaiting its moment; actual grace is its moment of fuller integration with God, self, others, the world. The gift of the Spirit is hidden within... Actual grace, God's operation from without, while not intermittent, comes to us in unique moments; habitual grace, God's operation from within, is the quiet but steady undertow in our lives that pulls us into the mysterious depth where alone the heart finds the fulfillment of its desire... Sanctifying or habitual grace... amounts to a participation in the divine life. It may be lost by serious sin and regained in penance.
>
> Dynamics, p.160-162

The basic end result of such heavy medieval metaphysics was that "Aquinas described the function of grace as both the healing of human nature wounded by sin, and as the elevating of human nature to participation in the divine life" (Catholicism, p.176). Saint Thomas Aquinas bridged the theological gap between Eastern/Greek Church and Western/Latin Church. Aquinas also bridges the chronological gap between the time of Jesus Christ and the time of modern Teens. Aquinas' theology of grace applied to the people in the 1st and 13th centuries, and it applies to Teens in the 21st century.

2.1 Mary Full of Grace

For example, it is hard to imagine a person in any age more full of grace, more holy, and more full of faith than Mary the Mother of Jesus. Using Aquinas' synthesized criteria for grace as healing the human nature and as elevating the human nature to God's divine life, Mary is the excellent model for "full of grace" in the 1st century. The grace of God healed Mary from sin (the Immaculate Conception) and elevated Mary to participate in divine life in the most special way as the Mother of Jesus, the Second Person of God. As a result, Mary is the Mother of Divine Grace, Jesus. Gabriel, the angel of God at the Annunciation of the holy birth of the Redeemer, declared the divine revelation to Mary with a divine communication: "Greetings, favored one! The Lord is with you" (NOAB/NRSV, Lk.1:28); and in another translation, "Rejoice, O highly favored daughter! The Lord is with you. Blessed are you among women" (NAB, Lk.1:28).

Luke freely composed the Gospel in the Greek language for his Greek readers. He chose two Greek verbs, "*chaire kecharitomene*," for the Annunciation expression of Angel Gabriel in the oldest extant biblical manuscripts. The two stem words closely related two verbs. *Chaire* was a verb that meant literally "rejoice." In everyday salutes, the Greek word meant, "hail, hello, good day, greetings." However, *kecharitomene* was from the verb "*charitoun*," and it meant "to make one favored, to give one grace." The verb had the same stem as the noun *charis*, "grace, favor."

Luke chose the ordinary Greek verb, *chaire*, for Gabriel the angel to say "hello." However, Luke chose the very unusual Greek verb, *kecharitomene*, for reference to Mary "as one who has been favored or graced by God" (Brown, Birth of the Messiah, p.326). The word, *kecharitomene*, was the highly charged theological word meaning the "favored one" which linguistically and theologically equals "full of grace." *Charitoun*, the root verb of *kecharitomene*, was a very rare verb used only twice in the New Testament (Lk.1:28; Eph.1:6), and "the verb occurs only about a dozen times in literature between the second century B.C. and the fifth century A.D. (Ibid., p.326, fn.86; p. 288, fn.28; 321-7; Catechism, n.2676).

With Luke's careful choice of words, his first century audience probably paused to feel and think about the dignity and the respect awarded to Mary, Mother of Jesus. The divine revelation of Gabriel, angel of God, communicated a high esteem of God for Mary with the vernacular greeting, "Hail, Mary, full of grace." And yet, it was Mary's choice to decide her reaction to the Angel Gabriel and to the grace of God. Mary decided with a real humility, "Here am I, the servant of the Lord; let it be with me according to your word" (Lk.1:38). Mary chose obedience to the will of God the Father. The obedience of Mary meant that the Most Holy Child historically named Jesus and theologically called Son of God entered salvation history of mankind.

Modern Teenagers may want to pause, think, feel the impact of grace from the virtue of obedience to the will of God. Jesus started his human life with the obedience of Mother Mary to the will of God the Father. Jesus ended his human life on the cross with his own obedience to the will of God the Father. From the first obedience of Mary to the last obedience of Jesus, God's will was done.

In the Middle Ages, Thomas Aquinas distinguished the healing and elevating functions of actual and sanctifying grace in retrospect to the Gospel of Luke in the first century. In the writings of Luke and in the definitions of Aquinas, Mary was full of grace. The Bishops at Vatican II professed in the twentieth century the same dignity and respect for Mary full of grace as Luke and Aquinas. In the Dogmatic Constitution of the Church (Lumen Gentium) the Bishops stated:

> ...she is endowed with the...dignity of the Mother of the Son of God...Because of this gift of sublime grace she far surpasses all creatures, both in heaven and on earth (n.53) ...the Fathers see Mary not merely as passively engaged by God, but as freely cooperating in the work of man's salvation through faith and obedience (n.56)... She conceived, brought forth, and nourished Christ, she presented him to the Father in the temple, shared her Son's sufferings as he died on the cross. Thus, in a wholly singular way she cooperated by her obedience, faith, hope and burning charity in the work of the Savior in restoring supernatural life to souls. For this reason

she is a mother to us in the order of grace (n.61)...Mary has by grace been exalted above all angels and men to a place second only to her Son, as the most holy mother of God who was involved in the mysteries of Christ... n.66

In definitions of grace from all ages, the first century Mother Mary is full of grace.

2.2 Teens Full of Grace

The genius of Saint Thomas Aquinas conveys to modern Teens that grace enables and empowers Teenagers to share the love of the Most Holy Trinity and to share a relationship of mutual friendship with God. Through prayers, thoughts, feelings about God the Teen may choose to live within sanctifying grace and to accept the spot help of actual grace in tough times. Sanctifying grace and actual grace fill a modern Teen with holiness. Teens have the potential to add "Saint" in front of their names. Based on free choices, Teenagers have the ability to conquer death, guilt, sin, evil spirits and to gain immortality with God through the special effects of God's grace. God waits on Teens to respond with action. Prayer with dignity and respect for the Most Holy Trinity activates dynamics of Teen spirituality and elevates Teen prayer-life above a kindergarten level.

The Almighty God, who did the actions of the physical creation, can do the two spiritual actions of healing Teenagers and elevating Teens to divine holiness. Actual grace is God's help for Teenagers to bow to God's divine moral authority. Sanctifying grace is God's life of love shared with Teens. Teens in grace share God's divine love. Holy Teens are full of grace just like Mother Mary.

Teens do not need to hold God's gift of grace hostage to God's gift of free choice. Grace and free choice co-exist. Teenagers can use freedom of choice to float between good and evil, or Teens can use freedom of choice to pray for the actual and sanctifying grace of God. One choice may make Teenagers popular with some peers, but the other choice makes Teens popular with God. One choice may make Teens rich, powerful, full of status in now time until the grave, but the other choice gives Teens the wealth of the divine friendship with the All Powerful God for all of God's time. One choice may make Teens temporarily surrender to the negative peer pressures, but the other choice makes Teens sensitive and perceptive to understand divine influences and directions. The choice to pray for grace is the choice to share the spiritual action of God.

Teenagers, who physically see and process in minds and hearts the beauty of the many shades of colors, have a potential to see and experience beautiful spirituality. God's blessings on all Teens include God's call to holy relationship with God. The dignity and respect of God for each Teenager includes instilling a holy longing for God in each Teen without deleting the Teen's individual freedom to choose good or evil. A delicate balance of God in the dynamics of Teenage spirituality empowers each Teenager to love God, self, and neighbor. God wants (but does not demand to the point of the Teen loss of free choice) a love relationship with each Teen. Potential exists in each Teen for the awesome spiritual reality of a love relationship with the Most Holy Trinity through the actual and sanctifying grace of God. Prayer is the basic connection of the Teenager with God. Prayers jump-start the "Dynamics of Teenage Spirituality." The choice of the Teen to pray establishes a dynamic connection between the Teen's freedom to respond and God's freedom to invite relationship.

c. *Most Holy Eucharist*

Sometimes Teenagers are so happy that they simply want to say thanks for the happy times. Sometimes Teenagers are so sad that they simply want to say I am sorry and please end the sad times. Sometimes Teens simply want to recognize and genuinely smile at the Power Person. Sometimes Teens simply want to ask the Power Person for some help. Teenagers see with their spiritual eyes that these are truly fine times to pray to the awesome God with prayers of thanksgiving, forgiveness, adoration, petitions.

Another fine time for the modern Teenager to pray is during the Mass. When the modern Teen wants to bring all types of prayers together with a choice to live daily prayers through actively knowing, loving, worshiping God and with a developed theology in centuries of spiritual thoughts from high-powered spiritual thinkers, there is the Eucharistic Prayer in the Mass. The Mass is simply a fine and holy time for modern Teens to pray.

The Mass is the public ritual prayer of the Catholic Church for the worship of God. It has for Teens the actual and sanctifying grace of God the Most Holy Trinity. The Mass is a spiritual platform for many combinations of positive thoughts and spiritual feelings for Teens. It has the Liturgy of the Word, which is the reading of Sacred Scripture from the writings of the prophets in the Old Testament and from the memoirs of the Apostles in the New Testament. The Mass also has the Liturgy of the Eucharist, which is consecration and Eucharistic conversion of bread and wine into the body and the blood of Jesus Christ. For 2,000 years the Catholic faith expressed the Divine and Real Presence of Jesus Christ in the Most Holy Eucharist as Mystery of the Divine Essence of God. For a modern Catholic Teenager the Mass has a Holy Communion with Jesus Christ the Second Person of God. In good and bad times, the Mass is God's grace to modern Teens. It has the potential for a dynamic spiritual reality in Teen life.

Today's Mass is the liturgical celebration for the Sacrament of the Eucharist. The Mass contains Eucharistic Prayers with ancient traditions that go all the way back to the beginnings of the Church.

Eucharist is the Greek word meaning "thanksgiving." At his Last Supper described in the New Testament, Jesus "gave thanks" in four Eucharistic Institution Narratives:

(1) <u>Mark 14:22-25</u>: During the meal he took bread, blessed and broke it, and gave it to them. "Take this," he said, "this is my body." He likewise took a cup, gave thanks and passed it to them, and they all drank from it. He said to them: "This is my blood, the blood of the covenant, to be poured out on behalf of many. I solemnly assure you, I will never again drink of the fruit of the vine until the day when I drink it new in the reign of God" (<u>NAB</u>);

(2) <u>Matthew 26:26-29</u>: During the meal Jesus took bread, blessed it, broke it, and gave it to his disciples. "Take this and eat it," he said, "this is my body." Then he took a cup, gave thanks, and gave it to them. "All of you must drink from it," he said, "for this is my blood, the blood of the covenant, to be poured out in behalf of many for the forgiveness of sins. I tell you, I will not drink this fruit of the vine from now until the day when I drink it new with you in my Father's reign" (<u>NAB</u>);

(3) <u>Luke 22:15-20</u>: He said to them: "I have greatly desired to eat this Passover with you before I suffer. I tell you, I will not eat again until it is fulfilled in the kingdom of God." Then taking a cup he offered a blessing in thanks and said: "Take this and divide it among you; I tell you, from now on I will not drink of the fruit of the vine until the coming of the reign of God." Then, taking bread and giving thanks, he broke it and gave it to them, saying: "This is my body to be given for you. Do this as a remembrance of me." He did the same with the cup after eating, saying as he did so: "This cup is the new covenant in my blood, which will be shed for you" (<u>NAB</u>);

(4) <u>1Corinthians 11:23-26</u>: ...the Lord Jesus on the night in which he was betrayed took bread, and after he had given thanks, broke it and said, "This is my body, which is for you. Do this in remembrance of me." In the same way, after the supper, he took the cup, saying, "This cup is the new covenant in my blood. Do this, whenever you drink it, in remembrance of me." Every time, then, you eat this bread and drink this cup, you proclaim the death of the Lord until he comes (<u>NAB</u>).

1.0 Most Holy Moment

Modern Teenagers hear the Eucharistic Prayers requested by the Vatican II Bishops and approved by Pope Paul VI in 1969. The Eucharistic Prayers are a synthesis of the four Eucharistic Institution Narratives in the New Testament, but the Prayers have the identical words of institution over the bread and the wine. Ordained Priests consecrate the bread and the wine in every Mass with the ancient words of Jesus:

> The day before he suffered he took bread in his sacred hands and looking up to heaven, to you, his almighty Father, he gave you thanks and praise. He broke the bread, gave it to his disciples, and said: Take this, all of you, and eat it: this is my body which will be given up for you. When supper was ended, he took the cup. Again he gave you thanks and praise, gave the cup to his disciples, and said: Take this, all of you, and drink from it: this is the cup of my blood, the blood of the new and everlasting covenant. It will be shed for you and for all so that sins may be forgiven. Do this in memory of me.   The Sacramentary, Eucharistic Prayer I

This is a most holy prayer in a most holy moment. Why? Catholics with the eyes of faith believe that the substance/essence of the consecrated bread and the consecrated wine is no longer bread and wine. At the moment of consecration due to "transubstantiation" the substance of the bread changes into the substance of the body of Christ, and the substance of the wine changes into the substance of the blood of Christ (Catechism, n.1376). In the Mystery of the Eucharist, Jesus Christ exists in the "Eucharistic Change" from bread and wine to the body and blood of Christ (Moloney, The Eucharist, p. 54-61). The Divine and Real Presence of Jesus Christ the Second Person of God is alive in the "Eucharistic conversion" from bread and wine to body and blood of Christ in the liturgy, the worship, the life of the Catholic Church (Pope Paul VI, Mysterium Fidei, n.38-9, 46, 51).

The physical sight of the consecrated bread and the consecrated wine does not look like the body and blood of the God of All Power. Remember, Teens, that the sight of Jesus hanging nailed to a Cross with 120 scourge marks on his body and 70 thorn marks on his head also did not look like the God of All Power. God is Divine Mystery. It sometimes takes humans a while to catch on to Divine Love.

When the Catholic Teenager chooses to receive the consecrated host in the Holy Communion, it is a most special communication with God. When the Catholic Teenager receives the Holy Eucharist, it is a living prayer of thanksgiving, adoration, forgiveness, petition with the Catholic traditions from centuries of knowing, loving, worshiping God in powerful spiritual thoughts. The Teen has a holy prayer in a holy moment. The Teen has a holy pause full of grace. The Teen is with a dignity and a respect for God the Most Holy Trinity in dynamic spirituality that elevates prayer-life. The Teen thinks and feels grace, love, hope, faith, humility, fortitude, trust, communion with the Most Holy God of Antiquity.

1.1 New Testament Eucharistic Institution Narratives

It is ancient Church tradition that Jesus and the Twelve Apostles shared his Last Supper as his Passover ritual meal and his farewell religious meal. The Twelve in turn honored his memorial command and shared Eucharistic meals with disciples and the early followers of Jesus. There were differences in the early churches as the belief in Jesus the Christ spread throughout the Roman Empire. However, the Eucharistic Prayers were vital parts of all early church traditions. The four Eucharistic Institution Narratives in the New Testament have the same basic structure. Father McBrien states: "The essential kernel of the various reports, however, is clearly part of a unanimous tradition in the New Testament churches... there is undeniable continuity between what happened at the Last Supper and what the disciples did together at meals after the resurrection" (Catholicism, p. 820, 822).

Jesus did not sit and chit chat with the Twelve Apostles about meaning and implications for his Eucharistic words of consecration at his Last Supper. Jesus moved to his prayers of agony in the garden. It was time for God's intervention into mankind's history with saving action of the Son's Passion, Crucifixion, Death, Resurrection. It was time for the Savior to redeem mankind from all sin and for the Divine Presence to restore the People of God to worthy relationship with the Most Holy God.

Prayers, thoughts, feelings about the meaning and implications of the Eucharistic words of Jesus came with the post-resurrectional faith of the Apostles and disciples. Theologians and biblical scholars studied the four New Testament Eucharistic Institution Narratives (Mk.14:22-4; Mt.26:26-8; Lk.22:19-20; 1Cor.11:23-5). The biblical scholars and theologians recognized two ancient traditions in four biblical texts of Eucharistic Institution Narratives. The Mark-Matthew Eucharistic tradition was primarily a theology of Jesus' redemptive sacrifice on the Cross for the forgiveness of sins. The Luke-Paul Eucharistic tradition was primarily a theology of eschatological (Gk., *eschatos*, "last") joy in a new covenant meal with Jesus the Messiah anticipating the final events at the end of mankind's time when the kingdom/rule of God would manifest itself for God's glory (Eucharist, p.21-2, 11-3). The four Eucharistic rituals in two early traditions were signs of the death and the Resurrection of Jesus Christ.

The Mark-Matthew sacrificial Eucharistic tradition found the Old Testament base in Exodus 24:1-18. The time frame was after Moses received the Ten Commandments but before he constructed the Ark of the Covenant to house them. At the ratification of the covenant, Moses and seventy elders of Israel went to the foot of Mount Sinai. "And Moses wrote down all the words of the Lord" (Ex.24:4). Moses built an altar to offer the holocausts and to sacrifice the young bulls as the burnt peace offerings. Moses put the blood of the animals in two bowls. He splashed the blood in the first bowl on the altar.

He read aloud to the people the book of the covenant containing the words of Yahweh written by Moses. The people agreed to obey the laws and ordinances of God. Moses sprinkled the blood in the second bowl on the people, while he said, "This is the blood of the covenant that the Lord has made with you in accordance with all these words of his" (NAB, Ex.24:8).

Moses proceeded with Aaron, his brother, and seventy elders up the mountain and "saw the God of Israel" (NOAB/ NRSV, Ex.24:10). Divine Holiness did not harm the leaders as they ate the covenant meal. "After gazing on God, they could still eat and drink" (NAB, Ex. 24:11). The Mark-Matthew Eucharistic tradition stressed that Jesus was the sacrifice of the new covenant for the forgiveness of sins.

Luke-Paul Eucharistic tradition with eschatological implications of the new covenant in the future final events at the end of mankind's time found the Old Testament support in Jeremiah 31:31-4. Prophet Jeremiah spoke after the utter destruction of Jerusalem in 587B.C. and during the Babylonian Captivity about a future "new covenant." God told Jeremiah and the exiled people that the Lord "will make a new covenant with the house of Israel" because Hebrew ancestors broke the Sinai Covenant (NOAB/NRSV, Jer.31:31-2). God said that in the new covenant "I will put my law within them, and I will write it on their hearts; and I will be their God, and they shall be my people" (Jer.31:33).

The new covenant of the Lord will last forever in the hearts of the People of God. All share the knowledge of God because "they shall all know me, from the least of them to the greatest, says the Lord; for I will forgive their iniquity, and remember their sin no more" (Jer.31: 34). The Luke-Paul Eucharistic tradition stressed the new covenant in a ritual meal that contained a future joy of final events within the glorious kingdom/rule of God. The eschatological rejoicing was in the human presence at the divine banquet of God the Father with the resurrected Messiah and the Holy Spirit of Jesus.

The modern Teen may see contrasts and similarities in the Old Testament biblical supports and in four New Testament Eucharistic Institution Narratives within the two ancient traditions. Clarifying the interrelationships of the four Eucharistic rituals in the Mark-Matthew and Luke-Paul traditions "must stress the basic unity amongst the four versions, greater than any diversity between them" (Eucharist, p.19). When the biblical scholars add the Eucharistic themes with eschatological implications in the Gospel of John (Jn.6:1-58; 13:1-34) to the four Eucharistic Institution Narratives, the Sacrament of the Most Holy Eucharist becomes the basic unity of early pluralistic churches and today's Catholic Church (Catechism, n.1324-7).

1.2 Eucharistic Themes in Gospel of John

Teenagers, please, note that John's Gospel has no Eucharistic Institution Narrative, but there are Eucharistic themes throughout the Gospel of John (Jn.13:1-34; 6:1-15, 47-58; 2:1-11; 17:1-26). At his Last Supper in John's Gospel, Jesus washed the feet of his disciples to set the premium example of humble service to others, and then Jesus commanded his disciples to love one another (Jn.13:1-17; 34-5). The biblical scholars and theologians puzzle over the absence of the Eucharistic Institution Narrative in the Gospel of John because the "Fourth Gospel, which is so permeated with a Eucharistic spirit, is the only one to draw a veil of silence over the institution of the sacrament" (Eucharist, p.63-4).

The author of John's Gospel wrote in c.90A.D. and was familiar with other Gospel narratives of the Last Supper. The discourse of Jesus at the Last Supper table in John's Gospel has the two major Eucharistic themes of love and unity (Jn.15:9-17; 13:34-5; 17:20-3). The scene also has the "High Priestly Prayer" of Jesus that is the theme of consecration central to Eucharistic Prayers (Jn.17:1-26; 17-9, NAB = "consecrate", NOAB/NRSV = "sanctify"). Nevertheless, the Gospel of John is silent with the actual words of Jesus instituting the Sacrament of Eucharist at his Last Supper.

Biblical scholars and theologians turn to Chapter 6 for the basic teaching on the Eucharist in John's Gospel. Jesus fed the hungry with the multiplication of the loaves of bread (Jn.6:1-14). Sacrament of Eucharist as the food for the spiritually hungry was a continuation of the power manifested by Jesus during his public ministry. But the discourse of Jesus on the "bread of life" produced a sacramental theology of Eucharist and also division among the disciples (Jn.6:25-70). Jesus prescribed that people work for "the food that endures for eternal life" and then have faith in the One whom God sent (Jn.6:27, 29). Jesus said: "I am the bread of life. Whoever comes to me will never be hungry, and whoever believes in me will never be thirsty... I am the living bread that came down from heaven. Whoever eats of this bread will live forever; and the bread that I will give for the life of the world is my flesh" (Jn.6:35, 51).

Jesus used symbolic language often in his public ministry, but this time, when the people took him literally, Jesus did not soften his language. Jesus insisted on realism to the point that cannibalism was not far distant: "Very truly, I tell you, unless you eat the flesh of the Son of Man and drink his blood, you have no life in you. Those who eat my flesh and drink my blood have eternal life, and I will raise them up on the last day; for my flesh is true food and my blood is true drink" (Jn.6:53-5). The Eucharistic teaching of Jesus was most difficult, shocking, provocative, and "because of this many of his disciples turned back and no longer went about with him" (Jn.6:66). Jesus asked the Twelve Apostles if they also wanted to leave him. Peter spoke with the pragmatic eyes of necessary faith: "Lord, to whom can we go? You have the words of eternal life. We have come to believe and know that you are the Holy One of God" (Jn.6:68-9).

Jesus of Nazareth, the Christ, did not tone down his theology of the Eucharist in the Gospel of John for popularity or the increase of followers. Father Moloney concludes:

That by the time of the Fourth Gospel such sensitivity can be set aside is indicative of how much has happened in the intervening years...the early Christians' grasp of the implications of Christ's resurrection strengthened...It would seem that the spiritual nature of this eating and drinking is now so clearly established that it can be taken for granted... The Eucharist is not cannibalism, because Christ's flesh and blood are made present in a sacramental way, not in a crudely physical sense. The eating and drinking are a means of union with the person, not for acquiring a particular quantity of sacred nourishment. <u>The Eucharist</u>, p.71

1.3 Holy Eucharist Elevates Prayer

Jesus Christ changed the way people worship God. Old Hebrew covenants had many bloody animal sacrifices, and the new Christian covenant has Christ's unbloody sacrifice in his Eucharistic Prayer. Jesus instituted his Eucharistic worship of God the Father based on Jewish table rituals with the blessings of Passover customs. Jesus' Eucharistic worship of God the Father gave a new meaning to the ancient memorial sacrifices and to ancient memorial ritual/religious meals. Jesus fused both sacrifice and meal into one complex sign of his bloody physical death and of his powerful bodily Resurrection (Ibid., p.10-12).

Love and Eucharistic unity distinguished the worship of the early Christ-based communities (Acts2:42,46). Mark-Matthew Eucharistic tradition emphasized that Jesus Christ was the offering and sacrifice of the new covenant for forgiveness of sins. Luke-Paul Eucharistic tradition highlighted the new covenant in a memorial ritual meal with connotations of a divine banquet in the company of God the Father, Jesus the suffering servant and resurrected Messiah, the Holy Spirit of Jesus, and the human People of God. Both traditions associated Eucharistic words of Jesus at his Last Supper with commemoration of his death.

The Eucharistic traditions in the Gospel of John contributed to the Eucharistic theology with emphasis on the Eucharist as the food and drink that gave eternal life (Jn.6:51-8). In the Gospel of John, eating the flesh and drinking the blood of Jesus Christ nourished the eternal life. Consequently, the Gospel of John "launched Christianity on the road to a distinctive sacramental theology whereby visible elements are signs communicating divine realities" (<u>Community</u>, p. 78-9, fn.145).

The same spiritual thinkers in the early Church, who thought, felt, prayed about the Holy Trinity and grace, also utilized spiritual energy concerning the Mystery of the Holy Eucharist. No one thought, felt, prayed in a spiritual void or vacuum. Spiritual viewpoints based on prayer moved and flowed within God the Holy Spirit toward the real development of understanding the vision of Jesus on how to live a love relationship with God and with neighbor. "These things God has revealed to us through the Spirit; for the Spirit searches everything, even the depths of God" (1Cor.2:10).

After the Apostles and the early disciples received God the Holy Spirit on Pentecost, they believed that the Holy Spirit helped them to make difficult decisions based on Jesus' vision (Acts2:1-4; 15:1- 29). Ultimately, the vision of Jesus taught Apostles, disciples, evangelists, Christians, spiritual thinkers, theologians, early Christian Churches, modern Teens how to worship God with total love of God's law and total obedience to God's will. Jesus taught us to pray with dignity and respect for God the Father. The Holy Spirit of Jesus moved the theology of the Holy Eucharist through actual and sanctifying grace of God to a beautiful prayer of worship with dignity and respect for the Most Holy Trinity.

Father Moloney wrote in The Eucharist:

> ...the fruits of the Eucharist, whether in Mass or in holy communion, are basically one. We can use different words to describe it, like love, union, life, grace, but always they come back to this: the Eucharist imparts that which it signifies, our ever deeper identity with that mystery of love which poured itself out on the cross and, at the resurrection, released into human history the very life of God...John opens up for us, in words of unforgettable mystery and awe, the wonder of the divinity as a drama of personal love, extended from the eternal Three to embrace all those who turn to Christ. One of the great advances in contemporary theology has been the recovery of the sense of grace as not just an accumulation of created graces but as ultimately the Uncreated Grace of Father, Son and Holy Spirit giving themselves to us and making their home in us (John 14: 17, 23). This is the sense in which divine grace is to be seen as the fruit of the Eucharist. It is the communion of Father, Son and Holy Spirit, shared with us in the mystery of sacramental communion. In a word, the Eucharist gives us the Trinity.
>
> p.237, 250

Teen prayers combined with the Holy Eucharist are holy prayers full of grace in a communion with the Most Holy Trinity. The Catholic Church considers the Mystery of the Holy Eucharist: (1) thanksgiving and praise to God the Father; (2) the true memorial sacrifice of Jesus Christ with his body and his blood; (3) real presence of Jesus Christ by the power of his word and of his Holy Spirit (Catechism, n.1358-81). The Eucharist is "the source and summit of the Christian life" because the essence of the Holy Eucharist is the Real Presence of Jesus through transubstantiation (Lumen Gentium, n.11).

God the Holy Spirit allowed the thoughts and spirituality of Saint Thomas Aquinas to understand the concepts of transubstantiation with the logic of medieval metaphysics. Aquinas said that God is the infinite action over the essence of nature, and consequently, in the Holy Eucharist God works change:

> ...And this is done by Divine power in this sacrament; for the whole substance of the bread is changed into the whole substance of Christ's body, and the whole substance of the wine into the whole substance of Christ's blood. Hence this is not a formal, but a substantial conversion; nor is it a kind of natural movement: but, with a name of its own, it can be called *transubstantiation*.   Summa Theologica, III, q.75, a.4

Aquinas cautioned that faith is necessary for humans on spiritual journeys because the Eucharistic substances and the Eucharistic conversions are supernatural:

> Christ's body is substantially present in this sacrament. But substance, as such, is not visible to the bodily eye, nor does it come under any one of the senses, nor under the imagination, but solely under the intellect... which is called the spiritual eye...since the way in which Christ is in this sacrament is entirely supernatural, it is visible in itself to a supernatural, i.e. the Divine, intellect, and consequently to a beatified intellect, of angel or of man, which, through the participated glory of the Divine intellect, sees all supernatural things in the vision of the Divine Essence. But it can be seen by a wayfarer through faith alone, like other supernatural things.   Ibid., III, q.76, a.7

Saint Thomas Aquinas recognized and acknowledged Jesus Christ with a certain dignity and respect for the Most Holy Eucharist:

> ...Absolutely speaking, the sacrament of the Eucharist is the greatest of all the sacraments...because it contains Christ Himself substantially...   Ibid., III, q.65, a.3
> ...the Eucharist is, as it were, the consummation of the spiritual life, and the end of all the sacraments...
> Ibid., III, q.73, a.3

Thomas Aquinas loved the Holy Eucharist so much that he wrote songs to worship God which Teens currently sing in adoration and benediction of the Most Blessed Sacrament ("Tantum Ergo"/Come Adore; "O Salutaris"/O Saving Victim).

Vatican II echoed Thomas Aquinas concerning the Real and the Divine Presence of Jesus Christ in the Most Holy Eucharist. All the sacraments and all the ministries bind to the Eucharist because "in the most blessed Eucharist is contained the whole spiritual good of the Church, namely Christ himself" (Decree on the Ministry and Life of Priests, n.5). Vatican II also teaches that Jesus Christ is present in the liturgical celebrations of the Church, in the Mass not only in the priest "but especially in the eucharistic species," in the Word of Holy Scriptures, in the community assembled for worship (Constitution on the Sacred Liturgy, n.7). However, the Eucharist is the sacrament of love in which "the mind is filled with grace" and "especially from the Eucharist, grace is poured forth upon us as from a fountain" (Ibid., n.47, 10).

Pope John Paul II continued the dignity and respect for the Most Holy Eucharist with authentic renewal of Vatican II in his encyclical On the Mystery and Worship of the Eucharist (Dominicae Cenae):

> This worship, given therefore to the Trinity of the Father and of the Son and of the Holy Spirit, above all accompanies and permeates the celebration of the Eucharistic Liturgy...since the Eucharistic Mystery was instituted out of love, and makes Christ sacramentally present, it is worthy of thanksgiving and worship...The Church and the world have a great need of eucharistic worship. Jesus waits for us in this sacrament of love. Let us be generous with our time in going to meet Him in adoration and in contemplation that is full of faith and ready to make reparation for the great faults and crimes of the world. May our adoration never cease.   n.3

> The authentic sense of the Eucharist becomes of itself the school of active love for neighbor...The Eucharist educates us to this love in a deeper way; it shows us, in fact, what value each person, our brother or sister, has in God's eyes, if Christ offers Himself equally to each one, under the species of bread and wine. If our Eucharistic worship is authentic, it must make us grow in awareness of the dignity of each person. The awareness of that dignity becomes the deepest motive of our relationship with our neighbor.   n.6

The epitome of divine action in relationship with modern Teens becomes the change of the substance of the bread and wine into the substance of the body and the blood of Jesus Christ because of the power of God in Transubstantiation, Eucharistic Change, Eucharistic Conversion. The Mystery of the Holy Eucharist is the Mystery of the Holy Trinity. The grace of the Holy Eucharist is the grace of the Holy Trinity. God calls the Catholic Teenager to relationship in the Holy Communion of God and Teen. The Catholic Teenager receives the divine love and the living grace of the Most Holy God of Antiquity in the awesome humility of the Holy Eucharist. With dignity and respect for the Most Holy God, the Teenager may elevate prayer-life off the kindergarten level and jump-start the dynamics of Teen spirituality through prayers of thanksgiving, forgiveness, adoration, petitions to the Most Holy Trinity of All Love, All Truth, All Grace in the Most Holy Eucharist.

C. PLEASE, CONSIDER THE FOLLOWING:

(1) Do a three-minute meditation with eyes closed, racket blocked out, thoughts/feelings concentrated on the focal point: I choose to pray, think, feel about...Most Holy Trinity of the Father the Creator, the Son the Redeemer, the Holy Spirit the Sanctifier...sanctifying and actual grace...the Most Holy Eucharist, the body and blood of Jesus the Christ...

(2) Create a mental list of thoughts and feelings pertaining to Mystery of the Holy Trinity, Mystery of Grace, Mystery of the Holy Eucharist... (change from a bad to a good person because of "slobber kiss"/love/ grace; pray/think/feel with dignity and respect for God the Most Holy Trinity; activate dynamics of Teen spirituality with personal choice to live daily prayer through efforts to increase knowledge, love, worship of God; elevate prayer-life off the kindergarten level with personal prayers of thanksgiving, forgiveness, adoration, petition; choose to pray for unity of East and West Christians; choose to pray for the increase in sanctifying and actual grace; choose to pray for the help of Mother Mary, full of grace; choose to pray for an increase of faith, trust, love in the Most Holy Trinity, grace, Most Holy Eucharist; etc.)

(3) Compose a homemade prayer to Almighty God concerning the Most Holy Trinity, God's grace, the Most Holy Eucharist which you can think and feel several times throughout the day...remember it's between you and your God...

(4) Try loving God and neighbor to the point that knowledge, love, worship concerning the Most Holy Trinity, God's grace, the Most Holy Eucharist mean something very special and very necessary in your mind and in your heart...

CHAPTER 6

SUMMARY: PRAYER IN ACTION SERVICE TO OTHERS

God is in all daily life whether the Teen has a mundane or exotic lifestyle. Travel to Europe or Egypt is not necessary to find the Most Holy God. Teens are gifted and blessed enough to find God in their everyday lives. God resides in the spirit of selfless acts within love for others. God is in the reason and in the feeling of self-sacrifice for the dignity, respect, honor, glory of God. My stories or Teen stories spin into God's stories and shared theology, not in the good or exotic story itself, but only when the Teen recognizes God as a living, daily, and Divine Presence in me, in other Teens, in self.

There is nothing wrong with the mundane, ordinary, unexciting existence because God is there with the Teen in the daily living. The Teen is not a "loser" when the Teen has the value and the meaning of God in the Divine Presence of daily Teen existence. Teens have spiritual perspectives that lead to the joy of God in daily life or to the human sorrow in unfulfilled egos. Is the bottle half full or half empty? When a Teen experiences the love of God, the Teen spiritual attitude becomes the recognition of God in all street scenes and in every life story. The search for God includes the recognition of God in others and in self. God has blessed most Teenagers with the gift of sight. Can the Teen sight the Most Holy God in others and in self?

Communication with God defines the concept and theology of prayer. Prayer is as easy for the Teen as the Teen ability to love. Prayer is as hard for Teenagers as maintaining a love relationship with meaning and longevity. When Teenagers choose to pray, high quality prayers in a small quantity of words are usually easy for the Teenager. Teen prayer formulas may include:

Prayers of Thanksgiving → "Thank you"
Prayers of Forgiveness → "I'm sorry"
Prayers of Adoration → "God is #1, I'm not"
Prayers of Petition → "Please."

In reality even these simple quality prayers are often hard to say with spiritual meaning from the mind and the heart especially without the premium virtues of humility and fortitude.

When Teens utilize God's marvelous gift of sight, Teens often think and feel the instant desire to pray in thanksgiving and adoration of God. Teenagers open eyes and see the wonderful creations of God such as flowers in bloom and birds in flight. When Teens grow in knowledge and see pretty flowers in bloom, Teenagers realize the intricate complexities of God's laws in nature within photosynthesis just to get the pretty bloom. A pretty flower has the power of God to change a foul Teen mood into worship of the glory and intelligence of God within the existence of the flower's life.

The same is true of the Teenage response to birds in flight. The Teenager sees the majesty of God in the flight of the bird. As Teens grow in knowledge,Teens understand that birds are descendents of the dinosaurs. For 90 million years, God nurtured and allowed the creation of birds in flight to evolve and to "defy" God's laws of gravity for the sake of survival. God also nurtured and allowed mankind to understand God's laws of gravity in the flight of a propeller-powered airplane. In 1903, the Wright brothers flew the first manned airplane for 12 seconds. Consequently, they proved in a mechanical machine the theories of flight that birds did naturally in living flesh through the wisdom and intelligence of God for 90 million years. Teens look at birds in flight with understanding and worship God.

Teens see the majesty of God's intelligence in flowers and birds, and Teenagers open eyes to give praise and thanksgiving to God the Creator. Jesus also utilized the birds in the air and the lilies of the fields to evoke praise, thanksgiving, love, trust of God the Creator (Lk.12:22-31; Mt.6:25-33). However, the acid tongues of peers often destroy the natural tendency of Teens to see God in nature and to choose praise of God the Creator in prayer. Teenagers often relax prayer-life until crunch time when negatives drive Teenagers to their knees to pray in desperation. The opportunities for the joy of a pure relationship with God in prayer exist well before and after the prayers said in the total desperation of crunch time.

Jesus Christ boiled the Ten Commandments and all laws of God down to love God above all things with whole heart, mind, soul and love neighbor as self. With the commands of Jesus to love totally, prayer takes priority in Teenage existence. It is simply too difficult to love unselfishly for any extended periods of time without prayer. The Teenager in relationship with God corrals his or her ego with prayer before the ego manipulates and blocks pure love of God. So to better maintain healthy love relationships, Teens need to communicate with God in private prayer and in community prayer (Mt.6:5-6;1Thes.5:16-17; Vat.II, Sacred Liturgy, n.12; Mt.18:20; Jn.6; 1Jn.4:20-1).

Teenagers make careful choices to prevent a blockage of their private and community prayers. Father Ronald Rolheiser makes this point in The Holy Longing:

> ...we, for every kind of reason, good and bad, are distracting ourselves into spiritual oblivion. It is not that we have anything against God, depth, and spirit...we are habitually too preoccupied to have any of these show up on our radar screens. We are more busy than bad, more distracted than nonspiritual, and more interested in the movie theater, the sports stadium, and the shopping mall and the fantasy life they produce in us than in church. Pathological busyness,

distraction, and restlessness are major blocks today within our spiritual lives. p.32-3

The commandments of Jesus to totally love interrelate with the private and the community prayers of Teens. Jesus told his disciples that if they loved him, they would keep his commandments (Jn.14; 15). Love of Jesus linked his followers with personal commandments to love God and to love neighbor. The followers of Jesus united in their community prayers of worship and in their moral/ethical way of life based on his commands to love. Father Rolheiser stated: "In the Gospels, fidelity in keeping the commandments is the only real criterion to tell real prayer from illusion...Jesus teaches this very clearly, that we cannot pretend to be loving if we are not keeping the commandments" (Holy Longing, p.62-3).

The foundations for early Christian church communities were to gather around the person of Jesus the Christ and to live in his Spirit. Sacred Scripture defines the Holy Spirit of Jesus as love, joy, peace, patient endurance, kindness, generosity, mildness, faith, and chastity (NAB, Gal.5:22-3). Father Rolheiser stated in The Holy Longing:

> Living in these virtues is what binds us into community in such a way that we are immune from separation by distance, temperament, race, color, gender, ideology, social status, history, creed, or even death. All who live in these virtues are one body with each other and constitute the church... it comprises the historical Christian churches, those that are visibly called into community by the word of Christ and the Eucharist that he left us. To be church is, therefore, to celebrate the word of Christ and the Eucharist... Spirituality is not a private search for what is highest in oneself but a communal search for the face of God. The call of God is double: Worship divinity and link yourself to humanity. There are two great, equal commandments: Love God and love your neighbor. p.120, 137

Teenage communication in private and community prayers to God maintains the healthy spiritual relationship of love for the Most Holy God of Antiquity.

However, Teens need to do the right thing for the right reasons. Take for example the two sons in Jesus' parable about the Prodigal Son (Lk.15:11-32). The younger brother broke relationship with the father through infidelity, weakness, too many wild and crazy parties. The attitude of the older brother also needed adjustment. The older brother always seemed to do the right thing, but he bluntly refused to welcome the younger brother home. The older brother did the right things for the right reasons for many years. Unfortunately, he threw away his connections to the Holy Spirit through joy, peace, patient endurance, mildness with his negative attitude toward his younger brother. As a result, the older brother also broke relationship with the father because of bitterness and anger directed toward the father's younger prodigal son.

Father Rolheiser commented about the attitude of the older son in The Holy Longing:

> His bitterness and unwillingness to take part in the celebration of his brother's return points to what he is still clinging to – life's unfairness, his own hurt, and his own unfulfilled fantasies. He is living in his father's house but he is no longer receiving the spirit of that house. Consequently, he is bitter, feels cheated, and lives joyously.   p.163

The older brother did the right things for the wrong reasons, and his latest actions with his brother produced negatives. Jesus wants Teens to emulate the compassion of the father for both sons (Ibid., p.67). Jesus wants Teens to do the right thing for the right reasons. Jesus wants Teen private and community prayers (the right things) to express thanksgiving, forgiveness, adoration, petition with dignity and respect for God (the right reasons).

Teenagers, like the older brother to the prodigal son, may need to change or to tweak attitudes toward private and community prayer to do the right spiritual things for the right spiritual reasons. All the changes and the tweaks to spiritual life are not automatically signs of bad news. People sometimes ask me why I write and target Teens. I answer by "tweaking" the Psalm verse from "Our help (hope) is in the name of the Lord, who made heaven and earth" (Ps.124: 8; 146: 5-6;121:2) to "Our help and hope is in the name of the Lord's Teens."

Teenagers are in natural change, and the changes are naturally good. Teenage bodies change; Teen emotions change; Teen minds change. Other authors could possibly substitute in this manuscript for the word "Teenager" with the words "old people" or "middle-aged people" or "mature adults," and then share the same exact legitimate thoughts and feelings about spirituality. However, "mature adults" sometimes choose not to change. It's like they open up their heads and fill them full of concrete. Then they open hearts and fill them full of concrete. The mental and emotional concrete sets, and so many adults have hard heads and hard hearts. Sometimes adults set in their ways, and there is no change.

But Teenagers are by nature in change. As the body, emotions, thoughts, heart, mind change, there are real opportunities for Teen spirituality to change for the better. Teen hearts and minds are not set in concrete...yet. Wouldn't it be a shame if Teen spirituality set in kindergarten concrete like so many adult hearts, minds, spiritualities? The faith journey demands and requires change, growth, conversion of mind and heart to God. Teens may do these things early in their lives because their way of life is change. Teens are already changing in so many areas of their existence that the Teenager only needs to recognize a holy longing for God to activate spiritual change, growth, and conversion of mind and heart to God. Teenagers may choose to eliminate the negative thoughts and negative feelings and to replace them with positive thoughts and positive feelings. Teens may choose spirituality because Teens are not set in their ways...yet.

God the Father creates Teens for God. God the Son redeems Teens for God. God the Holy Spirit sanctifies Teens for God. Every Teenager may choose to pray to God, communicate with God, and establish relationship with God. All Teenagers may choose to elevate prayer-life off a kindergarten level with their prayers of thanksgiving, prayers of forgiveness, prayers of adoration, prayers of petitions. All Teens may choose a dynamic Teen spirituality and then live prayer daily by better understanding the inner dynamics of Teen prayer as the progressive growth pattern of knowing, loving, and worshiping God. Every Teen may choose to pray with dignity and respect for the Most Holy God.

When the Teenager makes all these positive spiritual choices, the Teen may not set spirituality in mental and emotional concrete and bask in smugness. Teen spirituality is simply too dynamic to set in concrete once it is cranked up. To set Teen spirituality in mental and emotional concrete is disrespect for the God who gave Teens so much spiritual energy to do the right things for the right reasons.

Please, let me share examples while Teens think and feel deeply through optics of mind and heart. When filled with spiritual energy from the Holy Eucharist, elevated prayer-life, jump-started dynamics of Teen spirituality, activated dignity and respect for God the Holy Trinity, full of grace, Teens can not just set and do nothing like Libby Lou in her first fire drill, comatose Bully on new guinea-pig medicine, a boy holding the reins of a camel after beaten senseless by his own dad in hot Sahara sand, a little boy with a fly in the eye. Teens full of grace and the spiritual energy of God must do something positive (the right things) for the love of God and love of neighbor (the right reasons) like Colin Browne playing the trumpet and bringing joy in lightweight concerts to his friends, Bully trading french fries for sugar cubes for horses and choosing right behavior, Colin Browne patiently sitting in the big leather chair and cleverly pouncing on Headmaster's refusal for a swim, Bully lifting himself out of the mud and struggling forward because of love for horses, Colin Browne getting a smash in the face with a cricket ball and battling himself off gym floor, Colin Browne spending special time with his best friend Libby Lou because of the sound of her voice.

When filled with God's grace and God's fortitude, a Teen choice to set in mental and emotional concrete is not a viable option. Grace and fortitude from God are not the spiritual heebie-jeebies that will automatically go away if a Teen does nothing long enough. Grace and fortitude are the gifts of God to Teens to help Teens do the right things for the right reasons. Living a life of prayer produces positive Teen action, and prayerful action produces Teen service to others. Prayer in action is service to others.

The command of Jesus to totally love God and neighbor means that Teens make the efforts to sacrifice of self for God and neighbor. The command to totally love means action to do good stuff for God and others. The command to totally love God does not necessarily convey that Teens love family and friends any less by taking away or transferring love from others to God (Mt.10:37-9). The command of Jesus to totally love indicates that Teens continue to love others and to use this love as the baseline to love God even more than family and friends without deleting any love for others.

A genuine love means a genuine sacrifice of self. Jesus had total love for God the Father, total love for neighbors, total self-sacrifice for others. Jesus brought together his three expressions of genuine and total love on the cross. The ego of Jesus did not get in the way of the genuine and total love of Jesus. Consequently, Jesus obeyed the will of God the Father to totally love with his genuine sacrifice of self. Genuine love of God and others produces the positive action of total self-sacrifice.

Jesus Christ told disciples and modern Teenagers, "This is my commandment: love one another as I have loved you. There is no greater love than this: to lay down one's life for one's friends" (NAB, Jn.15:12-3). For Jesus, the verses meant crucifixion on the cross. For modern Teens, the verses mean the sacrifice of Teenage self for Teenage service to others. To give freely of self is love and charity to others. Prayer in action is service to others.

Jesus also said that the last judgment of people connects directly to love, charity, and self-sacrifice. When the Teen feeds the hungry, gives drink to the thirsty, welcomes the stranger, cloths the naked, comforts the sick, visits prisoners, Jesus Christ judges the individual Teen worthy of God's kingdom because "as often as you did it for one of my least brothers, you did it for me" (NAB, Mt.25:40, 31-46). Prayer in action is service to others.

The characteristic mark of disciples of Jesus is love: "I give you a new commandment, that you love one another. Just as I have loved you, you also should love one another. By this everyone will know that you are my disciples, if you have love for one another" (NOAB/ NRSV, Jn.13:34-5). Prayer in action is service to others.

The Bishops at Vatican II stated in the Decree on the Apostolate of Lay People (Apostolicam Actuositatem):

> Young people exert a very important influence in modern society: The circumstances of their life, their habits of thought, their relations with their families, have been completely transformed...The growth of their social

importance demands from them a corresponding apostolic activity; and indeed their natural character inclines them in this direction. Carried along by their natural ardor and exuberant energy, when awareness of their own personality ripens in them they shoulder responsibilities that are theirs and are eager to take their place in social and cultural life. If this enthusiasm is penetrated with the spirit of Christ, animated by a sense of obedience and love towards the pastors of the Church, a very rich harvest can be expected from it. The young should become the first apostles of the young, in direct contact with them, exercising the apostolate by themselves among themselves, taking account of their social environment ...The young, on their side, will treat their elders with respect and confidence; and though by nature inclined to favor what is new, they will have due esteem for praiseworthy traditions. n.12

The historical Jesus in the Gospels and the bishops in modern times ask Teens for service to others in the fulfillment of the personal commandment of Jesus to love. The more Teenagers know, love, and worship God the greater the internal call to help others through service. All Teens may choose private and community prayer in a spiritual framework. However, Jesus also calls all Teens to service in a temporal framework built on Teen spirituality. The Teen chooses to share valuable time when the Teenager decides to do service out of love of God and neighbors. Teen service becomes grace in action. Teen temporal service to others is Teen spiritual prayer in action.

Teens may volunteer to do many different activities for temporal service to elevate the dynamics of individual Teen spirituality. The creative imaginations of Teens are the only limits to a list of volunteer activities. The following items are suggestions, but certainly, the list is incomplete:

- help tutor little people
- help as assistant or head coach for little people in basketball, swimming, soccer, cheerleading, baseball, T-ball, etc.
- help Senior Citizens (carry groceries, mow lawn, rake leaves, talk on phone, play cards/scrabble, visits to homebound/nursing homes, e-mail family, bake cookies together, share computer skills, drive to shopping/haircut, drive to get ice cream, drive to/from Mass, etc.)
- help at homes for unwed or abused mothers (Mother Teresa Nuns, Catherine House, etc.)
- help children at orphanages
- help at homes for abused children
- help with mobility at blind school
- help at soup lines for homeless

- help at "Helping Hand" or organization to distribute food and clothing
- help at Catholic Social Services
- help teach English to Hispanic migrant workers' children
- help distribute food at homeless shelters during holidays
- help baby-sit at church
- help take neighbors' little people to zoo, movies, get ice cream
- help at YMCA
- help sing Christmas carols w/friends at nursing homes during season
- help friends to dress up like Santa Claus and bring candy/gifts to children in hospitals during Christmas season
- help at Big Brothers/Big Sisters
- help make a seasonal banner to hang in church
- help at hospitals
- help little people develop computer skills
- help at Boys and Girls Clubs of America.

Teenage lists of things to do for love of neighbor, service to others, prayers in action seem endless. Opportunities to do the right thing for the right reason exist for all Teens.

Teens, please, consider seriously the concept of tutoring the little people. One of the main reasons that I capitalize the "T" in Teenager is because of my experiences with the efforts of Teenagers in official Tutoring Programs. I think and feel strongly that the word "Teenager" designates a very special group of people within the human race. I base my opinion on 25 years of experience working with Teens that includes 18 years in Catholic Youth Ministry, 5 years with Boys and Girls Clubs of America, 13 years sharing theology in the structured classrooms, 15 years in Tutoring Programs. I saw and understood in four vastly different official Tutoring Programs that Teenagers have some of their finest moments working with little people who struggle miserably with homework.

My first exposure to official Tutoring Programs was as a student at the University of Notre Dame when Teen undergraduate students volunteered to tutor underprivileged elementary children in the South Bend public schools. The tutoring experience made a lasting positive impact on my life. I coordinated three different Tutoring Programs as the Director of Education at the North Little Rock Boys and Girls Club and then as Director of the Youth Ministry at two Catholic parishes.

Allow me, please, to share facts from some marvelous efforts of Teen tutors at the N.L.R. Boys and Girls Club. Mr. Jim Wetherington, Executive Director, totally supported Teen tutors with professional help, budgeted money, space in the Club's facilities, the commitment from the Club's Board of Directors, and most especially with his high energy. Mr. Jim truly had love, dignity, respect for his Teen tutors.

When his call for help with the Club's Tutoring Program went into the community, Teens from five area high schools responded to him. Because of his dedication to Teens, the Tutoring Program in its best year had 200 Teens volunteering to tutor one hour per week! When Teen Tutors matched up one-on-one with little people struggling with homework, there were 400 people in the N.L.R. Boys and Girls Club Tutoring Program!! In that academic school year, the Teen Tutors volunteered over 4,600 hours of time, energy, and talent!!! Because of the high quality Teenage efforts, the little people in the community experienced love of Teen tutors, good grades, better self-esteem. I know and understand that Teenagers do excellent work tutoring little people. As a result, I capitalize the "T" in the word Teenager.

In the ideal situation Teenage tutors work with sustained positive efforts because Teen tutors love and sacrifice for their little people. I think and feel that all Teenagers have the potential to tutor and to do excellent work with the kindergartner and first grade students. Teen tutors have the ability to put a well-deserved capitol "T" in Teenager for efforts filled with love and self-sacrifice for the little people. Teen tutors live a service to others and prayers in action. Teenagers help little people who often struggle miserably alone and without hope for good grades on homework. Teen tutors fill terribly negative academic gaps in the little people's lives with pure love, genuine concern, and self-sacrifice. Teens laugh with the little people instead of laughing at them like at school. Teen tutors supply laughter where there is no laughter. Teens share talents and fill the little people with so many positive thoughts and positive emotions.

Teen tutors understand quickly that no matter how much Teens struggle with their own math classes, every Teen counts, subtracts, adds better than kindergartners and first graders. Teen tutors realize that regardless of their grade in English, all Teens read better than little people. Teen tutors know that no matter how discombobulated their emotional relationships with each other, every Teen is more together emotionally and psychologically than a kindergartner or a first grader. Little people simply do not care how smart or what kind of grades their tutor makes. Little people only care to see and spend time with their favorite Teen tutor.

Consequently, Teenage tutors bring in humble honesty their true selves with their strengths and their weaknesses to the little people. Little people respond with a pure love for their Teen tutor. Because Teens are closer in age to the little people and spend quality time one-on-one, Teenage tutors often get the academic results from the little people that marvel teachers and parents. Teen tutors express sensitivity, intelligence, and love for the little people. Teenage tutors often choose to change behavior around little people in the tutoring programs by deleting acid tongues. Little people and their parents might very well say, "Our help is in the name of the Lord's Teens."

In addition, spiritually mature adults might very well pray to God for a blessing on all Teens:

> May God, who allowed people to stand upright in humanity with essential knowledge of right and wrong and with the fundamental option to choose between good and evil, allow all Teens in a world of constant misery and depression to stand upright in a united Teen prayer for a world change to peace and love in the Divine Presence of the Most Holy God of Antiquity.

Teen service to others is Teen prayer in action. Teen prayer in action elevates Teenage prayer-life. Elevated Teenage prayer-life is dynamic Teen spirituality. Dynamic Teen spirituality is the Teenage relationship of love with dignity and respect for the Most Holy God. The Teenage relationship of love with dignity and respect for the Most Holy God is the Teen basis for total love of God, total love of neighbor, pure trust of the Divine Presence in Teen life. The Teen basis for total love of God, total love of neighbor, pure trust of the Divine Presence in Teen life is prayer. Prayer is communication with the Most Holy God of Love through prayers of thanksgiving, prayers of forgiveness, prayers of adoration, prayers of petition. Prayers of thanksgiving elevate Teen prayer-life off the kindergarten level with ease because Teens see the blessings of God such as eyesight.

May the Most Holy God of Antiquity continue to bless all Teens.

Bibliography

Anderson, Bernhard W. Understanding the Old Testament. 4th ed. Englewood Cliffs: Prentice-Hall, 1986.

Aquinas, O.P., Rev. Thomas. Basic Writings of Saint Thomas Aquinas. 2 vols. Ed. Anton C. Pegis. Indianapolis: Hackett Publishing Co., 1997.

"Astronomy." Microsoft Encarta '98 Encyclopedia. 1998 ed.

Baldick, Robert, et al., eds. The Koran. Trans. N.J. Dawood. Baltimore: Penguin Books, Inc., 1968.

Barbet, M.D., Pierre. A Doctor at Calvary: The Passion of Our Lord Jesus Christ as Described by a Surgeon. Fort Collins: Roman Catholic Books, 1949.

Bishop, M.C., ed. The Production and Distribution of Roman Military Equipment: Proceedings of the Second Roman Military Equipment Research Seminar. Oxford: B.A.R. Publications, 1985.

Brown, S.S., Rev. Raymond E. Biblical Exegesis & Church Doctrine. New York: Paulist Press, 1985.

Brown, S.S., Rev. Raymond E. The Birth of the Messiah: A Commentary on the Infancy Narratives in the Gospels of Matthew and Luke. New Updated Ed. New York: Doubleday, 1999.

Brown, S.S., Rev. Raymond E. The Churches the Apostles Left Behind. New York: Paulist Press, 1984.

Brown, S.S., Rev. Raymond E. The Community of the Beloved Disciple: The Life, Loves, and Hates of an Individual Church in New Testament Times. New York: Paulist Press, 1979.

Brown, S.S., Rev. Raymond E. The Death of the Messiah: From Gethsemane to the Grave: A Commentary on the Passion Narratives in the Four Gospels. 2 vols. New York: Doubleday, 1998.

Brown, S.S., Rev. Raymond E. An Introduction to New Testament Christology. New York: Paulist Press, 1994.

Brown, S.S., Rev. Raymond E. Jesus God and Man: Modern Biblical Reflections. New York: Macmillan Publishing Co., Inc., 1967.

Brown, S.S., Rev. Raymond E., and Rev. Joseph A. Fitzmyer, S.J., and Rev. Roland E. Murphy, O.Carm., eds. The New Jerome Biblical Commentary. Englewood Cliffs: Prentice-Hall, 1990.

Brown, S.S., Rev. Raymond E. Priest and Bishop: Biblical Reflections. Eugene: Wipf and Stock Publishers, 1970.

Brown, S.S., Rev. Raymond E. The Virginal Conception & Bodily Resurrection of Jesus. New York: Paulist Press, 1973.

Budge, E.A. Wallis. The Egyptian Book of the Dead: (The Papyrus of Ani) Egyptian Text Transliteration and Translation. New York: Dover Publications, Inc., 1967.

"Calendar." Microsoft Encarta '98 Encyclopedia. 1998 ed.

Cary, M. A History of Rome: Down to the Reign of Constantine. 2nd ed. London: Macmillan, 1967.

Cassius Dio Cocceianus. Dio's Roman History: With an English Translation by Earnest Cary on the Basis of the Version of Herbert Baldwin Foster in Nine Volumes V. The Loeb Classical Library (Greek Authors), No. 82. Ed. G.P. Goold. 1917. Cambridge: Harvard University Press, 1989.

"Chronology." Microsoft Encarta '98 Encyclopedia. 1998 ed.

Cook, S.A., eds. et al. The Cambridge Ancient History. X: The Augustan Empire 44B.C. – 70A.D. 1963 ed.

Coriden, James A., and Thomas J. Green, and Donald E. Heintschel, eds. The Code of Canon Law: A Text and Commentary. New York: Paulist Press, 1985.

"Cosmology." Microsoft Encarta '98 Encyclopedia. 1998 ed.

Duffy, Stephen J. The Dynamics of Grace: Perspectives in Theological Anthropology. Collegeville: Liturgical Press, 1993.

"Earth." Microsoft Encarta '98 Encyclopedia. 1998 ed.

Edersheim, Alfred. Sketches of Jewish Social Life. Updated ed. Peabody: Hendrickson Publishers, Inc., 1994.

Faulkner, Raymond, and James Wasserman. The Egyptian Book of the Dead: The Book of Going Forth By Day. San Francisco: Chronicle Books, 1998.

Fitzmyer, S.J., Rev. Joseph A. <u>The Dead Sea Scrolls and Christian Origins</u>. Grand Rapids: William B. Eerdmans Publishing Co., 2000.

Fitzmyer, S.J., Rev. Joseph A. <u>Saint Joseph in Matthew's Gospel</u>. Philadelphia: Saint Joseph's University Press, 1997.

Flannery, O.P., Rev. Austin, ed. <u>Vatican Council II: Volume 1: The Conciliar and Post Conciliar Documents</u>. New Revised 4th ed. Northport: Costello Publishing Co., Inc., 1998.

Frank, Tenney. <u>An Economic History of Rome</u>. 1927. New York: Gordon Press, 1973.

Frank, Tenney, eds., et al. <u>An Economic Survey of Ancient Rome</u>. 6 vols. Paterson: Pageant Books, Inc., 1959.

Garza-Valdes, Dr. Leoncio A. <u>The DNA of God?</u> New York: Doubleday, 1999.

"Geologic Time." <u>Microsoft Encarta '98 Encyclopedia</u>. 1998 ed.

Gorman, C.P., Rev. Ralph. <u>The Last Hours of Jesus</u>. New York: Sheed & Ward, 1960.

Gurrieri, Rev. John A., Ex. Dir. Liturgy. <u>The Sacramentary</u>. New York: Catholic Book Publishing Co., 1985.

Hadas, Moses. <u>A History of Rome</u>. Garden City: Doubleday & Co., 1956.

Haight, S.J., Rev. Roger. <u>The Experience and Language of Grace</u>. New York: Paulist Press, 1979.

Hartman,C.SS.R., Rev. Louis, ed., et al. <u>The New American Bible</u>. Nashville: Thomas Nelson Publishers, 1980.

Huebsch, Bill. <u>A Spirituality of Wholeness: The New Look at Grace</u>. 4th ed. Mystic: Twenty-Third Publications, 1992.

"Illuminated Manuscripts." <u>Microsoft Encarta '98 Encyclopedia</u>. 1998 ed.

John Paul II, His Holiness Pope. <u>Dominicae Cenae: On the Mystery and Worship of the Eucharist</u>. www.vatican.va [then click: The Holy See, Archive (circle logo), The Holy Father, John Paul II, Letters, Dominicae Cenae (Feb. 24,1980)].

John Paul II, His Holiness Pope. The Holy Shroud. www.vatican.va [then click: The Holy See, Archive (circle logo), The Holy Father, John Paul II, Travels, Vercelli and Turin (1998), The Holy Shroud (Turin, 24 May 1998)].

Josephus, Flavius. Josephus: The Complete Works. Trans. William Whiston, A.M. Nashville: Thomas Nelson Publishers, 1998.

Judaeus, Philo. The Works of Philo: Complete and Unabridged New Updated Version. Trans. C.D.Yonge. 1993. Peabody: Hendrickson Publishers, Inc., 2000.

Kelley, C.P., Rev. Bennet, ed. The New Saint Joseph Baltimore Catechism. Official Revised ed. No. 2. New York: Catholic Book Publishing Co., 1969.

Laymon, Charles M., ed. Interpreter's Concise Commentary. 8 vols. Nashville: Abingdon Press, 1983.

Lewis, Naphtali, and Meyer Reinhold, eds. Roman Civilization: Sourcebook I: The Republic; Sourcebook II: The Empire. 2 vols. New York: Harper & Row, Publishers, 1966.

"Light Year." Microsoft Encarta '98 Encyclopedia. 1998 ed.

Livy. History of Rome (Ab Urbe Condita): With an English Translation by B.O. Foster in Fourteen Volumes III, With an English Translation by Evan T. Sage IX. The Loeb Classical Library (Latin Authors), No. 172, 295. Ed. G.P. Goold. Cambridge: Harvard University Press, 1924, 1935.

Marien, Rev. Roy C. Letter to Philip Joseph Balest. 11 August 2001.

McBrien, Rev. Richard P. Catholicism: New Edition. San Francisco: HaperCollins Publishers, 1994.

McBrien, Rev. Richard P., eds., et al. The HaperCollins Encyclopedia of Catholicism. San Francisco: HaperCollins Publishers, 1995.

Mély, Fernand de, and Paul Édouard Didier, Comte, Riant. Exuviae Sacrae Constantinopolitanae: La Croix Des Premiers Croisés La Sainte Lance La Sainte Couronne. Vol. III. 3 vols. Paris: Ernest Leroux, 1904.

Metzger, Bruce M., and Roland E. Murphy, eds. The New Oxford Annotated Bible with the Apocryphal and Deuterocanonical

Books: New Revised Standard Version. New York: Oxford University Press, 1991.

"Milky Way." Microsoft Encarta '98 Encyclopedia. 1998 ed.

Moldenke, Harold N., and Alma L. Moldenke. Plants of the Bible. New York: Ronald Press Co., 1952.

Moloney, S.J., Rev. Raymond. The Eucharist. Collegeville: Liturgical Press, 1995.

"Moses." Encyclopaedia Judaica. Ed. Cecil Roth. Jerusalem: Keter Publishing House, 1973.

Page II, Charles R. Jesus & the Land. Nashville: Abingdon Press, 1995.

"Paleolithic Art." Microsoft Encarta '98 Encyclopedia. 1998 ed.

Paul VI, His Holiness Pope. Mysterium Fidei: Encyclical of Pope Paul VI on the Holy Eucharist. www.vatican.va [then click: The Holy See, Archive (circle logo), The Holy Father, Paul VI, Encyclicals, Mysterium Fidei (Sept. 3, 1965)].

Plutarch. The Parallel Lives: With an English Translation by B. Perrin in Eleven Volumes VII. The Loeb Classical Library (Greek Authors), No. 99. Ed. G.P. Goold. Cambridge: Harvard University Press, 1919.

Polybius. The Histories: With an English Translation by W.R. Paton in Six Volumes III, V. The Loeb Classical Library (Greek Authors), No. 138, 160. Ed. G.P. Goold. Cambridge: Harvard University Press, 1923, 1926.

Rahner, S.J., Rev. Karl. Foundations of Christian Faith: An Introduction to the Idea of Christianity. Trans. William Dych. New York: Crossroad Publishing Co., 1998.

Ratzinger, Joseph Cardinal, ed. (Imprimi Potest). Catechism of the Catholic Church. New York (Citta del Vaticano): Catholic Book Publishing Co. (Libreria Editrice Vaticana), 1994.

Rolheiser, O.M.I., Rev. Ronald. The Holy Longing: The Search for a Christian Spirituality. New York: Doubleday, 1999.

"Sadat." Microsoft Encarta '98 Encyclopedia. 1998 ed.

"Second." Microsoft Encarta '98 Encyclopedia. 1998 ed.

Smith, Sir William. A Smaller Dictionary of Greek and Roman Antiquities. 13th ed. London: John Murray, 1885.

"Star." Microsoft Encarta '98 Encyclopedia. 1998 ed.

Stravinskas, Rev. Peter M.J., ed. Our Sunday Visitor's Catholic Encyclopedia. Huntington: Our Sunday Visitor, Inc., 1991.

Tacitus, Cornelius. The Annals: With an English Translation by John Jackson in Five Volumes III. The Loeb Classical Library (Latin Authors), No. 249. Ed. G.P. Goold. Cambridge: Harvard University Press, 1931.

Thurston, Herbert. "Crown of Thorns." The Catholic Encyclopedia. 1908 ed.

"Time." Microsoft Encarta '98 Encyclopedia. 1998 ed.

Ulrich, Eugene. The Dead Sea Scrolls and the Origins of the Bible. Grand Rapids: William B. Eerdmans Publishing Co., 1999.

VanderKam. James C. The Dead Sea Scrolls Today. Grand Rapids: William B. Eerdmans Publishing Co., 1994.

VanderKam. James C. Enoch: A Man For All Generations. Columbia: University of South Carolina Press, 1995.

Vaux, O.P., Rev. Roland de. Ancient Israel: Its Life and Institutions. Trans. John McHugh. Grand Rapids: William B. Eerdmans Publishing Co., 1997.

Vermes, Geza. The Complete Dead Sea Scrolls in English. 1962. New York: Penguin Books, 1997.

Walker, Winifred. All the Plants of the Bible. New York: Harper & Brothers Publishers, 1957.

Wilson, Ian. The Bible Is History. Washington, DC: Regnery Publishing, Inc., 1999.

Wilson, Ian. The Blood and the Shroud: New Evidence That the World's Most Sacred Relic Is Real. New York: Simon & Schuster, 1998.

Wilson, Ian. Holy Faces, Secret Places: An Amazing Quest for the Face of Jesus. New York: Doubleday, 1991.

Wilson, Ian. Jesus: The Evidence. San Francisco: HarperCollins, 1984.

Wilson, Ian. The Mysterious Shroud. New York: Doubleday & Company, Inc., 1986.

Wilson, Ian. The Shroud of Turin: The Burial Cloth of Jesus Christ? Garden City: Doubleday & Company, Inc., 1978.

www.britannica.com

www.newadvent.org/cathen... /doc

www.shroud.com

www.sindone.org.

www.touregypt.net

www.vatican.va

"Yom Kippur War." Microsoft Encarta '98 Encyclopedia. 1998 ed.

Notes

Notes

Please, e-mail author

pjbalest@aol.com

with your name and address to purchase gift

**<u>With Dignity and Respect...
Dynamics of Teenage Spirituality:
How Teens May Elevate Prayer-Life</u>**

for Teen friends and Teens in extended family.

Thanks!